GREAT
AMERICAN
HORSE
STORIES

GREAT

AMERICAN

HORSE

STORIES

EDITED BY

SHARON B. SMITH

GUILFORD
CONNECTICUT

An imprint of Globe Pequot

Distributed by NATIONAL BOOK NETWORK

Copyright © 2017 by Rowman & Littlefield

British Library Cataloguing in Publication Information Available

Library of Congress Cataloging-in-Publication Data

ISBN 978-1-4930-2987-7 (paperback)
ISBN 978-1-4930-2988-4 (e-book)

♾™ The paper used in this publication meets the minimum requirements of American National Standard for Information Sciences—Permanence of Paper for Printed Library Materials, ANSI/NISO Z39.48-1992.

Printed in the United States of America

EDITOR'S NOTE

Several of these stories include minor changes in punctuation to improve readability for modern readers. There are no alterations in the sometimes-dated vocabulary chosen by the authors, with the exception of some of the dialogue in Bret Harte's "Chu Chu." Harte's use of Spanish dialect is excessive even for the 1890s. I have changed the most extreme examples to standard English to avoid distractions for today's readers.

CONTENTS

INTRODUCTION

The histories of North America and the horse are so interwoven that it's impossible to imagine one without the other. The earliest ancestors of equines, little fox-sized, single-toed animals, first appeared in the Americas fifty million years ago. They evolved into fully modern horses before traveling west over the land bridge between Alaska and Asia around the same time fully modern humans were traveling in the other direction. This happened about 13,000 years ago.

Horses and humans didn't meet again in North America until Spanish conquistadores arrived with riding and packhorses in the early sixteenth century. At that moment, the special relationship between American horses and humans began. Within a few decades, Native Americans began acquiring horses of their own, utterly transforming the culture of the Indians of the Great Plains and the American Southwest. In the early seventeenth century, French and English settlers in the east began transporting horses from northern Europe.

The rapid European expansion to the West would have been impossible without horses. On the other hand, settlement would have been considerably easier for European Americans if the Indians hadn't already obtained horses of their own. The clash of cultures on the American frontier led to some of the most captivating tales in world folklore.

The earliest stories were unwritten anecdotes and fables, told around Native campfires across the continent—legends of shape-shifting wild horses, of creatures half-man and half-horse, of white stallions who couldn't be captured. The settlers had horse stories of their own, often related and intertwined with the Native legends. Settlers—and the cowboys who evolved from them—had their own yarns of extraordinary wild stallions, of horses who were loved companions as well as workers, of horses who were the objects of greed and competition.

The legends of western horses found their way east just as the short story joined the novel as the most popular forms of fiction in North America. Most of the best writers in the late nineteenth and early twentieth centuries wrote about horses, including Bret Harte and Zane Grey, and their stories found an enthusiastic and massive audience. Some writers specialized in sagas that capitalized on the allure of the West, although most later expanded into other facets of the relationship between horses and Americans.

They produced exciting adventure stories, informative historical fiction, and even ghost stories. The great authors enjoyed writing about horses and their audiences certainly enjoyed reading about them.

Journalism was also important during the nineteenth and early twentieth centuries and the horse was a frequent subject in nonfiction as well. The growth of professional sports and the importance of horse racing ensured extensive coverage in the thousands of newspapers and magazines published in the Americas. During most of that era, racing drew more spectators and earned more coverage than any other sport. The illustrious horses and celebrated races were talked about in private parlors, on street corners, and in country stores, thanks to newspaper stories and magazine articles. Nearly everyone knew about the great sectional match races that took place during the years before the Civil War. They knew about the champion horses and their accomplishments. Jockeys were often household names.

This collection includes samples from these histories, memoirs, novels, short stories, and journalism. In each case a horse is either the center of the story or is a significant supporting player. While to us, horses mostly provide pleasurable entertainment, at the time the stories first appeared, they were a vital part of daily life. These stories provide us not just diversion but an understanding of our American past.

I

THE HORSE RETURNS TO AMERICA

1

MEMOIRS OF CONQUISTADOR BERNAL DÍAZ DEL CASTILLO

BY BERNAL DÍAZ DEL CASTILLO;
TRANSLATED BY
JOHN INGRAM LOCKHART (1844)

Although North America was home to its ancestors, the horse had evolved, migrated, and become extinct in its homeland by the time the Spanish conquistadores arrived in the late fifteenth century. Columbus was the first to return the horse to the Americas when he landed at the Caribbean island of Marie-Galante in 1493 on his second voyage to the New World. The first identifiable Spanish horses to set foot on the North American continent were the fifteen mounts of the soldiers of Hernan Cortes, who arrived to conquer Mexico in February 1519. Historian and soldier Bernal Díaz del Castillo, who came along for the conquest, leaves us descriptions of the individual horses in his history of the expedition.

CHAPTER 23

For memory's sake I will here likewise describe the horses and mares which we took with us on our expedition. Cortes had a dark chestnut stallion, which died afterwards at St. Juan de Ulua. Pedro de Alvarado and Hernando Lopez d'Avila had jointly an excellent brown mare, which had been broken in for the field of battle as well as for tournaments.

After our arrival in New Spain, Alvarado bought Lopez's share, or perhaps took forcible possession of it. Alonso Hernandez Puertocarrero had a gray-colored mare, which Cortes had purchased for him with the golden borders of his state robe; it was capitally trained for the field of battle. Juan Velasquez de Leon's mare was of the same color, a noble and powerful animal, full of fire and eager for battle: we commonly termed it the "short tail."

Christobal de Oli had a dark brown fine-spirited horse. Francisco de Montejo and Alonso de Avila had between them a sorrel-colored horse, but of little use in battle. Francisco de Morla had likewise a dark chestnut stallion, one full of fire and wonderfully swift. The light-colored horse of Juan de Escalante was not worth much. The gray-colored mare of Diego de Ordas, which would never foal, was neither very swift. Gonzalo Dominiguez had a small dark-brown nag, a very swift and noble animal.

Also the brown-colored horse of Pedro Gonzalez de Truxillo was a swift animal. Moron, who was a native of Vaimo, had a small horse, which was pretty well trained. Vaena, of Trinidad, had a darkish-colored horse, though a bad leaper. The light-colored chestnut galloway of De Lares was, on the other hand, a splendid animal and a capital runner.

Ortiz, the musician, and a certain Bartolome Garcia, who had applied himself to the art of mining, had between them a very good dark-colored horse, which they named the Arriero (mule driver), and was one of the best animals of the whole corps. Juan Sedeño, of the Havana, had a fine chestnut mare, which foaled on board. This Sedeño was considered to be the most wealthy man amongst us; for he had a ship of his own, a horse, a few Negroes to attend upon him, and his own lading of cassava and cured bacon. Just about this time horses and Negroes were only to be purchased for very high prices, which accounts for the small number of the former we had with us on this expedition.

Later Diaz explains how the conquistadores used their horses. On March 12, 1519, Cortes and his retinue anchored off the Yucatán Peninsula. The following day warriors from the village of Potonchán attacked the handful of dismounted soldiers who had disembarked. The Spaniards managed to fight off the attackers and capture the town. Diaz picks up the story.

CHAPTER 33

Cortes being now certain that the Indians would renew the attack, immediately ordered all our horses to be brought on shore, and every one, our wounded not excepted, to hold himself in readiness. When our horses, which had been such a length of time at sea, now stepped on firm ground again, they appeared very awkward and full of fear; however, the day following, they had regained their usual liveliness and agility. There were also six or seven of our men, all young and otherwise strong fellows, who were attacked with such severe pains in the groins that they could not walk without support. No one could guess the cause of this; it was only said they had lived too freely at Cuba, and that the pain was occasioned by the heat, and the weight of their arms; Cortes, therefore, ordered them again on board. The cavaliers, who were to fight on horseback, were commanded to hang bells around their horses' necks, and Cortes impressed on their minds not to rush at the Indians with their lances before they had been dispersed, and then even to aim at their faces only. The following men were selected to fight on horseback:

Christobal de Oli, Pedro de Alvarado, Alonso Hernandez Puerto-carrero, and Juan de Escalante. Francisco de Montejo and Alonso de Avila were to use the horses of Ortiz the musician, and of a certain Bartolome Garcia, though neither was worth much. Further, there were Velasquez de Leon, Francisco de Morla, and one of the Lares (for there was another excellent horseman among us of that name), and Gonzalo Dominiguez, both superior horsemen; lastly, there were Moron de Bayamo and Pedro de Truxillo. Then comes Cortes, who placed himself at their head. Mesa had charge of the artillery, while the rest of our men were commanded by Diego de Ordas, who, though he knew nothing of the cavalry service, excelled as a crossbow man and musketeer.

The morning following, which was the day of annunciation to the holy Virgin, we attended mass very early, and arranged ourselves under our ensign Antonio de Villareal. We now put ourselves in motion, and marched towards some extensive bean fields, where Francisco de Lugo and Pedro de Alvarado had fought the previous battle.

There was a village in this neighborhood called Cintla, belonging to the Tabascans, which lay about four miles from our headquarters. Cortes, on account of the bogs, which our horses could not pass, was obliged to take a circuitous route. Our other troops, however, under

Diego de Ordas, came up with the Indians near Cintla, where they had arranged themselves on the plain: if they felt equal ardor for the combat as we did, they could now satisfy themselves, for this was a battle in every sense of the word which we here fought, fearful in the extreme, as will be seen.

What followed was the Battle of Cintla. In the midst of close combat between dismounted Spaniards and a full force of Mayans, the natives appeared repeatedly to be gaining the upper hand.

CHAPTER 34

In one of these moments Cortes came galloping up with the horse. Our enemies being still busily engaged with us did not immediately observe this, so that our cavalry easily dashed in among them from behind. The nature of the ground was quite favorable for its maneuvers and as it consisted of strong active fellows, most of the horses being, moreover, powerful and fiery animals, our small body of cavalry in every way made the best use of their weapons. When we, who were already hotly engaged with the enemy, espied our cavalry, we fought with renewed energy, while the latter, by attacking them in the rear at the same time, now obliged them to face about. The Indians, who had never seen any horses before, could not think otherwise than that horse and rider were one body. Quite astounded at this to them so novel a sight, they quitted the plain and retreated to a rising ground.

The Spanish victory at Cintla was an important step to the conquest of the Aztec Empire. That happened eleven months later.

II

NATIVE
AMERICAN
HORSES

2

THE DUN HORSE

BY GEORGE BIRD GRINNELL

As the founder of the National Audubon Society, naturalist George Bird Grinnell may be best known for his love of American birds. But his admiration for Native American culture was equally important to him. He devoted much of his life to gathering the histories and legends of several tribes of the Great Plains, including the Pawnee, who honored him with the name "White Wolf." Grinnell's 1899 compilation of the Pawnee legends included the story of a dun pony who saved his master from ridicule and starvation and then assured him a future of prosperity and respect.

Many years ago there lived in the Pawnee tribe an old woman and her grandson, a boy about sixteen years old. These people had no relations and were very poor. They were so poor that they were despised by the rest of the tribe. They had nothing of their own; and always, after the village started to move the camp from one place to another, these two would stay behind the rest, to look over the old camp and pick up anything that the other Indians had thrown away as worn out or useless. In this way they would sometimes get pieces of robes, worn out moccasins with holes in them, and bits of meat.

Now, it happened one day, after the tribe had moved away from the camp, that this old woman and her boy were following along the trail behind the rest, when they came to a miserable old worn-out dun horse, which they supposed had been abandoned by some Indians. He was thin and exhausted, was blind of one eye, had a bad sore back, and one of his forelegs was very much swollen. In fact, he was so worthless that none of the Pawnees had been willing to take the trouble to try to drive him along with them. But when the old woman and her boy came along, the boy said, "Come now, we will take this old horse, for we can make him carry our pack." So the old woman put her pack on the horse, and drove him along, but he limped and could only go very slowly.

The tribe moved up on the North Platte until they came to Court House Rock. The two poor Indians followed them and camped with the others. One day while they were here, the young men who had been sent out to look for buffalo came hurrying into camp and told the chiefs that a large herd of buffalo were near and that among them was a spotted calf.

The Head Chief of the Pawnees had a very beautiful daughter, and when he heard about the spotted calf, he ordered his old crier to go about through the village and call out that the man who killed the spotted calf should have his daughter for his wife. For a spotted robe is ti-war'-uks-ti—big medicine.

The buffalo were feeding about four miles from the village, and the chiefs decided that the charge should be made from there. In this way, the man who had the fastest horse would be the most likely to kill the calf. Then all the warriors and the young men picked out their best and fastest horses, and made ready to start. Among those who prepared for the charge was the poor boy on the old dun horse. But when they saw him, all the rich young braves on their fast horses pointed at him and said, "Oh, see; there is the horse that is going to catch the spotted calf"; and they laughed at him, so that the poor boy was ashamed, and rode off to one side of the crowd, where he could not hear their jokes and laughter.

When he had ridden off some little way the horse stopped and turned his head round, and spoke to the boy. He said, "Take me down the creek, and plaster me all over with mud. Cover my head and neck and body and legs." When the boy heard the horse speak, he was afraid; but he did as he was told. Then the horse said, "Now mount, but do not ride back to the warriors, who laugh at you because you have such a poor horse. Stay right here until the word is given to charge." So the boy stayed there.

And presently all the fine horses were drawn up in line and pranced about, and were so eager to go that their riders could hardly hold them in; and at last the old crier gave the word, "Loo-ah!—Go!" Then the Pawnees all leaned forward on their horses and yelled, and away they went.

Suddenly, away off to the right, was seen the old dun horse. He did not seem to run. He seemed to sail along like a bird. He passed all the fastest horses, and in a moment he was among the buffalo. First he picked out the spotted calf, and charging up alongside of it, U-ra-rish! Straight flew the arrow. The calf fell. The boy drew another arrow, and killed a fat cow that was running by. Then he dismounted and began to skin the calf, before any of the other warriors had come up. But when the rider got off the old dun horse, how changed he was! He pranced about and would hardly stand still near the dead buffalo. His back was all right again; his legs were well and fine; and both his eyes were clear and bright.

The boy skinned the calf and the cow that he had killed, and then he packed all the meat on the horse, and put the spotted robe on top of the load, and started back to the camp on foot, leading the dun horse. But even with this heavy load the horse pranced all the time, and was scared at everything he saw. On the way to camp, one of the rich young chiefs of the tribe rode up by the boy and offered him twelve good horses for the spotted robe, so that he could marry the Head Chief's beautiful daughter; but the boy laughed at him and would not sell the robe.

Now, while the boy walked to the camp leading the dun horse, most of the warriors rode back, and one of those that came first to the village went to the old woman and said to her, "Your grandson has killed the spotted calf." And the old woman said, "Why do you come to tell me this? You ought to be ashamed to make fun of my boy, because he is poor." The warrior said, "What I have told you is true," and then he rode away. After a little while another brave rode up to the old woman, and said to her, "Your grandson has killed the spotted calf." Then the old woman began to cry, she felt so badly because every one made fun of her boy, because he was poor.

Pretty soon the boy came along, leading the horse up to the lodge where he and his grandmother lived. It was a little lodge, just big enough for two, and was made of old pieces of skin that the old woman had picked up, and was tied together with strings of rawhide and sinew. It was the meanest and worst lodge in the village. When the old woman saw her boy leading the dun horse with the load of meat and the robes on it, she was very surprised. The boy said to her, "Here, I have brought you plenty of meat to eat, and here is a robe, that you may have for yourself. Take the meat off the horse." Then the old woman laughed, for her heart was glad. But when she went to take the meat from the horse's back, he snorted and jumped about, and acted like a wild horse. The old woman looked at him in wonder, and could hardly believe that it was the same horse. So the boy had to take off the meat, for the horse would not let the old woman come near him.

That night the horse spoke again to the boy and said, "Wa-ti-hes Chah'-ra-rat wa-ta. Tomorrow the Sioux are coming—a large war party. They will attack the village, and you will have a great battle. Now, when the Sioux are all drawn up in line of battle, and are all ready to fight, you jump on to me, and ride as hard as you can, right into the middle of the Sioux, and up to their Head Chief, their greatest warrior, and count coup on him, and kill him, and then ride back. Do this four times, and count coup on four of the bravest Sioux, and kill them, but don't go again. If you go the fifth time, maybe you will be killed, or else you will lose me. La-ku'-ta-chix—remember." So the boy promised.

The next day it happened as the horse had said, and the Sioux came down and formed in line of battle. Then the boy took his bow and arrows, and jumped on the dun horse, and charged into the midst of them. And when the Sioux saw that he was going to strike their Head Chief, they all shot their arrows at him, and the arrows flew so thickly across each other that they darkened the sky, but none of them hit the boy. And he counted coup on the Chief, and killed him, and then rode back. After that he charged again among the Sioux, where they were gathered thickest, and counted coup on their bravest warrior, and killed him. And then twice more, until he had gone four times as the horse had told him.

But the Sioux and the Pawnees kept on fighting, and the boy stood around and watched the battle. And at last he said to himself, "I have been four times and have killed four Sioux, and I am all right, I am not hurt anywhere; why may I not go again?" So he jumped on the dun horse, and charged again. But when he got among the Sioux, one Sioux warrior drew an arrow and shot. The arrow struck the dun horse behind the forelegs and pierced him through. And the horse fell down dead. But the boy jumped off, and fought his way through the Sioux, and ran away as fast as he could to the Pawnees.

Now, as soon as the horse was killed, the Sioux said to each other: "This horse was like a man. He was brave. He was not like a horse." And they took their knives and hatchets, and hacked the dun horse and gashed his flesh, and cut him into small pieces.

The Pawnees and Sioux fought all day long, but toward night the Sioux broke and fled.

The boy felt very badly that he had lost his horse, and, after the fight was over, he went out from the village to where it had taken place, to mourn for his horse. He went to the spot where the horse lay, and gathered up all the pieces of flesh, which the Sioux had cut off, and the legs and the hoofs, and put them all together in a pile. Then he went off to the top of a hill near by, and sat down and drew his robe over his head, and began to mourn for his horse.

As he sat there, he heard a great windstorm coming up, and it passed over him with a loud rushing sound, and after the wind came a rain. The boy looked down from where he sat to the pile of flesh and bones, which was all that was left of his horse, and he could just see it through the rain. And the rain passed by, and his heart was very heavy, and he kept on mourning.

And pretty soon came another rushing wind, and after it a rain; and as he looked through the driving rain toward the spot where the pieces lay, he thought that they seemed to come together and take shape, and that the pile looked like a horse lying down, but he could not see well for the thick rain.

After this came a third storm like the others; and now when he looked toward the horse he thought he saw its tail move from side to side two or three times, and that it lifted its head from the ground. The boy was afraid, and wanted to run away, but he stayed. And as he waited, there came another storm. And while the rain fell, looking through the rain, the boy saw the horse raise himself up on his fore-legs and look about. Then the dun horse stood up.

The boy left the place where he had been sitting on the hilltop, and went down to him. When the boy had come near to him, the horse spoke and said: "You have seen how it has been this day; and from this you may know how it will be after this. But Ti-ra'-wa has been good, and has let me come back to you. After this, do what I tell you; not any more, not any less." Then the horse said: "Now lead me off, far away from the camp, behind that big hill, and leave me there tonight, and in the morning come for me," and the boy did as he was told.

And when he went for the horse in the morning, he found with him a beautiful white gelding, much more handsome than any horse in the tribe. That night the dun horse told the boy to take him again to the place behind the big hill, and to come for him the next morning; and when the boy went for him again, he found with him a beautiful black gelding. And so for ten nights, he left the horse among the hills, and each morning he found a different colored horse, a bay, a roan, a gray, a blue, a spotted horse, and all of them finer than any horses that the Pawnees had ever had in their tribe before.

Now the boy was rich, and he married the beautiful daughter of the Head Chief, and when he became older he was made Head Chief himself. He had many children by his beautiful wife, and one day when his oldest boy died, he wrapped him in the spotted calf robe and buried him in it. He always took good care of his old grandmother, and kept her in his own lodge until she died. The dun horse was never

ridden except at feasts, and when they were going to have a doctors'
dance, but he was always led about with the Chief wherever he went.
The horse lived in the village for many years, until he became very old.
And at last he died.

3

THE WOMAN WHO BECAME A HORSE

BY GEORGE A. DORSEY

During the late nineteenth and early twentieth century, Harvard-educated anthropologist George Amos Dorsey collected hundreds of legends from the tribes of the Great Plains, primarily the Arapahoe, Cheyenne, and Pawnee. Among them was the story of a Skidi Pawnee woman who met a beautiful spotted pony. She soon discovered that she preferred the pony to her husband.

There was a village, and the men decided to go on a warpath. So these men started, and they journeyed for several days toward the south. They came to a thickly wooded country. They found wild horses, and among them was a spotted pony.

One man caught the spotted pony and took care of it. He took it home, and instructed his wife to look after it, as if it were their chief.

This she did, and, further, she liked the horse very much. She took it where there was good grass. In the wintertime she cut young cottonwood shoots for it, so that the horse was always fat. In the night, if it was stormy, she pulled a lot of dry grass, and when she put the blanket over the horse and tied it up, she stuffed the grass under the blanket, so the horse never got cold. It was always fine and sleek.

One summer evening she went to where she had tied the horse, and she met a fine-looking man, who had on a buffalo robe with a spotted horse pictured on it. She liked him; he smelt finely.

She followed him until they came to where the horse had been, and the man said, "You went with me. It is I who was a horse."

She was glad, for she liked the horse. For several years they were together, and the woman gave birth, and it was a spotted pony. When the pony was born, the woman found she had a tail like that of a horse. She also had long hair. When the colt sucked, the woman stood up.

For several years they roamed about, and had more ponies, all spotted. At home the man mourned for his lost wife. He could not make out why she should go off.

People went on a hunt many years afterward, and they came across these spotted ponies. People did not care to attack them, for among them was a strange looking animal. But, as they came across them now and then, they decided to catch them. They were hard to catch, but at last they caught them, all but the woman, for she could run fast; but as they caught her children, she gave in and was caught.

People said, "This is the woman who was lost."

And some said, "No, it is not."

Her husband was sent for, and he recognized her. He took his bow and arrows out and shot her dead, for he did not like to see her with the horse's tail. The other spotted ponies were kept, and as they increased, they were spotted. So the people had many spotted ponies.

4

~~

THE COMANCHES' MANNER OF CAPTURING WILD HORSES

BY HENRY INMAN

Henry Inman was a professional soldier, a veteran of the Civil War and the conflicts of the Great Plains, when he turned to journalism in the 1870s. Fame came to Inman a decade later when he began compiling selections of his newspaper stories into popular books about life in the West. Indians and their horses made up an important part of Inman's work.

Inman's The Delahoydes: Boy Life on the Old Santa Fe Trail *is a mix of fiction and nonfiction, narrative and sketch. It's the tale of two ranch boys and their friends who venture out onto the Santa Fe Trail in the late 1860s in search of adventure and buffalo. The boys are captured by a band of Comanches, who teach them a great deal about life on the Plains, including their methods of increasing their pony herds.*

At the time of the capture of the young buffalo hunters, the Comanches were in all probability the most formidable and bloodthirsty savages of the Great Plains. They were the most perfect equestrians in the world. Forever on horseback, forever at war, they roamed restlessly from one point of the great prairies to another in search of the buffalo, which supported them. They acknowledged no superior to that of their own tribe.

They robbed indiscriminately all who ventured through their inhospitable hunting grounds, murdering the defenseless who were so unfortunate as to fall under their hatred. They were a dangerous, implacable, cunning, brutal and treacherous enemy, half centaur, half demon, living but to kill and eat.

They were trained in warlike feats from their infancy. When perfected in the art of their splendid horseback riding, they would dash along at full speed, then suddenly drop over the side of their animal, leaving no part of their person visible but the sole of one foot, which was fastened over the horse's back, as a purchase by which the rider could pull himself to an upright position. In that attitude they could ride any distance, and at the same time use their bow or fourteen-foot lance with deadly effect. One of their favorite methods of attack was to ride swiftly at the top of their animal's speed toward the enemy, and then, just before they came within range, drop on the opposite side of the horse, dash past, and pour into the surprised foe a shower of arrows delivered from under the animal's neck or even under his belly. It was useless for the enemy to return the shots, as the whole body of the Comanche was hidden behind that of his horse. There was nothing to aim at but the sole of the savage's foot, just projecting over the horse's back.

Often the Comanches would try to steal upon their enemies by leaving their lances behind them, slinging themselves along the sides of their horses, and approaching carelessly, as though these horses were nothing but a troop of animals without riders. A quick eye was necessary to detect this ruse, which was generally betrayed by the fact that the horses always kept the same side toward the looker-on, which would seldom be the case were they wild and unrestrained in their movements.

Every Comanche warrior had one favorite horse, which he never mounted except for the warpath or for hunting the buffalo, always using an inferior upon ordinary occasions. Swiftness was the chief quality for which the steed was selected, and for no price would the owner part with his favorite animal. Like all uncivilized peoples, the Comanche treated his horse with a strange mixture of cruelty and kindness. While engaged in a hunt, for example, he spurred and whipped the animal in the cruelest manner; but as soon as he returned, he carefully turned the valued beast over to his squaw, who stood ready to receive it as if it were a cherished member of the family.

The manner in which the Comanches replenished their stock of horses was remarkable. In many portions of the central regions of the continent, until within a few years ago (there may be some yet left in remote places), horses had become so perfectly acclimatized, had run wild for so many decades, that they had lost all traces of domestication, and were as truly wild as the buffalo or antelope, and assembled in immense herds led by the strongest and swiftest stallions.

It was from these immense droves that the Comanches supplied themselves with horses, which were so absolutely necessary to them. When a warrior wished a fresh animal he mounted his best that he had at home, provided himself with a lasso, and started out in search of the nearest herd of wild ones. When he arrived as closely as possible without being in danger of discovery, he dashed at them at full speed, and singling out one of the animals that suited him (which, hampered by the multitude of its companions, ran on), he soon threw his lasso over its neck. As the noose became firmly settled, the Indian jumped off his own animal. The pony was trained to stand where left, and allowed himself to be dragged by the frightened horse he had taken, and which shortly fell by the choking the leather cord effected. As soon as the horse had gone to the ground, the savage came up to it very cautiously, keeping the lasso tight enough to prevent it breathing perfectly, and yet loose enough to guard against complete strangulation, and at last was able to place one hand over its eyes and the other on its nostrils. The horse was now at the Indian's mercy. Then, in order to impress upon the animal the fact of its servitude, he hobbled together its fore feet for a time, and fastened a noose to its lower jaw; but within a wonderfully short period he was able to remove the hobbles, and to ride the conquered animal into camp. Of course, during the time occupied in taming the horse it jumped and struggled in the wildest manner; but after the one attempt for the mastery it gave up, and became the willing slave of its captor.

One of the most astonishing things in the whole process was the rapidity with which the operation of taming was accomplished. An experienced hunter would chase, capture and break a wild horse within an hour, and do it so effectually that almost before the herd was out of sight the wild animal was ridden as easily as if it had been born in servitude.

The Comanche, cruel master as he generally was, always took special care not to break the spirit of his horse, and prided himself on the jumps and the bucking which the animal indulged in whenever it received its rider upon its back.

Of course, the very best animals were never captured from the herd. It was impossible to capture them, because they always placed themselves at the head of the troop, assuming the position of leaders, and dashed off at full speed as soon as they feared danger. Consequently they were often a half-mile or more in advance of their fellows, so that an Indian stood no chance of overtaking them on a horse impeded by the weight of the rider.

When the Indians began to receive firearms and had learned how to use them, they adopted a new method for capturing wild horses, called "creasing." Taking his rifle, the hunter crept as near the herd as he could get, and watched until he decided which horse he wanted. He waited until the horse stood with its side toward him, then aimed carefully at the top of its neck and fired. If the shot was correctly guided, the bullet just grazed the ridge of the neck and the horse fell as if dead, stunned for a moment by the shock. It recovered within a very short time, however; but before it had regained its feet, the Indian was able to go up to it, hobble and secure it. It was a very effectual method of wild horse catching, but always broke the spirit of the animal, and deprived it of that fire and animation which the warrior prized so highly; therefore the Indians resorted to it only occasionally.

After a year and a half of captivity the Delahoyde boys and their friends escape from the Comanche. Years later they find themselves drawn to the places they traveled with the tribe, camping for weeks at a time along the now safe and peaceful Santa Fe Trail.

III

WESTERN
HORSES

5

THE CAMP OF THE WILD HORSE

BY WASHINGTON IRVING

White Americans also hunted wild horses. Their techniques were different, as were the uses they had for the animals they captured. The famous New York writer Washington Irving, who had lived abroad for seventeen years, returned to the United States in 1832 with an urge to see his country and prove he hadn't lost his feeling for his native land. Irving, already renowned for his stories "Rip van Winkle" and the "Legend of Sleepy Hollow," immediately embarked on a tour of what is now Oklahoma. He turned the journals he kept on the trip into A Tour on the Prairies, *a masterpiece of early western travel literature. In this chapter, he describes the exhilaration of the wild horse hunt.*

We had encamped in a good neighborhood for game, as the reports of rifles in various directions speedily gave notice. One of our hunters soon returned with the meat of a doe tied up in the skin and slung across his shoulders. Another brought a fat buck across his horse. Two other deer were brought in, and a number of turkeys. All the game was thrown down in front of the captain's fire, to be portioned out among the various messes. The spits and camp kettles were soon in full employ, and throughout the evening there was a scene of hunters' feasting and profusion.

We had been disappointed this day in our hopes of meeting with buffalo, but the sight of the wild horse had been a great novelty and gave a turn to the conversation of the camp for the evening. There were several anecdotes told of a famous gray horse that has ranged the prairies of this neighborhood for six or seven years, setting at naught any attempt of the hunters to capture him. They say he can pace and rack (or amble) faster than the fleetest horses can run. Equally marvelous accounts were given of a black horse on the Brazos, who grazed the prairies on that river's banks in Texas. For years he outstripped all pursuit. His fame spread far and wide; offers were made for him to the amount of a thousand dollars; the boldest and most hard-riding hunters tried incessantly to make prize of him, but in vain. At length he fell a victim to his gallantry; being decoyed under a tree by a tame mare, and a noose dropped over his head by a boy perched among the branches.

The capture of the wild horse is one of the most favorite achievements of the prairie tribes; and, indeed, it is from this source that the Indian hunters chiefly supply themselves. The wild horses that range those vast grassy plains, extending from the Arkansas to the Spanish settlements, are of various forms and colors, betraying their various descents. Some resemble the common English stock, and are probably descended from horses that have escaped from our border settlements. Others are of a low but strong make, and are supposed to be of the Andalusian breed, brought out by the Spanish discoverers.

Some fanciful speculatists have seen in them descendants of the Arab stock brought into Spain from Africa, and thence transferred to this country; and have pleased themselves with the idea that their sires may have been of the pure coursers of the desert, that once bore Mahomet and his warlike disciples across the sandy plains of Arabia!

The habits of the Arab seem to have come with the steed. The introduction of the horse on the boundless plains of the far West changed the whole mode of living of their inhabitants. It gave them that facility of rapid motion, and of sudden and distant change of place, so dear to the roving propensities of man. Instead of lurking in the depths of gloomy forests, and patiently threading the mazes of a tangled wilderness on foot, like his brethren of the north, the Indian of the west is a rover of the plain; he leads a brighter and more sun-shiny life, almost always on horseback, on vast flowery prairies and under cloudless skies.

I was lying by the captain's fire late in the evening, listening to stories about these coursers of the prairies and weaving speculations of my own, when there was a clamor of voices and a loud cheering at the other end of the camp, and word was passed that Beatte, the half-breed, had brought in a wild horse.

In an instant every fire was deserted; the whole camp crowded to see the Indian and his prize. It was a colt about two years old, well grown, finely limbed, with bright prominent eyes, and a spirited yet gentle demeanor. He gazed about him with an air of mingled stupe-faction and surprise at the men, the horses, and the campfires; while the Indian stood before him with folded arms, having hold of the other end of the cord which noosed his captive, and gazing on him with a most imperturbable aspect. Beatte, as I have before observed, has a greenish olive complexion; with a strongly-marked countenance not unlike the bronze casts of Napoleon; and as he stood before his captive horse, with folded arms and fixed aspect, he looked more like a statue than a man.

If the horse, however, manifested the least restiveness, Beatte would immediately worry him with the lariat, jerking him first on one side then on the other, so as almost to throw him on the ground; when he had thus rendered him passive, he would resume his statue-like attitude and gaze at him in silence.

The whole scene was singularly wild: the tall grove partially illumined by the flashing fires of the camp; the horses tethered here and there among the trees; the carcasses of deer hanging around; and in the midst of all the wild huntsman and his wild horse, with an admiring throng of rangers, almost as wild.

In the eagerness of their excitement, several of the young rangers sought to get the horse by purchase or barter, and even offered extravagant terms; but Beatte declined all their offers. "You give great price now," said he; "tomorrow you take back, and say, 'D——d Indian!'"

The young men importuned him with questions about the mode in which he took the horse, but his answers were dry and laconic; he evidently retained some pique at having been undervalued and sneered at by the young rangers, and at the same time looked down upon them with contempt as greenhorns, little versed in the noble science of woodcraft.

Afterwards, however, when he was seated by our fire, I readily drew from him an account of his exploit; for, though taciturn among strangers, and little prone to boast of his actions, yet his taciturnity, like that of all Indians, had its times of relaxation.

He informed me that, on leaving the camp, he had returned to the place where we had lost sight of the wild horse. Soon getting upon its track, he followed it to the banks of the river. Here, the prints being more distinct in the sand, he perceived that one of the hoofs was broken and defective, so he gave up the pursuit.

As he was returning to the camp, he came upon a gang of six horses, which immediately made for the river. He pursued them across the stream, left his rifle on the river bank, and, putting his horse to full speed, soon came up with the fugitives. He attempted to noose one of them; but the lariat hitched on one of his ears, and he shook it off. The horses dashed up a hill; he followed hard at their heels; when, of a sudden, he saw their tails whisking in the air, indicating that they were plunging down a precipice. It was too late to stop. He shut his eyes, held in his breath, and went over with them—neck or nothing. The descent was between twenty and thirty feet, but they all came down safe upon a sandy bottom.

He now succeeded in throwing his noose round a fine young horse. As he galloped alongside of him, the two horses passed each side of a sapling, and the end of the lariat was jerked out of his hand. He regained it, but an intervening tree obliged him again to let it go. Having once more caught it, and coming to a more open country, he was enabled to play the young horse with the line until he gradually checked and subdued him, so as to lead him to the place where he had left his rifle.

He had another formidable difficulty in getting him across the river, where both horses stuck for a time in the mire, and Beatte was nearly unseated from his saddle by the force of the current and the struggles of his captive. After much toil and trouble, however, he got across the stream, and brought his prize safe into the camp.

For the remainder of the evening the camp remained in a high state of excitement: nothing was talked of but the capture of wild horses; every youngster of the troop was for this harum-scarum kind of chase; every one promised himself to return from the campaign in triumph, bestriding one of these wild coursers of the prairies. Beatte had suddenly risen to great importance; he was the prime hunter, the hero of the day; offers were made him by the best mounted rangers to let him ride their horses in the chase, provided he would give them a share of the spoil. Beatte bore his honors in silence, and closed with none of the offers. Our stammering, chattering, gasconading little Frenchman, however, made up for his taciturnity by vaunting as much upon the subject as if it were he that had caught the horse. Indeed, he held forth so learnedly in the matter, and boasted so much of the many horses he had taken, that he began to be considered an oracle, and some of the youngsters were inclined to doubt whether he were not superior even to the taciturn Beatte.

The excitement kept the camp awake later than usual. The hum of voices, interrupted by occasional peals of laughter, was heard from the groups around the various fires, and the night was considerably advanced before all had sunk to sleep.

With the morning dawn the excitement revived, and Beatte and his wild horse were again the gaze and talk of the camp. The captive had been tied all night to a tree, among the other horses. He was again led forth by Beatte, by a long halter, or lariat, and, on his manifesting the least restiveness, was, as before, jerked and worried into passive submission. He appeared to be gentle and docile by nature, and had a beautifully mild expression of the eye. In his strange and forlorn situation, the poor animal seemed to seek protection and companionship in the very horse that had aided to capture him.

Seeing him thus gentle and tractable, Beatte, just as we were about to march, strapped a light pack upon his back, by way of giving him the first lesson in servitude. The native pride and independence of the animal took fire at this indignity. He reared, and plunged, and kicked, and tried in every way to get rid of the degrading burden. The Indian was too potent for him. At every paroxysm he renewed the discipline of the halter, until the poor animal, driven to despair, threw himself prostrate on the ground, and lay motionless, as if acknowledging himself vanquished. A stage hero representing the despair of a captive prince could not have played his part more dramatically. There was absolutely a moral grandeur in it.

The imperturbable Beatte folded his arms, and stood for a time looking down in silence upon his captive, until, seeing him perfectly subdued, he nodded his head slowly, screwed his mouth into a sardonic smile of triumph, and, with a jerk of the halter, ordered him to rise. He obeyed, and from that time forward offered no resistance. During that day he bore his pack patiently and was led by the halter; but in two days he followed voluntarily at large among the supernumerary horses of the troop.

I could not but look with compassion upon this fine young animal, whose whole course of existence had been so suddenly reversed. From being a denizen of these vast pastures, ranging at will from plain to plain and mead to mead, cropping of every herb and flower, and drinking of every stream, he was suddenly reduced to perpetual and painful servitude, to pass his life under the harness and the curb, amid, perhaps, the din and dust and drudgery of cities. The transition in his lot was such as sometimes takes place in human affairs, and in the fortunes of towering individuals: one day, a prince of the prairies; the next day, a packhorse!

6

CHU CHU

BY BRET HARTE

Bret Harte, born Francis Brett Harte in Albany, New York, in 1836, was one of the most famous writers in North America during the last quarter of the nineteenth century. Magazines paid the unheard of sum of $1,000 each for some of his colorful short stories of life in the rowdy mining camps and isolated ranches of California. Harte came by the color honestly, having worked in the gold camps, as a guard on a stage-coach line, and as a reporter and editor for several western newspapers.

Bret Harte had great affection for both horses and Californios, the descendants of the aristocratic Spanish settlers of the early part of the nineteenth century. Both are featured in "Chu Chu," the story of a beautiful wild mare who was never quite tamed.

I do not believe that the most enthusiastic lover of that "useful and noble animal," the horse, will claim for him the charm of geniality, humor, or expansive confidence. Any creature who will not look you squarely in the eye, whose only oblique glances are inspired by fear, distrust, or a view to attack; who has no way of returning caresses, and whose favorite expression is one of head-lifting disdain, may be "noble" or "useful," but can be hardly said to add to the gaiety of nations. Indeed, it may be broadly stated that, with the single exception of goldfish, of all animals kept for the recreation of mankind the horse is alone capable of exciting a passion that shall be absolutely hopeless. I deem these general remarks necessary to prove that my unreciprocated affection for Chu Chu was not purely individual or singular. And I may add that to these general characteristics she brought the waywardness of her capricious sex.

She came to me out of the rolling dust of an emigrant wagon, behind whose tailboard she was gravely trotting. She was a half-broken filly in which character she had at different times unseated everybody in the train and, although covered with dust, she had a beautiful coat and the most lambent gazelle-like eyes I had ever seen. I think she kept these latter organs purely for ornament, apparently looking at things with her nose, her sensitive ears, and, sometimes, even a slight lifting of her slim near foreleg. On our first interview I thought she favored me with a coy glance, but as it was accompanied by an irrelevant "Look out!" from her owner, the teamster, I was not certain.

I only know that after some conversation, a good deal of mental reservation, and the disbursement of considerable coin, I found myself standing in the dust of the departing emigrant wagon with one end of a forty-foot riata in my hand, and Chu Chu at the other. I pulled invitingly at my own end, and even advanced a step or two towards her. She then broke into a long disdainful pace, and began to circle round me at the extreme limit of her tether. I stood admiring her free action for some moments, not always turning with her, which was tiring until I found that she was gradually winding herself up on me.

Her frantic astonishment when she suddenly found herself thus brought up against me was one of the most remarkable things I ever saw and nearly took me off my legs. Then, when she had pulled against the riata until her narrow head and prettily arched neck were on a perfectly straight line with it, she as suddenly slackened the tension and condescended to follow me, at an angle of her own choosing. Sometimes it was on one side of me, sometimes on the other.

Even then the sense of my dreadful contiguity apparently would come upon her like a fresh discovery, and she would become hysterical. But I do not think that she really saw me. She looked at the riata and sniffed it disparagingly; she pawed some pebbles that were near me tentatively with her small hoof; she started back with a Robinson Crusoe–like horror of my footprints in the wet gully, but my actual personal presence she ignored. She would sometimes pause, with her head thoughtfully between her forelegs, and apparently say: "There is some extraordinary presence here: animal, vegetable, or mineral I can't make out which but it's not good to eat, and I loathe and detest it."

When I reached my house in the suburbs, before entering the "fifty vara" lot enclosure, I deemed it prudent to leave her outside while I informed the household of my purchase, and with this object I tethered her by the long riata to a solitary sycamore which stood in the center of the road, the crossing of two frequented thoroughfares. It was not long, however, before I was interrupted by shouts and screams from that vicinity, and on returning thither I found that Chu Chu, with the assistance of her riata, had securely wound up two of my neighbors to the tree, where they presented the appearance of early Christian martyrs. When I released them it appeared that they had been attracted by Chu Chu's graces, and had offered her overtures of affection, to which she had characteristically rotated, with this miserable result.

I led her, with some difficulty, warily keeping clear of the riata, to the enclosure from whose fence I had previously removed several bars. Although the space was wide enough to have admitted a troop of cavalry she affected not to notice it, and managed to kick away part of another section on entering. She resisted the stable for some time, but after carefully examining it with her hoofs and an affectedly meek outstretching of her nose, she consented to recognize some oats in the feed-box without looking at them and was formally installed. All this while she had resolutely ignored my presence. As I stood watching her she suddenly stopped eating; the same reflective look came over her.

"Surely I am not mistaken, but that same obnoxious creature is somewhere about here," she seemed to say, and shivered at the possibility.

It was probably this which made me confide my unreciprocated affection to one of my neighbors, a man supposed to be an authority on horses, and particularly of that wild species to which Chu Chu belonged. It was he who, leaning over the edge of the stall where she was complacently and, as usual, obliviously munching, absolutely dared to toy with a pet lock of hair which she wore over the pretty star on her forehead.

"Ye see, Captain," he said, with jaunty easiness, "Hosses is like women; ye don't want ter use any standoffishness or shyness with them; a steady but careless sort o' familiarity, a kind o' free but firm handlin', just like this, to let her see who's master."

We never clearly knew how it happened, but when I picked up my neighbor from the doorway, amid the broken splinters of the stall rail, and a quantity of oats that mysteriously filled his hair and pockets, Chu Chu was found to have faced around the other way, and was contemplating her forelegs, with her hind ones in the other stall.

My neighbor spoke of damages while he was in the stall, and of physical coercion when he was out of it again. But here Chu Chu, in some marvelous way, righted herself, and my neighbor departed hurriedly with a brimless hat and an unfinished sentence.

My next intermediary was Enriquez Saltello, a youth of my own age, and the brother of Consuelo Saltello, whom I adored. As a Spanish Californian he was presumed, on account of Chu Chu's half-Spanish origin, to have superior knowledge of her character, and I even vaguely believed that his language and accent would fall familiarly on her ear. There was the drawback, however, that he always preferred to talk in a marvelous English, combining Castilian precision with what he fondly believed to be California slang.

"To confer then as to this horse, which is not observe me a Mexican plug! Ah, no! you can your boots bet on that. She is of Castilian stock, believe me, and strike me dead! I will myself at different times overlook and affront her in the stable, examine her as to the assault, and why she should do this thing. When she is of the exercise I will also accost and restrain her. Remain tranquil, my friend! When a few days shall pass much shall be changed, and she will be as another. Trust your uncle to do this thing! Comprehend me? Everything shall be lovely, and the goose hang high!"

Conformably with this he "overlooked" her the next day, with a cigarette between his yellow-stained finger tips, which made her sneeze in a silent pantomimic way, and certain Spanish blandishments of speech, which she received with more complacency. But I don't think she ever even looked at him. In vain he protested that she was the "dearest" and "littlest" of his "little loves"; in vain he asserted that she was his patron saint and that it was his soul's delight to pray to her; she accepted the compliment with her eyes fixed upon the manger. When he had exhausted his whole stock of endearing diminutives, adding a few playful and more audacious sallies, she remained with her head down, as if inclined to meditate upon them. This he declared was at least an improvement on her former performances. It may have been my own jealousy, but I fancied she was only saying to herself, "Gracious! can there be two of them?"

"Courage and patience, my friend," he said, as we were slowly quitting the stable. "This horse is young and has not yet the habitude of the person. Tomorrow, at another season, I shall give to her a foundling ('fondling,' I have reason to believe, was the word intended by Enriquez) and we shall see. It shall be as easy as to fall away from a log. A little more of this chin music which your friend Enriquez possesses, and some tapping of the head and neck, and you are there. You are ever the right side up. Houpla! But let us not precipitate this thing. The more haste, we do not so much accelerate ourselves." He appeared to be suiting the action to the word as he lingered in the doorway of the stable.

"Come on," I said.

"Pardon," he returned, with a bow that was both elaborate and evasive, "but you shall yourself precede me. The stable is yours."

"Oh, come along!" I continued, impatiently. To my surprise he seemed to dodge back into the stable again. After an instant he reappeared.

"Pardon! But I am restrain! Of a truth, in this instant I am grasp by the mouth of this horse in the coattail of my dress! She will that I should remain. It would seem"—he disappeared again—"that"—he was out once more—"the experiment is a success! She reciprocate. She is, of a truth, gone on me. It is love!"

A stronger pull from Chu Chu here sent him in again but he was out now triumphantly with half his garment torn away. "I shall coquet."

Nothing daunted, however, the gallant fellow was back next day with a Mexican saddle and attired in the complete outfit of a *vaquero*.

Overcome though he was by heavy deerskin trousers, open at the side from the knees down, and fringed with bullion buttons, an enormous flat sombrero and a stiff, short, embroidered velvet jacket, I was more concerned at the ponderous saddle and equipments intended for the slim Chu Chu. That these would hide and conceal her beautiful curves and contour, as well as overweight her, seemed certain; that she would resist them all to the last seemed equally clear.

Nevertheless, to my surprise, when she was led out, and the saddle thrown deftly across her back, she was passive. Was it possible that some drop of her old Spanish blood responded to its clinging embrace? She did not either look at it or smell it. But when Enriquez began to tighten the "cinch" or girth a more singular thing occurred. Chu Chu visibly distended her slender barrel to twice its dimensions; the more he pulled the more she swelled, until I was actually ashamed of her. Not so Enriquez. He smiled at us, and complacently stroked his thin moustache.

"It is ever so! She is the child of her grandmother! Even when you shall make saddle this old Castilian stock, it will make large. It will become a balloon! It is a trick. It is a little game believe me. For why?"

I had not listened, as I was at that moment astonished to see the saddle slowly slide under Chu Chu's belly, and her figure resume, as if by magic, its former slim proportions. Enriquez followed my eyes, lifted his shoulders, shrugged them, and said smilingly, "Ah, you see!"

When the girths were drawn in again with an extra pull or two from the indefatigable Enriquez, I fancied that Chu Chu nevertheless secretly enjoyed it, as her sex is said to appreciate tight lacing. She drew a deep sigh, possibly of satisfaction, turned her neck, and apparently tried to glance at her own figure—Enriquez promptly withdrawing to enable her to do so easily. Then the dread moment arrived. Enriquez, with his hand on her mane, suddenly paused, and with exaggerated courtesy lifted his hat and made an inviting gesture.

"You will honor me to precede."

I shook my head laughingly.

"I see," responded Enriquez, gravely. "You have to attend the obsequies of your aunt, who is dead, at two of the clock. You have to meet your broker, who has bought you fifty share of the Comstock Lode at this moment or you are loss! You are excuse! Attend! Gentlemen, make your bets! The band has arrived to play! Here we are!"

With a quick movement the alert young fellow had vaulted into the saddle. But, to the astonishment of both of us, the mare remained perfectly still. There was Enriquez, bolt upright in the stirrups, completely overshadowing, by his saddle-flaps, leggings, and gigantic spurs, the fine proportions of Chu Chu, until she might have been a placid Rosinante, bestridden by some youthful Quixote. She closed her eyes; she was going to sleep! We were dreadfully disappointed. This clearly would not do. Enriquez lifted the reins cautiously! Chu Chu moved forward slowly—then stopped, apparently lost in reflection.

"Affront her on this side."

I approached her gently. She shot suddenly into the air, coming down again on perfectly stiff legs with a springless jolt. This she instantly followed by a succession of other rocket-like propulsions, utterly unlike a leap, all over the enclosure. The movements of the unfortunate Enriquez were equally unlike any equitation I ever saw. He appeared occasionally over Chu Chu's head, astride of her neck and tail, or in the free air, but never in the saddle. His rigid legs, however, never lost the stirrups but came down regularly, accentuating her springless hops. More than that, the disproportionate excess of rider, saddle, and accoutrements was so great that he had at times the appearance of lifting Chu Chu forcibly from the ground by superior strength, and of actually contributing to her exercise.

As they came towards me, a wild, tossing, and flying mass of hoofs and spurs, it was not only difficult to distinguish them apart, but to ascertain how much of the jumping was done by Enriquez separately. At last Chu Chu brought matters to a close by making for the low-stretching branches of an oak tree which stood at the corner of the lot. In a few moments she emerged from it—but without Enriquez!

I found the gallant fellow disengaging himself from the fork of a branch in which he had been firmly wedged, but still smiling and confident, and his cigarette between his teeth. Then for the first time he removed it, and seating himself easily on the branch with his legs dangling down, he blandly waved aside my anxious queries with a gentle reassuring gesture.

"Remain tranquil, my friend. This does not count! I have conquer—you observe—for why? I have never for once arrive at the ground! Consequent she is disappoint! She will ever that I should! But I have got her when the hair is not long! Your uncle Henry"—with an angelic wink—"is fly! He is ever a bully boy, with the eye of glass! Believe me. Behold! I am here! Big Injun! Whoop!"

He leaped lightly to the ground. Chu Chu, standing watchfully at a little distance, was evidently astonished at his appearance. She threw out her hind hoofs violently, shot up into the air until the stirrups crossed each other high above the saddle, and made for the stable in a succession of rabbit-like bounds, taking the precaution to remove the saddle on entering by striking it against the lintel of the door.

"You observe," said Enriquez, blandly, "she would make that thing of *me*. Not having the good occasion, she is dissatisfied. Where are you now?"

Two or three days afterwards he rode her again with the same result—accepted by him with the same heroic complacency. As we did not, for certain reasons, care to use the open road for this exercise, and as it was impossible to remove the tree, we were obliged to submit to the inevitable. On the following day I mounted her—undergoing the same experience as Enriquez, with the individual sensation of falling from a third-story window on top of a counting-house stool, and the variation of being projected over the fence. When I found that Chu Chu had not accompanied me, I saw Enriquez at my side.

"More than ever it is become necessary that we should do this thing again," he said, gravely, as he assisted me to my feet. "Courage, my noble General! God and Liberty! Once more on to the breach! Charge, Chestare, charge! Come on, Don Stanley! 'Ere we are!"

He helped me none too quickly to catch my seat again, for it apparently had the effect of the turned peg on the enchanted horse in the "Arabian Nights," and Chu Chu instantly rose into the air. But she came down this time before the open window of the kitchen, and I alighted easily on the dresser. The indefatigable Enriquez followed me.

"Won't this do?" I asked, meekly.

"It is better for you arrive not on the ground," he said, cheerfully, "but you should not once but a thousand times make trial! Ha! Go and win! Never die and say so! There you are!"

Luckily, this time I managed to lock the rowels of my long spurs under her girth, and she could not unseat me. She seemed to recognize the fact after one or two plunges, when, to my great surprise, she suddenly sank to the ground and quietly rolled over me. The action disengaged my spurs, but, righting herself without getting up, she turned her beautiful head and absolutely looked at me, still in the saddle. I felt myself blushing. But the voice of Enriquez was at my side.

"Arise, my friend; you have conquer! It is she who has arrive at the ground. You are all right. It is done; believe me, it is finish. No more shall she make this thing. From this instant you shall ride her as the cow as the rail of this fence and remain tranquil. For she is broke! Ta-ta! Regain your hats, gentlemen! Pass in your checks! It is over! How are you now?" He lit a fresh cigarette, put his hands in his pockets, and smiled at me blandly.

For all that, I ventured to point out that the habit of alighting in the fork of a tree, or the disengaging of oneself from the saddle on the ground, was attended with inconvenience, and even ostentatious display. But Enriquez swept the objections away with a single gesture.

"It is the principal—the bottom fact—at which you arrive. The next come of himself! Many horse have achieve to mount the rider by the knees, and relinquish after this same fashion. My grandfather had a barb of this kind—but she has gone dead, and so have my grandfather. Which is sad and strange! Otherwise I shall make of them both an instant example!"

I ought to have said that although these performances were never actually witnessed by Enriquez's sister—for reasons which he and I thought sufficient—the dear girl displayed the greatest interest in them, and, perhaps aided by our mutually complimentary accounts of the other, looked upon us both as invincible heroes. It is possible also that she over-estimated our success, for she suddenly demanded that I should ride Chu Chu to her house, that she might see her.

It was not far; by going through a back lane I could avoid the trees which exercised such a fatal fascination for Chu Chu. There was a pleading, child-like entreaty in Consuelo's voice that I could not resist, with a slight flash from her lustrous dark eyes that I did not care to encourage. So I resolved to try it at all hazards. My equipment for the performance was modeled after Enriquez's previous costume, with the addition of a

few fripperies of silver and stamped leather, out of compliment to Consuelo, and even with a faint hope that it might appease Chu Chu. She
certainly looked beautiful in her glittering accoutrements, set off by
her jet-black shining coat. With an air of demure abstraction she permitted me to mount her, and even for a hundred yards or so indulged
in a mincing maidenly amble that was not without a touch of coquetry.
Encouraged by this, I addressed a few terms of endearment to her,
and in the exuberance of my youthful enthusiasm I even confided to
her my love for Consuelo, and begged her to be "good" and not disgrace herself and me before my Dulcinea. In my foolish trustfulness I
was rash enough to add a caress, and to pat her soft neck. She stopped
instantly with a hysteric shudder. I knew what was passing through her
mind; she had suddenly become aware of my baleful existence.

The saddle and bridle Chu Chu was becoming accustomed to, but
who was this living, breathing object that had actually touched her?
Presently her oblique vision was attracted by the fluttering movement
of a fallen oak leaf in the road before her. She had probably seen many
oak leaves many times before; her ancestors had no doubt been familiar with them on the trackless hills and in field and paddock; but this
did not alter her profound conviction that I and the leaf were identical, that our baleful touch was something indissolubly connected. She
reared before that innocent leaf, she revolved round it, and then fled
from it at the top of her speed.

The lane passed before the rear wall of Saltello's garden. Unfortunately, at the angle of the fence stood a beautiful Madroño tree, brilliant with its scarlet berries and endeared to me as Consuelo's favorite
haunt, under whose protecting shade I had more than once avowed
my youthful passion. By the irony of fate Chu Chu caught sight of
it, and with a succession of spirited bounds instantly made for it. In
another moment I was beneath it, and Chu Chu shot like a rocket

into the air. I had barely time to withdraw my feet from the stirrups, to throw up one arm to protect my glazed sombrero and grasp an overhanging branch with the other, before Chu Chu darted off. But to my consternation, as I gained a secure perch on the tree, and looked about me, I saw her—instead of running away—quietly trot through the gate into Saltello's garden.

Need I say that it was to the beneficent Enriquez that I again owed my salvation? Scarcely a moment elapsed before his bland voice rose in a concentrated whisper from the corner of the garden below me. He had divined the dreadful truth!

"For the love of God, collect to yourself many kinds of this berry! All you can! Your full arms round! Rest tranquil. Leave to your old uncle to make for you a delicate exposure. At the instant!"

He was gone again. I gathered, wonderingly, a few of the larger clusters of parti-colored fruit and patiently waited. Presently he reappeared, and with him the lovely Consuelo, her dear eyes filled with an adorable anxiety.

"Yes," continued Enriquez to his sister, with a confidential lowering of tone but great distinctness of utterance, "it is ever so with the American! He will ever make *first* the salutation of the flower or the fruit, picked to himself by his own hand, to the lady where he call. It is the custom of the American hidalgo! My God!—what will you! *I* make it not—it is so! Without doubt he is in this instant doing this thing. That is why he have let go his horse to precede him here; it is always the etiquette to offer this things on the feet. Ah, I behold! It is he!—Don Francisco! Even now he will descend from this tree! Ah! You make the blush, little sister! (archly). I will retire. I am discreet; two is not company for the one. I make tracks. I am gone."

How far Consuelo entirely believed and trusted her ingenious brother I do not know, nor even then cared to inquire. For there was a pretty mantling of her olive cheek as I came forward with my offering, and a certain significant shyness in her manner that were enough to throw me into a state of hopeless imbecility. And I was always miserably conscious that Consuelo possessed an exalted sentimentality and a predilection for the highest medieval romance, in which I knew I was lamentably deficient. Even in our most confidential moments I was always aware that I weakly lagged behind this daughter of a gloomily distinguished ancestry in her frequent incursions into a vague but poetic past. There was something of the dignity of the Spanish *châtelaine* in the sweetly grave little figure that advanced to accept my specious offering. I think I should have fallen on my knees to present it, but for the presence of the all-seeing Enriquez. But why did I even at that moment remember that he had early bestowed upon her the nickname of "Pomposa"? This, as Enriquez himself might have observed, was "sad and strange."

I managed to stammer out something about the Madroño berries being at her "disposicion" (the tree was in her own garden), and she took the branches in her little brown hand with a soft response to my unutterable glances. But here Chu Chu, momentarily forgotten, executed a happy diversion. To our astonishment she gravely walked up to Consuelo, and, stretching out her long slim neck, not only sniffed curiously at the berries, but even protruded a black underlip towards the young girl herself. In another instant Consuelo's dignity melted. Throwing her arms around Chu Chu's neck she embraced and kissed her. Young as I was, I understood the divine significance of a girl's vicarious effusiveness at such a moment and felt delighted. But I was the more astonished that the usually sensitive horse not only submitted to these caresses, but actually responded to the extent of affecting to nip my mistress's little right ear.

This was enough for the impulsive Consuelo. She ran hastily into the house, and in a few moments reappeared in a bewitching riding skirt gathered round her waist. In vain Enriquez and myself joined in earnest entreaty; the horse was hardly broken for even a man's riding yet; the saints alone could tell what the nervous creature might do with a woman's skirt flapping at her side! We begged for delay, for reflection, for at least time to change the saddle but with no avail. Consuelo was determined, indignant, distressingly reproachful! Ah, well! If Don Pancho (an ingenious diminutive of my Christian name) valued his horse so highly—if he were jealous of the evident devotion of the animal to herself, he would—But here I succumbed! And then I had the felicity of holding that little foot for one brief moment in the hollow of my hand, of readjusting the skirt as she threw her knee over the saddle horn, of clasping her tightly only half in fear as I surrendered the reins to her grasp. And to tell the truth, as Enriquez and I fell back, although I had insisted upon still keeping hold of the end of the riata, it was a picture to admire. The petite figure of the young girl, and the graceful folds of her skirt, admirably harmonized with Chu Chu's lithe contour, and as the mare arched her slim neck and raised her slender head under the pressure of the reins, it was so like the lifted velvet-capped toreador crest of Consuelo herself that they seemed of one race.

"I would not that you should hold the riata," said Consuelo, petulantly.

I hesitated. Chu Chu looked, certainly, very amiable. I let go. She began to amble towards the gate, not mincingly as before, but with a freer and fuller stride. In spite of the incongruous saddle, the young girl's seat was admirable. As they neared the gate she cast a single mischievous glance at me, jerked at the rein, and Chu Chu sprang into the road at a rapid canter. I watched them fearfully and breathlessly, until at the end of the lane I saw Consuelo rein in slightly, wheel easily, and come flying back. There was no doubt about it; the horse was under perfect control. Her second subjugation was complete and final.

Overjoyed and bewildered, I overwhelmed them with congratulations; Enriquez alone retaining the usual brotherly attitude of criticism and a superior toleration of a lover's enthusiasm. I ventured to hint to Consuelo (in what I believed was a safe whisper) that Chu Chu only showed my own feelings towards her.

"Without doubt," responded Enriquez, gravely. "She have of herself assist you to climb to the tree to pull to yourself the berry for my sister." But I felt Consuelo's little hand return my pressure, and I forgave and even pitied him.

From that day forward Chu Chu and Consuelo were not only firm friends but daily companions. In my devotion I would have presented the horse to the young girl, but with flattering delicacy she preferred to call it mine.

"I shall ride it for you, Pancho," she said. "I shall feel," she continued, with exalted although somewhat vague poetry, "that it is of *you*. You love the beast—it is therefore of a necessity *you*, my Pancho! It is *your* soul I shall ride like the wings of the wind—your love in this beast shall be my only cavalier forever."

I would have preferred something whose vicarious qualities were less uncertain than I still felt Chu Chu's to be, but I kissed the girl's hand submissively. It was only when I attempted to accompany her in the flesh, on another horse, that I felt the full truth of my instinctive fears. Chu Chu would not permit anyone to approach her mistress's side. My mounted presence revived in her all her old blind astonishment and disbelief in my existence; she would start suddenly, face about, and back away from me in utter amazement, as if I had been only recently created, or with an affected modesty as if I had been just guilty of some grave indecorum towards her sex which she really could not stand. The frequency of these exhibitions in the public highway were not only distressing to me as a simple escort, but as it had the effect on the casual spectators of making Consuelo seem to participate in Chu Chu's objections, I felt that, as a lover, it could not be borne. Any attempt to coerce Chu Chu ended in her running away. And my frantic pursuit of her was open to equal misconstruction.

"Go it, miss, the little dude is gainin' on you!" shouted by a drunken teamster to the frightened Consuelo, once checked me in mid-career. Even the dear girl herself saw the uselessness of my real presence, and after a while was content to ride with "my soul."

Notwithstanding this, I am not ashamed to say that it was my custom, whenever she rode out, to keep a slinking and distant surveillance of Chu Chu on another horse, until she had fairly settled down to her pace. A little nod of Consuelo's round black-and-red toreador hat, or a kiss tossed from her riding whip was reward enough!

I remember a pleasant afternoon when I was thus awaiting her in the outskirts of the village. The eternal smile of the Californian summer had begun to waver and grow less fixed; dust lay thick on leaf and blade; the dry hills were clothed in russet leather; the trade winds were shifting to the south with an ominous warm humidity. A few days longer and the rains would be here.

It so chanced that this afternoon my seclusion on the roadside was accidentally invaded by a village belle—a Western young lady somewhat older than myself and of a flirtatious reputation. As she persistently, and—as I now have reason to believe—mischievously lingered, I had only a passing glimpse of Consuelo riding past at an unaccustomed speed which surprised me at the moment. But as I reasoned later that she was only trying to avoid a merely formal meeting, I thought no more about it.

It was not until I called at the house to fetch Chu Chu at the usual hour and found that Consuelo had not yet returned that a recollection of Chu Chu's furious pace again troubled me. An hour passed—it was getting towards sunset but there were no signs of Chu Chu nor her mistress. I became seriously alarmed. I did not care to reveal my fears to the family, for I felt myself responsible for Chu Chu. At last I desperately saddled my horse and galloped off in the direction she had taken. It was the road to Rosario, and the *hacienda* of one of her relations, where she sometimes halted.

The road was a very unfrequented one, twisting like a mountain river; indeed, it was the bed of an old watercourse, between brown hills of wild oats, and debouching at last into a broad blue lake-like expanse of alfalfa meadows. In vain I strained my eyes over the monotonous level; nothing appeared to rise above or move across it. In the faint hope that she might have lingered at the *hacienda*, I was spurring on again, when I heard a slight splashing on my left. I looked around. A broad patch of fresher-colored herbage and a cluster of dwarfed alders indicated a hidden spring. I cautiously approached its quaggy edges, when I was shocked by what appeared to be a sudden vision! Mid-leg deep in the center of a greenish pool stood Chu Chu! But without a strap or buckle of harness upon her—as naked as when she was foaled.

For a moment I could only stare at her in bewildered terror. Far from recognizing me, she seemed to be absorbed in a nymph-like contemplation of her own graces in the pool. Then I called "Consuelo!" and galloped frantically around the spring. But there was no response, nor was there anything to be seen but the all-unconscious Chu Chu. The pool, thank Heaven, was not deep enough to have drowned anyone; there were no signs of a struggle on its quaggy edges. The horse might have come from a distance! I galloped on, still calling. A few hundred yards farther I detected the vivid glow of Chu Chu's scarlet saddle blanket in the brush near the trail. My heart leaped—I was on the track. I called again; this time a faint; reply, in accents I knew too well, came from the field beside me.

Consuelo was there, reclining beside a manzanita bush which screened her from the road, in what struck me, even at that supreme moment, as a judicious and picturesquely selected couch of scented Indian grass and dry tussocks. The velvet hat with its balls of scarlet plush was laid carefully aside; her lovely blue-black hair retained its tight coils undishevelled; her eyes were luminous and tender. Shocked as I was at her apparent helplessness, I remember being impressed with the fact that it gave so little indication of violent usage or disaster.

I threw myself frantically on the ground beside her. "You are hurt, Consita! For Heaven's sake! What has happened?"

She pushed my hat back with her little hand and tumbled my hair gently. "Nothing. *You* are here, Pancho—it is enough! What shall come after this—when I am perhaps gone among the grave—make nothing! *You* are here I am happy. For a little, perhaps—not much."

"But," I went on, desperately, "was it an accident? Were you thrown? Was it Chu Chu?"—for somehow, in spite of her languid posture and voice, I could not, even in my fears, believe her seriously hurt.

"Beat not the poor beast, Pancho. It is not from *her* comes this thing. She have make nothing—believe me! I have come upon your assignation with Miss Smith! I make but to pass you—to fly—to never come back! I have say to Chu Chu, "Fly!" We fly many miles. Sometimes together, sometimes not so much! Sometimes in the saddle, sometimes on the neck. Many things remain in the road; at the end, I myself remain! I have say, 'Courage, Pancho will come!' Then I say, 'No, he is talk with Miss Smith!' I remember not more. I have creep here on the hands. It is finish!"

I looked at her distractedly. She smiled tenderly and slightly smoothed down and rearranged a fold of her dress to cover her delicate little boot.

"But," I protested, "you are not much hurt, dearest. You have broken no bones. Perhaps," I added, looking at the boot, "only a slight sprain. Let me carry you to my horse; I will walk beside you home. Do, dearest Consita!"

She turned her lovely eyes towards me sadly. "You comprehend not, my poor Pancho! It is not of the foot, the ankle, the arm, or the head that I can say, 'she is broke!' I would it were even so. But"—she lifted her sweet lashes slowly—"I have derange my inside. It is an affair of my family. My grandfather have once tumble over the bull at a rodeo. He speak no more; he is dead. For why? He has derange his inside. Believe me, it is of the family. You comprehend? The Saltellos are not as the other peoples for this. When I am gone, you will bring to me the berry to grow upon my tomb, Pancho, the berry you have picked for me. The little flower will come too, the little star will arrive, but Consuelo, who loves you, she will come not more! When you are happy and talk in the road to the Smith, you will not think of me. You will not see my eyes, Pancho; this little grass"—she ran her plump little fingers through a tussock—"will hide them; and the small animals in the black coats that live here will have much sorrow but you will not. It is better so! My father will not that I, a Catholique, should marry into a camp-meeting, and live in a tent, and make howl like the coyote." (It was one of Consuelo's bewildering beliefs that there was only one form of dissent—Methodism!) "He will not that I should marry a man who possesses not the many horses, ox, and cow, like him. But I care not. *You* are my only religion, Pancho! I have enough of the horse, and ox, and cow when *you* are with me! Kiss me, Pancho. Perhaps it is for the last time—the finish! Who knows?"

There were tears in her lovely eyes; I felt that my own were growing dim; the sun was sinking over the dreary plain to the slow rising of the wind; an infinite loneliness had fallen upon us, and yet I was miserably conscious of some dreadful unreality in it all. A desire to laugh, which I felt must be hysterical, was creeping over me; I dared not speak. But her dear head was on my shoulder, and the situation was not unpleasant.

Nevertheless, something must be done! This was the more difficult as it was by no means clear what had already been done. Even while I supported her drooping figure I was straining my eyes across her shoulder for succor of some kind. Suddenly the figure of a rapid rider appeared upon the road. It seemed familiar. I looked again it was the blessed Enriquez! A sense of deep relief came over me. I loved Consuelo; but never before had lover ever hailed the irruption of one of his beloved's family with such complacency.

"You are safe, dearest; it is Enriquez."

I thought she received the information coldly. Suddenly she turned upon me her eyes, now bright and glittering. "Swear to me at the instant, Pancho, that you will not again look upon Miss Smith, even for once."

I was simple and literal. Miss Smith was my nearest neighbor, and, unless I was stricken with blindness, compliance was impossible. I hesitated but swore.

"Enough—you have hesitate—I will no more." She rose to her feet with grave deliberation.

For an instant, with the recollection of the delicate internal organization of the Saltellos on my mind, I was in agony lest she should totter and fall, even then, yielding up her gentle spirit on the spot. But when I looked again she had a hairpin between her white teeth, and was carefully adjusting her toreador hat. And beside us was Enriquez cheerful, alert, voluble, and undaunted.

"Eureka! I have found! We are all here! It is a little public—eh! A little too much of a front seat for a *tête-à-tête*, my young friends," he said, glancing at the remains of Consuelo's bower, "but for the accounting of taste there is none. What will you? The meat of the one man shall envenom the meat of the other. But," (in a whisper to me) "as to this horse—this Chu Chu, which I have just pass—why is she undress? Surely you would not make an exposition of her to the traveler to suspect! And if not, why so?"

I tried to explain, looking at Consuelo, that Chu Chu had run away, that Consuelo had met with a terrible accident, had been thrown, and I feared had suffered serious internal injury. But to my embarrassment, Consuelo maintained a half scornful silence, and an inconsistent freshness of healthful indifference, as Enriquez approached her with an engaging smile.

"Ah, yes, she have the headache and the molligrubs. She will sit on the damp stone when the gentle dew is falling. I comprehend. Meet me in the lane when the clock strike nine! But," in a lower voice, "of this undress horse I comprehend nothing! Look you—it is sad and strange."

He went off to fetch Chu Chu, leaving me and Consuelo alone. I do not think I ever felt so utterly abject and bewildered before in my life. Without knowing why, I was miserably conscious of having in some way offended the girl for whom I believed I would have given my life, and I had made her and myself ridiculous in the eyes of her brother. I had again failed in my slower Western nature to understand her high romantic Spanish soul. Meantime she was smoothing out her riding habit, and looking as fresh and pretty as when she first left her house.

"Consita," I said, hesitatingly, "you are not angry with me?"

"Angry?" she repeated haughtily, without looking at me. "Oh, no! Of a possibility it is Miss Smith who is angry that I have interrupt her *tête-à-tête* with you, and have send here my brother to make the same with me."

"But," I said, eagerly, "Miss Smith does not even know Enriquez!"

Consuelo turned on me a glance of unutterable significance. "Ah!" she said, darkly, "you *think!*"

Indeed I *knew*. But here I believe I understood Consuelo and was relieved. I even ventured to say gently, "And are you better?"

She drew herself up to her full height, which was not much. "Of my health, what is it? A nothing. Yes! Of my soul, let us not speak."

Nevertheless, when Enriquez appeared with Chu Chu she ran towards her with outstretched arms. Chu Chu protruded about six inches of upper lip in response—apparently under the impression, which I could quite understand, that her mistress was edible. And, I may have been mistaken, but their beautiful eyes met in an absolute and distinct glance of intelligence!

During the home journey Consuelo recovered her spirits, and parted from me with a magnanimous and forgiving pressure of the hand. I do not know what explanation of Chu Chu's original escapade was given to Enriquez and the rest of the family; the inscrutable forgiveness extended to me by Consuelo precluded any further inquiry on my part. I was willing to leave it a secret between her and Chu Chu. But, strange to say, it seemed to complete our own understanding and precipitated, not only our lovemaking, but the final catastrophe which culminated that romance. For we had resolved to elope. I do not know that this heroic remedy was absolutely necessary from the attitude of either Consuelo's family or my own; I am inclined to think we preferred it, because it involved no previous explanation or advice. Need I say that our confidant and firm ally was Consuelo's brother—the alert, the linguistic, the ever-happy, ever-ready Enriquez! It was understood that his presence would not only give a certain mature respectability to our performance but I do not think we would have contemplated this step without it. During one of our riding excursions we were to secure the services of a Methodist minister in the adjoining county, and later, that of the Mission Padre—when the secret was out.

"I will give her away," said Enriquez confidently. "It will on the instant propitiate the old shadbelly who shall perform the affair, and withhold his jaw. A little chin-music from your uncle Harry shall finish it! Remain tranquil, and forget not a ring! One does not always, in the agony and dissatisfaction of the moment, a ring remember. I shall bring two in the pocket of my dress."

If I did not entirely participate in this roseate view, it may have been because Enriquez, although a few years my senior, was much younger-looking, and with his demure devilry of eye, and his upper lip close shaven for this occasion, he suggested a depraved acolyte rather than a responsible member of a family. Consuelo had also confided to me that her father—possibly owing to some rumors of our previous escapade—had forbidden any further excursions with me alone. The innocent man did not know that Chu Chu had forbidden it also, and that even on this momentous occasion both Enriquez and myself were obliged to ride in opposite fields like out-flankers. But we nevertheless felt the full guilt of disobedience added to our desperate enterprise.

Meanwhile, although pressed for time, and subject to discovery at any moment, I managed at certain points of the road to dismount and walk beside Chu Chu (who did not seem to recognize me on foot), holding Consuelo's hand in my own, with the discreet Enriquez leading my horse in the distant field. I retain a very vivid picture of that walk—the ascent of a gentle slope towards a prospect as yet unknown, but full of glorious possibilities; the tender dropping light of an autumn sky, slightly filmed with the promise of the future rains, like foreshadowed tears; and the half-frightened, half-serious talk into which Consuelo and I had insensibly fallen.

And then, I don't know how it happened, but as we reached the summit Chu Chu suddenly reared, wheeled, and the next moment was flying back along the road we had just traveled, at the top of her speed! It might have been that, after her abstracted fashion, she only at that moment detected my presence, but so sudden and complete was her evolution that before I could regain my horse from the astonished Enriquez she was already a quarter of a mile on the homeward stretch, with the frantic Consuelo pulling hopelessly at the bridle.

We started in pursuit. But a horrible despair seized us. To attempt to overtake her, to even follow at the same rate of speed, would not only excite Chu Chu, but endanger Consuelo's life. There was absolutely no help for it—nothing could be done. The mare had taken her determined, long, continuous stride, the road was a straight, steady descent all the way back to the village, Chu Chu had the bit between her teeth, and there was no prospect of swerving her. We could only follow hopelessly, idiotically, furiously, until Chu Chu dashed triumphantly into the Saltellos' courtyard, carrying the half-fainting Consuelo back to the arms of her assembled and astonished family.

It was our last ride together. It was the last I ever saw of Consuelo before her transfer to the safe seclusion of a convent in Southern California. It was the last I ever saw of Chu Chu, who in the confusion of that rencontre was overlooked in her half-loosed harness, and allowed to escape through the back gate to the fields. Months afterwards it was said that she had been identified among a band of wild horses in the Coast Range, as a strange and beautiful creature who had escaped the brand of the rodeo and had become a myth.

There was another legend that she had been seen, sleek, fat, and gorgeously caparisoned, issuing from the gateway of the Rosario, before a lumbering Spanish cabriole in which a short, stout matron was seated but I will have none of it. For there are days when she still lives, and I can see her plainly still climbing the gentle slope towards the summit, with Consuelo on her back, and myself at her side, pressing eagerly forward towards the illimitable prospect that opens in the distance.

7

A CHESTNUT PONY

BY S. CARLETON JONES

Susan Morrow Jones was an enigma. Her novels and short stories appeared under so many pseudonyms, including a masculine-sounding version of her married name, that her career remains difficult to trace. The pen names carefully hid the fact that her subjects were highly unsuitable for a society woman from Nova Scotia during the first decades of the twentieth century. Jones wrote of divorce, a scandalous topic for a woman of her time and place. She wrote of the West, to her a region of crime and menace inhabited by rough and dangerous men.

Out of Drowning Valley, *published under the name of S. Carleton Jones, is filled with violence and peril, greed and longing. In chapter 12 there also appears a beautiful chestnut pony who holds the key to a mystery.*

Charles Edgerley Scarlett and his companion Billy Halliday have discovered the legendary gold deposits of Drowning Valley, knowing they must work fast before the spring rain causes a deadly river rise. There's a good reason for the valley's name.

Scarlett pays a brief visit to the mining town of Janesville to sell the first of his newly acquired nuggets, carefully telling the people in town that they came from a well-known and nearly played-out site named Tabeak. But Scarlett attracts the attention of three old enemies: a bandit named Eldon, a French-Canadian adventurer known as Sabarin, and a thief named Inkster. They follow him back to the caves of Drowning Valley.

The criminals are convinced that Scarlett has discovered a significant gold deposit and they will stop at nothing to get to it. Scarlett's return trip to Drowning Valley is hampered by the sudden illness of the chestnut pack pony he had acquired in town. He knows that he should simply leave the pony to die, or shoot it to put it out of its misery. But it's a beautiful pony and he finds himself unable to destroy it. At a roadhouse between the town and Drowning Valley, Scarlett meets a blond woman named Athol who agrees to care for the chestnut pony, hiding him from anybody who comes along asking questions.

Scarlett correctly assumes his pursuers will make a wrong turn and he reaches Drowning Valley safely, reuniting with Halliday. But, as they prepare to resume digging, they hear what sounds like fighting deep in the caves at their site. It must, Halliday thinks, be members of the Eldon gang who have found another entrance to the treacherous caves of Drowning Valley.

But as it happened, Halliday, climbing and sweating after Scarlett in the darkness of Drowning Valley caves, was wrong. If any one were fighting in the depths of that tortuous place, it was not Eldon, nor any of his gang.

At the precise moment Inkster and the Frenchman sat in the one tent of their outfit, dead beat from an exhausting—and useless—

search of the road to Tabeak. Scarlett's guess about their overshooting the turn into the pasture had been right; they had not even glanced at so simple and open a place as they thundered past it to Tabeak. Coming back in the early morning their luck had been no better, and they sat now in sullen silence—Inkster in a black rage, and Sabarin subdued to cringing.

Hope was dead in both of them. There was not likely to be another chance to track Scarlett to his gold, and, on Inkster's part, the Frenchman's story of having seen him at the roadhouse seemed apparently a plain lie. Yet both men, hearing the tramp of a leg-weary horse through the willows, pricked their ears. It could only be Eldon coming back from Janesville, and it was not Eldon's way to return empty-handed when he went out for news. But neither his face nor his manner invited inquiry.

For a moment he sat motionless in his saddle in the natural clearing where his camp was set, and his string of horses hobbled, taking in the faces of the two men awaiting him. Then he swung himself down.

"I needn't ask what luck you've had," he remarked contemptuously. "So you didn't even see Scarlett!"

"No," Inkster snarled, "nor smell him, either. It's my opinion that he was never here. We've been all the way to Tabeak, and he hadn't been there, either; and, what's more, there wasn't a track leading off the road anywhere between here and there that he could have gone off by."

"Not that a grown man could find!" Eldon threw his saddle on the ground and let his horse go loose, without so much as a glance at its mired legs and spurred sides. "I'll send a child next time."

"You'd better preach about your own luck before you take to sneering," retorted Inkster darkly. "P'r'aps you shook hands with Scarlett in Janesville!"

"He hadn't been there," answered Eldon slowly.

"How d'ye know?"

Eldon made no reply but a scowl. Janesville had been interested neither in him, nor his inquiries for a friend named Scarlett. The whole town had gone mad over the rumor of some gold brought in by a man from Tabeak, and every soul in it who had the use of his legs was getting ready to go over there. None of them had ever seen such gold. Harris's assayer had been given more drinks than any one man had a use for, so long as it pleased him to hold forth on its purity, its color, and its worth.

No one seemed to have seen or noticed the man who had brought it in. He had sold his gold, bought a bay and a chestnut pack pony, and departed to Tabeak without so much as mentioning his claim there: it was the assayer who had done that. The man himself he, too, did not happen to have seen, but Janesville cared little for the man. It was gold like his its citizens wanted, and they talked of nothing else.

Eldon, in the back of the hotel bar, listened with a curious, growing excitement. He knew Tabeak—lock, stock, and barrel—and the gold that was setting Janesville agog had never come out of it. There was but one place in the country where such gold could have been found, and that was Drowning Valley. It was just possible, taking the French-man's story for truth, that the strange man who had been in Janesville was Scarlett; and that he had crept, under Eldon's very nose in the dark, back to whence he came—which was certainly not Tabeak. Yet the two pack ponies bought in Janesville were against it.

Sabarin had sworn to seeing Scarlett that very morning, but he had also sworn he was riding a buckskin horse. The stories did not tally, yet a biting hope gnawed at Eldon. He turned abruptly from the assayer and the citizens of Janesville, and repaired to the bank, with a face that was calm enough if his nostrils had not quivered.

The bank must know if Scarlett had been in Janesville. No one knew better than Eldon that Scarlett and Halliday had been down to their last six cents when they left Blaze Creek, and, if Scarlett had been the strange man who paid in money for two pack ponies, he must have gone to the bank to do it. But at the bank Eldon got his first check.

The almost forgotten name of Edgerley had served Scarlett better there than he knew. To Eldon's inquiry, as to a friend named Scarlett, the teller merely jerked his head towards the ledger keeper, who snapped that he knew no such person. Mr. Harris, happening to stand in the door of his own office, had cared neither for the too-guileless countenance of Mr. Eldon nor for the way in which he was inspecting the physical geography of the bank. He announced stiffly that no one named Scarlett was a customer of his, nor had sold him any gold; and that if his questioner had any business of his own he could state what it was.

But Eldon had none, except to turn and go out. And to his further inquiries round a preoccupied Janesville as to a man having ridden a buckskin out of it the day before, he got nothing but profane denials. No such man or no such horse had been seen, and the only person who had left that center had been the Tabeak man with his recently acquired pack ponies.

Eldon had cursed and spurred all the way home. For all that he had discovered the Tabeak man might be real, and the Frenchman's story of Scarlett a lie, and the latter seemed the more likely.

"Well," said Inkster, driven desperate by his silence, "I suppose you know if Scarlett was there or he wasn't! Get it out."

Eldon turned on him and the Frenchman with the fury he had been obliged to repress all day. "The United Bank staff told me he hadn't been there, and nobody had even seen a man on a buckskin. By heaven, Sabarin," he cried thickly, "if you've brought me here all the way from Blaze Creek with a lie, and you've lied again about having seen Scarlett yesterday morning, I'll put a bullet through your head!" And he meant it: the Janesville road would tell no tales.

Sabarin sprang to his feet, but Eldon's hard fist sent him down again. "I tell no lies," he screeched from the ground. "I did see Scarlett! If he doesn't go to Janesville, is that my fault? He was *here*, at the roadhouse!"

"Riding a buckskin, I suppose?" Eldon sneered into the glaring, terrified eyes, and Ba'tiste Sabarin knew suddenly that death stood at his elbow. Terror lent him coherence and instinct told him to make time.

"Can I help it that you miss him?" he asked hoarsely. "I track Scarlett into the lower end of Drowning Valley like you say," summing up his case like a man tried for his life, "I hear him arrange with that Indian how he'd come out at this end, between Tabeak and Janesville. I see him ride out of that roadhouse yard with my own eyes yesterday morning. That accursed young cat of a girl over there locked me up till the road was tramped all over the tracks of him and his pack pony, but . . ."

"His what?" snapped Eldon. "You didn't say he'd pack ponies!" His hand came out of his hip pocket. "What were they like?"

"There was only one," answered the Frenchman sullenly. "It was a bay."

Eldon's strong nerves jerked incontinently through his body. One of the ponies sold at Janesville had been a bay, the other a chestnut with two white legs. If he could find the pack ponies, he had found Scarlett in the man all Janesville had thought came from Tabeak.

"His other horse?" he roared.

"I told you—it was a buckskin."

"Get out what's in your head, Eldon," Inkster cut in impatiently. But when he heard it his face fell.

"P'r'aps Sabarin's Ethel-girl lent him the buckskin," he observed doubtfully.

The Frenchman would have lied, but he did not dare. "She had no buckskin," he said.

Eldon cut him off with an uplifted finger. "Was it that girl you meant when you said some one had tramped up all the road?" he asked.

"There was nobody else to do it! Nobody passed. She knew Scarlett. He and she stood whispering—whispering—yesterday morning," the Frenchman answered viciously.

Eldon, for a long minute, sat absolutely still. "I met a girl on the road just now," he said at last, "kind of yellow about the head, and talking to an old vegetable on a saddle that was held together with packthread. She looked at me as if I were dirt. Was that your Ethel-girl?"

"Yes. She talked to the uncle come back from Tabeak. We passed them on the road."

"So that's her"—Eldon gave a sudden jerking laugh—"that's her! And she was whispering to Scarlett. By heaven," irrelevantly, "she had eyes!"

Inkster cast down the pipe he was smoking, in a sudden access of rage. "There you go," he said bitterly, "running off on girls when we've come all the way from Blaze Creek for nothing! There's not one thing to say that Scarlett was the man who took that gold to Janesville; bay ponies are as common as dirt! Whether Ba'tiste's lied about seeing him here or not doesn't matter, either, as far as we're concerned. What does is that we're not a foot nearer the gold he's stealing—and that's what I'm after if you're not! I don't care a darn for something that happened 'way back when you were colts, and fool revenges on Scarlett. I want to get after his mine!"

Eldon laughed in his face. "He and his mine are in Drowning Valley," he said, "and *if* he was the man that girl I saw was whispering to, we've got both of them!"

"I don't see how we've got them," growled Inkster. "I guess for all we'll ever see of Scarlett and his gold—if it *was* Scarlett here and in Janesville, and not some fool from Tabeak—we may as well go home. Where are you going?" he added sharply. For Eldon had risen and was turning away.

"Visiting," returned the other sententiously. "You sit here till I come back, and if Sabarin's got any intention of leaving you snick a bullet through him. He's seeing this thing through till I find out if he's lied, and make up *my* mind," with a sneer, "to go home! If the trail's false, it's false; but, if it isn't, I bet I'm on Scarlett's heels."

He grinned enigmatically in Inkster's stupid face, and disappeared in the willows that hid his camp from the Janesville road. The Frenchman's "Ethel-girl" had acquired a new significance for him since he had seen her.

"Kind of yellow about the head" he had called her, when, in sober truth, the molten gold of her hair in the sun had burned into his senses; the cold eyes she had lifted for one moment to his started the fierce passion that stood for attraction with him. He was a man to whom every girl was fair game, till he had tired of her, a man, too, who had usually only to hold up his finger to any woman of the kind he was wont to meet. Beauty like the "Ethel-girl's"—at a roadhouse—would probably not even require that lifted finger. It was not the first time Eldon had used a girl to track a man, yet he walked slowly toward the roadhouse, and thought hard.

This girl was his only chance, of course, of finding out whether the man who had left her house in the red dawn had or had not been

Scarlett; but, though to make love to her might be the quickest way to discover it, there might be—others!

"If Scarlett hadn't been burned to a char by a woman he'd be back to see this kind of a girl," he thought coarsely, "but Scarlett won't even remember her. If it's another man, he'll"—and he swore over it—"come back! I would, if she'd whispered to me. But I guess I won't have to wait long to find out which it was—from a roadhouse girl!"

His grin and his thoughtful progress stopped dead. From the road-house yard had come the crack of a rifle. It was so unexpected, and Mr. Eldon knew so little about the inhabitants that he could not be blamed for thinking it might have a personal significance. He took cover abruptly behind a gatepost, peered round it, and laughed sheepishly.

In the yard, with their backs toward him, stood a tall, slack-jointed man apparently trying a new rifle, and beside him was the "Ethel-girl"! Eldon heard her laugh as Welsh fired again at something, and missed. Then he stepped casually forward and hailed the shooter. He explained glibly that he and a friend were camping across the road, resting up a string of horses for Janesville, and that they were out of salt.

Jim Welsh turned with shy cordiality. Drunk or sober, and over half his time he was the former, his fellow creatures were welcome to him, even such as chose to camp instead of patronizing his roadhouse. Not that the latter thought occurred to him; keeping a roadhouse at all was too much of an accident to be taken seriously. It had been just a backwoods farm till the Janesville road cut past it, and stray travelers, wishing to stay there, stayed.

"Glad to see you," he said simply. He had been an educated man when first he buried himself in the wilderness, and when he was not drinking he was one still. "You can have all the salt you want. Athol—my niece here—has plenty."

Athol! The unusual name struck Eldon oddly: to have found her a real "Ethel-girl" would have suited him better. But as she turned he forgot the trifle of her name. Scarlett had merely realized that she was beautiful. Eldon took in her every point like a slave dealer.

Her hair that was pure gold threaded with copper, her apricot-flushed skin, her arrow-straight figure, and her eyes, which were blue, set in black lashes. They met his—and checked them. For their glance was hard as a man's and far more searching. Eldon realized with a shock that, however she came there, she was no roadhouse girl. He turned to Welsh with an effort.

"New gun?" he drawled, glancing at the rifle.

"Yes! Throws a trifle high. Want to try it?"

Eldon could shoot, and he knew it. An angry impulse made him want the girl who had turned away from him with that one hard look to know it, too. Half an old bottle glittered in the sun, not too far off. Eldon took up Welsh's rifle and fired the instant it touched his shoulder. The bottle shivered, and Welsh said something civil, but without the astonishment at his quickness and apparent lack of aim to which Eldon was used.

"Your turn next, Athol," he added to the girl; and it struck Eldon oddly that, so far, she had never said a word.

"Oh, why?" she returned carelessly. "But if you like," as Welsh's face fell, "I'll write my name on the fence."

It was fifty yards further off than Eldon's bottle, and he smiled incredulously as she lifted the rifle—but the smile died. He was quick as men go—but he had never imagined such quickness as this girl's. Five shots had rung out almost as one, and in the fence-rail stood an "A," pierced with the five bullets. Looking at her shooting, Eldon liked still less her silence when she had put down the rifle.

"It's no sort of distance for her," said Welsh with proud apology. "But there's no chance of mistake in Athol's shooting."

Eldon needed no telling. He was too sore at having been beaten by a girl. Oddly enough, it sowed in his mind the first seeds of a curious hatred for her that was to crush out all thought of her beauty. He stood wishing viciously that he could pick her up bodily and shake the truth out of her as to whether or not Sabarin's stranger had been Scarlett when he saw her start past him, just as a horse might start under the sudden cut of a whip.

With Welsh's coming she had had no chance to keep the stable key and Welsh, going unnoticed behind her and Eldon, had flung the stable door wide open.

"The salt's in the house, Uncle Jim," she cried sharply, "if Mr. Eldon wants salt!"

As she spoke she had pushed the door shut, and in a breath was leaning against it, but it was too late. Inside the stable, clear in the hot light, Eldon had seen a chestnut pony, white on two legs from the hock down—the pony which had been bought in Janesville! It was no sham miner from Tabeak who had left it here, but Scarlett: and the girl with the hard eyes knew it.

For there had been one—just one—half-second when Athol's look had met his with fear, and—what was worse—comprehension. She had gripped herself to stolidity almost instantly, but the mischief was done. Eldon sucked in both cheeks between his strong teeth before he spoke. He had taken Jim Welsh in from head to heels, and Jim Welsh's testimony should clinch what his niece's face had betrayed.

"I just need a little man's salt, not horse's," he said mildly. "That chestnut yours, Mr. Welsh?"

"No, it's a stranger," returned Welsh carelessly. He had heard nothing of Scarlett beyond the bare fact of an unknown man having stayed a night and was not interested. "A man left it here because it was sick. He's coming back for it shortly."

"Oh!" The hand that held Eldon's cigarette jerked infinitesimally. "One of the Tabeak rush, I suppose! I hear there's been a strike there."

"Tabeak rush!" Welsh stared. "There's no rush in Tabeak," he exclaimed, "it's the deadest place I ever saw! I've just been there, and there hasn't been a man made a dollar a day out of a claim. Don't let anybody tell you differently, because it isn't so."

Eldon had hoped it, if he had not dared to believe it. He had to keep his eyes on the ground to hide the triumph in them. Welsh's niece might be a high and mighty, contemptuous lady, but Scarlett had been the man who had left the pony, and he knew it, if Welsh did not. And Scarlett, who would never come back for a woman, would come back twice over for a horse.

It seemed to Mr. Eldon that even Inkster would not go home just yet, not without the Drowning Valley gold, and that he had made no unfounded boast himself when he announced his fingers were already on Red Scarlett. He looked up so suddenly that for the second time he caught Athol Gray with unguarded eyes full on his face—and for once Eldon stood taken aback, with a new light cast on his calculations.

"It isn't the horse Scarlett's coming back for," he thought, and it was pure intuition; "*it's the girl.*"

Then and there he gave up all intention of making love to her. Even if he had not really taken a dislike to her, she was not the kind who would listen to his speeches, and besides, the sight of the pack pony had put something else into his head. All he had to do now to get Scarlett would be to stay beside it and the girl, and wait till he came.

But to the assortment of weapons that already adorned his body Mr. Eldon added that night, and thoughtfully, a rawhide rope—after he had tried a few experiments with it on Sabarin, whom, as was well known except by Scarlett, no rope could hold.

8

WILDFIRE

BY ZANE GREY

For a man who became the most famous of the western writers, the Ohio-born Zane Grey began life with an improbable name and in unlikely circumstances. His parents named him Pearl Zane Gray. He dropped the "Pearl," changed the spelling of his surname, and shed his career as a dentist as he began to sell stories to outdoor and hunting magazines.

The turning point of Grey's professional life came in 1905 when he traveled to California on his honeymoon. It was the first of many trips out West and provided him with his first look at a life and landscape that he had been only able to imagine. Before he was finished, Zane Grey produced fifty-six western novels, making him the first million-aire author in American publishing history.

Although his westerns were filled with menacing villains and worthy heroes, most also included a charming heroine. A romance was often at the heart of a Zane Grey novel. Almost all included horses, usually as secondary characters. Sometimes a horse was at the heart of the story, as in Wildfire.

Lucy Bostil is the eighteen-year-old daughter of John Bostil, a rancher who has made himself rich in the wild borderlands of Utah and Arizona. Bostil loves horses almost as much as he loves Lucy, but the enemies he has made over the years threaten both his horses and his daughter.

The rival Creech family hovers nearby, with young Joel Creech hoping for Lucy's attention and his father refusing to part with the one horse in the region that could challenge Bostil's great racer Sage King. Also nearby is a horse thief named Cordts, who hopes to acquire Sage King, legally or otherwise.

Lucy, one of the most competent riders at Bostil's Ford, is out almost every day aboard the best of her father's horses. One day, aboard Sage King, she comes across a beautiful wild stallion struggling against a rope, with cactus tearing his shiny red coat. She soon finds the man who roped him, the injured wild horse hunter Lin Slone. Lucy helps both man and horse.

Over the next several weeks, Lucy returns again and again to help Slone break and train the horse they now call Wildfire. She decides that Wildfire will challenge Sage King in her father's annual race day.

~~~~~~

CHAPTER 7

Bostil slept that night, but his sleep was troubled, and a strange, dreadful roar seemed to run through it, like a mournful wind over a dark desert. He was awakened early by a voice at his window. He listened. There came a rap on the wood.

"Bostil! . . . Bostil!" It was Holley's voice.

Bostil rolled off the bed. He had slept without removing any apparel except his boots.

"Jane, what's got into her?" asked Bostil, appealing to his sister.

"Bostil, she's in fun, of course," declared Aunt Jane. "Still, at that, there's some sense in what she says. Come to your breakfast, now."

Bostil took his seat at the table, glad that he could once more be amiable with his womenfolk. "Lucy, tomorrow'll be the biggest day Bostil's Ford has ever seen," he said.

"It sure will be, Dad. The biggest *surprising* day the Ford ever had," replied Lucy.

"Surprisin'?"

"Yes, Dad."

"Who's goin' to get surprised?"

"Everybody."

Bostil said to himself that he had been used to Lucy's banter, but during his moody spell of days past he had forgotten how to take her or else she was different.

"Brackton tells me you've entered a hoss against the field."

"It's an open race, isn't it?"

"Open as the desert, Lucy," he replied. "What's this hoss Wildfire you've entered?"

"Wouldn't you like to know?" taunted Lucy.

"If he's as good as his name you might be in at the finish. . . . But, Lucy, my dear, talkin' good sense now—you ain't a-goin' to go up on some unbroken mustang in this big race?"

"Dad, I'm going to ride a horse."

"But, Lucy, ain't it a risk you'll be takin'—all for fun?"

"Fun! . . . I'm in dead earnest."

Bostil liked the look of her then. She had paled a little; her eyes blazed; she was intense. His question had brought out her earnestness, and straightway Bostil became thoughtful. If Lucy had been a boy she would have been the greatest rider on the uplands; and even girl as she was, superbly mounted, she would have been dangerous in any race.

"Wal, I ain't afraid of your handlin' of a hoss," he said, soberly. "An' as long as you're in earnest I won't stop you. But, Lucy, no bettin'. I won't let you gamble."

"Not even with you?" she asked.

Bostil stared at the girl. What had gotten into her? "What'll you bet?" he queried, with blunt curiosity.

"Dad, I'll go you a hundred dollars in gold that I finish one—two—three."

Bostil threw back his head to laugh heartily. What a chip of the old block she was. "Child, there's some fast hosses that'll be back of the King. You'd be throwin' money away."

Blue fire shone in his daughter's eyes. She meant business, all right, and Bostil thrilled with pride in her.

"Dad, I'll bet you two hundred, even, that I beat the King!" she flashed.

"Wal, of all the nerve!" ejaculated Bostil. "No, I won't take you up. Reckon I never before turned down an even bet. Understand, Lucy, ridin' in the race is enough for you."

"All right, Dad," replied Lucy, obediently.

At that juncture Bostil suddenly shoved back his plate and turned his face to the open door. "Don't I hear a runnin' hoss?"

Aunt Jane stopped the noise she was making, and Lucy darted to the door. Then Bostil heard the sharp, rhythmic hoofbeats he recognized. They shortened to clatter and pound—then ceased somewhere out in front of the house.

"It's the King with Van up," said Lucy, from the door. "Dad, Van's jumped off—he's coming in . . . he's running. Something has happened. . . . There are other horses coming—riders—Indians."

"A-huh!" grunted Bostil. "Right you are."

"Dad, can't anything be done to help Creech now?" appealed Lucy, going close to her father.

Bostil put his arm around her and felt immeasurably relieved to have the golden head press close to his shoulder.

"Child, we can't fly acrost the river. Now don't you cry about Creech's hosses. They ain't starved yet. It's hard luck. But mebbe it'll turn out so Creech'll lose only the race. An', Lucy, it was a dead sure bet he'd have lost that anyway."

Bostil fondled his daughter a moment, the first time in many a day, and then he turned to his rider at the door. "Van, how's the King?"

"Wild to run, Bostil, just plumb wild. There won't be any hoss with the ghost of a show tomorrow."

Lucy raised her drooping head. "Is *that* so, Van Sickle? . . . Listen here. If you and Sage King don't get more wild running tomorrow than you ever had I'll never ride again!" With this retort Lucy left the room.

Van stared at the door and then at Bostil. "What'd I say, Bostil?" he asked, plaintively. "I'm always rilin' her."

"Cheer up, Van. You didn't say much. Lucy is fiery these days. She's got a hoss somewhere an' she's goin' to ride him in the race. She offered to bet on him—against the King! I've a hunch there's a dark hoss goin' to show up here, Van. So don't underrate Lucy an' her mount, whatever he is. She calls him Wildfire. Ever see him?"

"I sure haven't. Fact is, I haven't seen Lucy for days an' days. As for the hunch you gave, I'll say I was figurin' Lucy for some real race. Bostil, she doesn't *make* a hoss run. He'll run just to please her. An' Lucy's lighter 'n a feather. Why Bostil, if she happened to ride out there on Blue Roan or some other hoss as fast I'd—I'd just wilt."

Bostil uttered a laugh full of pride in his daughter. "Wal, she won't show up on Blue Roan," he replied, with grim gruffness. "That's sure as death. . . . Come on out now. I want a look at the King."

Bostil went into the village. All day long he was so busy with a thousand and one things referred to him, put on him, undertaken by him, that he had no time to think. Back in his mind, however, there was a burden of which he was vaguely conscious all the time. He worked late into the night and slept late the next morning.

Never in his life had Bostil been gloomy or retrospective on the day of a race. In the press of matters he had only a word for Lucy, but that earned a saucy, dauntless look. He was glad when he was able to join the procession of villagers, visitors, and Indians moving out toward the sage.

The racecourse lay at the foot of the slope, and now the gray and purple sage was dotted with more horses and Indians, more moving things and colors, than Bostil had ever seen there before. It was a spectacle that stirred him. Many fires sent up blue columns of smoke from before the hastily built brush huts where the Indians cooked and ate. Blankets shone bright in the sun; burros grazed and brayed; horses whistled piercingly across the slope; Indians lolled before the huts or talked in groups, sitting and lounging on their ponies; down in the valley, here and there, were Indians racing, and others were chasing the wiry mustangs. Beyond this gay and colorful spectacle stretched the valley, merging into the desert marked so strikingly and beautifully by the monuments.

Bostil was among the last to ride down to the high bench that overlooked the home end of the racecourse. He calculated that there were a thousand Indians and whites congregated at that point, which was the best vantage-ground to see the finish of a race. And the occasion

once she slipped out of that skirt she could ride with any rider there. He saw that she had become the center toward which all eyes shifted. It pleased him. She was his, like her mother, and as beautiful and thoroughbred as any rider could wish his daughter.

"Lucy, where's your hoss?" he asked, curiously.

"Never you mind, Dad. I'll be there at the finish," she replied.

"Red's your color for today, then?" he questioned, as he put a big hand on the bright-colored head.

She nodded archly.

"Lucy, I never thought you'd flaunt red in your old Dad's face. Red, when the color of the King is like the sage out yonder. You've gone back on the King."

"No. Dad. I never was for Sage King, else I wouldn't wear red today."

"Child, you sure mean to run in this race—the big one?"

"Sure and certain."

"Wal, the only bitter drop in my cup today will be seein' you get beat. But if you run second I'll give you a present that'll make the purse look sick."

Even the Indian chiefs were smiling. Old Horse, the Navajo, beamed benignly upon this daughter of the friend of the Indians. Silver, his brother chieftain, nodded as if he understood Bostil's pride and regret. Some of the young riders showed their hearts in their eyes. Farlane tried to look mysterious, to pretend he was in Lucy's confidence.

"Lucy, if you are really goin' to race I'll withdraw my hoss so you can win," said Wetherby, gallantly.

Bostil's sonorous laugh rolled down the slope.

"Miss Lucy, I sure hate to run a hoss against yours," said old Cal Blinn. Then Colson, Sticks, Burthwait, the other principals, paid laughing compliments to the bright-haired girl.

Bostil enjoyed this hugely until he caught the strange intensity of regard in the cavernous eye of Cordts. That gave him a shock. Cordts had long wanted this girl as much probably as he wanted Sage King. There were dark and terrible stories that stained the name of Cordts. Bostil regretted his impulse in granting the horse-thief permission to attend the races. Sight of Lucy's fair, sweet face might inflame this Cordts—this Kentuckian who had boasted of his love of horses and women. Behind Cordts hung the little dust-colored Sears, like a coiled snake, ready to strike. Bostil felt stir in him a long-dormant fire—a stealing along his veins, a passion he hated.

"Lucy, go back to the women till you're ready to come out on your hoss," he said. "An' mind you, be careful today!"

He gave her a meaning glance, which she understood perfectly, he saw, and then he turned to start the day's sport.

The Indian races ran in twos and threes, and on up to a number that crowded the racecourse; the betting and yelling and running; the wild and plunging mustangs; the heat and dust and pounding of hoofs; the excited betting; the surprises and defeats and victories; the trial tests of the principals, jealously keeping off to themselves in the sage; the endless moving, colorful procession, gaudy and swift and thrilling—all these Bostil loved tremendously.

But they were as nothing to what they gradually worked up to—the climax—the great race.

It was afternoon when all was ready for this race, and the sage was bright gray in the westering sun. Everybody was resting, waiting. The tense quiet of the riders seemed to settle upon the whole assemblage. Only the thoroughbreds were restless. They quivered and stamped and tossed their small, fine heads. They knew what was going to happen. They wanted to run. Blacks, bays, and whites were the predominating colors, and the horses and mustangs were alike

"A wild stallion!" echoed Bostil. "A-huh! An' she calls him Wildfire. Where'd she get him? . . . Gimme that glass."

But all Bostil could make out was a blur. His eyes were wet. He realized now that his first sight of Lucy on the strange horse had been clear and strong, and it was that which had dimmed his eyes.

"Holley, you use the glass—an' tell us what comes off," said Bostil, as he wiped his eyes with his scarf; he was relieved to find that his sight was clearing. "My God! If I couldn't see this finish!"

Then everybody watched the close, dark mass of horses and riders down the valley. And all waited for Holley to speak. "They're linin' up," began the rider. "Havin' some muss, too, it 'pears. . . . Bostil, that red hoss is raisin' hell! He wants to fight. There! He's up in the air. . . . Boys, he's a devil—a hoss killer like all them wild stallions. He's plungin' at the King—strikin'! There! Lucy's got him down. She's handlin' him. . . . Now they've got the King on the other side. That's better. But Lucy's hoss won't stand. Anyway, it's a runnin' start. . . . Van's got the best position. Foxy Van! . . . He'll be leadin' before the rest know the race's on. . . . Them Indian mustangs are behavin' scandalous. Guess the red stallion scared 'em. Now they're all lined up back of the post. . . . Ah! Gun-smoke! They move. . . . It looks like a go."

Then Holley was silent, strained in watching. So were all the watchers silent. Bostil saw far down the valley, a moving, dark line of horses.

"*They're off! They're off!*" called Holley, thrillingly.

Bostil uttered a deep and booming yell, which rose above the shouts of the men round him and was heard even in the din of Indian cries. Then as quickly as the yells had risen they ceased.

Holley stood up on the rock with leveled glass.

"Mac's dropped the flag. It's a sure go. Now! . . . Van's out there front—inside. The King's got his stride. Boss, the King's stretchin' out! . . . Look! Look! See that red hoss leap! . . . Bostil, he's runnin' down the King! I knowed it. He's like lightnin'. He's pushin' the King over—off the course! See him plunge! Lord! Lucy sticks like a burr. Good, Lucy! Hang on! . . . My Gawd, Bostil, the King's thrown! He's down! . . . He comes up, off the course. The others flash by. . . . Van's out of the race! . . . An', Bostil—an', gentlemen, there ain't anything more to this race than a red hoss!"

Bostil's heart gave a great leap and then seemed to stand still. He was half cold, half hot.

What a horrible, sickening disappointment. Bostil rolled out a cursing query. Holley's answer was short and sharp. The King was out! Bostil raved. He could not see. He could not believe. After all the weeks of preparation, of excitement, of suspense—only this! There was no race. The King was out! The thing did not seem possible. A thousand thoughts flitted through Bostil's mind. Rage, impotent rage, possessed him. He cursed Van, he swore he would kill that red stallion. And someone shook him hard. Someone's incisive words cut into his thick, throbbing ears: "Luck of the game! The King ain't beat! He's only out!"

Then the rider's habit of mind asserted itself and Bostil began to recover. For the King to fall was hard luck. But he had not lost the race! Anguish and pride battled for mastery over him. Even if the King were out it was a Bostil who would win the great race.

"He ain't beat!" muttered Bostil. "It ain't fair! He's run off the track by a wild stallion!"

His dimmed sight grew clear and sharp. And with a gasp he saw the moving, dark line take shape as horses. A bright horse was in the lead. Brighter and larger he grew. Swiftly and more swiftly he came on. The bright color changed to red. Bostil heard Holley calling and Cordts calling—and other voices. But he did not distinguish what was said. The line of horses began to bob, to bunch. The race looked close,

IV

MILITARY
HORSES

before. Once more, returning home, it was the gray colt from whose bridle fluttered the honorable blue ribbon.

But by the time another year had come around County Fairs had begun to seem little things indeed compared with the big national events and interests and the rumors of war that were stirring the country. Stable boys and farm hands, masters and chance guests, talked of little else. If the gray colt were to see more of the world it was likely indeed now to be more than the Lewisburg Fair. Instead of dusty vehicles creaking on their slow way, he might have cantered any day to the meadow bars to look at troops of soldiers riding past, or at an occasional messenger in military garb galloping on in haste.

One day one of these messengers stopped. He was a quartermaster of the Third Regiment of Infantry of the Wise legion, then camped at and near Big Sewell Mountain; and he came in search of a horse of the Greenbrier stock for the use, during the war, of his brother, a major in the same regiment.

The best horses in the stables and meadow were shown him. He considered them all carefully; then he considered the gray colt a little more carefully, put a few questions, stroked him and considered again. Finally, the others were led back by the stable boys. Some gold was counted out by the soldier, and saddle and bridle were put on "Jeff Davis."

As the gray colt and the soldier rode away, as the road turned and the mountains folded in, shutting the home lands from view, they were shutting in at the same time all the treasures of peace, of home meadow and the quiet, dewy mornings and the cool, untroubled evenings. But the gray colt did not look back. His gait was rapid, his head high; he sniffed from side to side in eager contentment. "Jeff Davis" himself was off to the war. If he had been heretofore a companion to peaceful days and stable boys, here was indeed a new outlook.

When the quartermaster drew rein and dismounted, "Jeff Davis" found himself in the midst of a camp. Those about him were soldiers, all of them. Groups of Confederates admired his fine points, his easy gait, and asked where he came from. In time he became known among them by the name of his home county, "Greenbrier." Scarcely a day went by when someone did not have a word of praise or admiration for him.

One autumn day General Lee arrived in camp. The gray colt had never seen the commander, although there had been plenty of talk about him among men and officers. When he did see him he saw a man of gentle but soldierly bearing, who looked at him not critically, as had the quartermaster and the judges at the county fair; not so critically as kindly, and with a sort of gentle comradeship; and who stroked him and said to "Greenbrier's" master: "Major, I shall need that horse before the war is over."

After that they met often. The General always had a kind word to say to "my colt," as he called the proud stepping gray. But this was not to last long as General Lee soon left camp to take up his command in South Carolina. Several months later, however, the Third Regiment was also ordered to that state.

It was the quartermaster who rode the gray colt now, for the major, ill of a fever, had remained in Virginia. One day, near Pocotaligo, General Lee chanced to see the major's horse again. There was the usual greeting and praise. The general's liking for "Greenbrier" was by this time so well known that the quartermaster ventured to offer the colt as a gift. This the commander declined; but if the major would be willing to sell the horse—in that case General Lee would like to use him for a week to become acquainted with his qualities. The following day "Greenbrier" was led to the stables of General Lee.

he had known in '61 were worn and hunger-stricken. The proud ranks were for the most part torn and decimated. The men who cheered now as he passed had faces furrowed with hunger and suffering; many of them staggered from weakness; their clothes were tattered and the feet of many were bare and bleeding. Their cause was already a lost cause. Yet for another winter still the brilliant fight continued. Along the lines of defenses from the Chickahominy, north of Richmond, to Hatcher's Run, south of the Appomattox, "Traveller" was to be seen daily. Heavy odds were closing in. The war was nearing its end. The stricken South could hold her own but little longer. One day the last stand was taken; the last struggle made; the last smoke of battle cleared away. Defense was no longer possible. The cause which had led so many must be abandoned.

The story of Lee's surrender at Appomattox need not be retold. If "Traveller" himself could have told it we should have heard most, no doubt, of the few brief words of farewell which his master spoke to his tattered soldiers; and of how the ragged men crowded, sobbing, to touch their General's hand, or his uniform, or just to lay hands on good old "Traveller."

From that day on there was no more war, but only the memory of war, for the "Confederate Gray." From Appomattox "Traveller" carried his beloved master, now a prisoner of war on parole, to Richmond. As the well-known horse and rider came unexpected through the streets, Southern citizens and Northern soldiers, recognizing them, raised their hats in silent respect or emotion as the two passed by. At East Franklin Street, where General Lee dismounted and made his way to his waiting family, sympathetic crowds gathered around the gray horse who had carried him so well and so long, and some put their arms about "Traveller's" neck and sobbed there and kissed him.

After the war, when General Lee took up his duties at Lexington, "Traveller" was still his master's beloved friend and companion. When work for the day was finished "Traveller" would be brought from the stable and his master would ride in paths now of memory and quietness. Or in the summer "Traveller" would sometimes carry General Lee to the mountains of the White Sulphur in Greenbrier. There the gray horse saw once more his old haunts of quiet and peace; once more he took his way along the very mountain roads where, as a proud young colt, he had in former years returned from the Lewisburg Fair with the blue ribbon, his first honor, fluttering from his bridle knot.

There were honors in plenty for him now. His master often rode him on visits to friends and relatives on the plantations throughout Virginia. Everywhere he was welcomed royally. As war had taught him courage, so peace taught him now the gentler virtues and softer honors of life. He learned to know the loving touch of women's hands, the glad welcome and caresses of little children, and all the quiet, daily lovelinesses that still bloomed in a land so lately visited by war.

So quiet pleasure followed on quiet pleasure until 1870. In the autumn of that year his master lay stricken and on his deathbed. The physicians, making an effort to rouse him, reminded him that he must make haste to get well, for old "Traveller" had been standing in the stable and needed exercise. But General Lee, knowing that his end was near, shook his head. "Traveller" still waited. And the kind hand and gentle voice did not come to him again. From then on he was to miss the familiar touch on his bridle.

After that he was petted even more than before. He might browse as he chose about his master's house, or stand at the veranda whinnying softly for the caresses and attentions he had grown to love.

But "Traveller" did not long survive his master.

10

HOW MISS LAKE'S CIRCUS HORSES WERE RESTORED

BY THOMAS WALLACE KNOX

The Lake family, performers and part owners of a traveling circus, kept themselves busy and their audiences entertained during the Civil War. They had little regard for the political and military circumstances of the places they visited. Then, in Nashville in December of 1864, an occupying Federal force under General James H. Wilson turned the circus upside down. Fifteen-year-old Alice Lake was the one to put it upright again.

Here is the story of Alice and her circus horses, as told by the journalist Thomas Wallace Knox. He served in the Civil War, but probably did not hear this story firsthand, since he was wounded and discharged during the first months of the war. Knox specialized in adventure stories for boys, but the story of Alice Lake certainly appealed to girls as well.

One of the stories told during the evening was about the seizure of some circus horses in Nashville, Tennessee, at the time of the American Civil War. Lake and North's Circus was performing there during the winter of 1864, while the town was held by the Northern army and threatened by the Confederates.

At 9 o'clock on the morning of the 6th of December the company was in the practice ring, drilling for a new grand entry. They had nineteen ring horses, including three black stallions, which Miss Lake, the daughter of one of the proprietors, used to drive in a manège act, and which she had trained herself on her father's Kentucky farm, and loved as a Kentucky girl will love her horses.

The band had just finished the first bar when in stalked an officer of the army, and called Lake aside. "You have nineteen horses here, I see," he said; "one of them is lame; we don't want him, but the others are confiscated. Rather a fine lot. Suppose we say a hundred apiece for them."

Then he made out a requisition on the Treasury for $1800—handed it to Lake, called in his men, and in five minutes left the company with a show on its hands and only one lame horse to do all the equestrian business.

Miss Lake cried and some of the men used hard language, but all the same, for four days they gave a show twice a day with that one lame horse. Then Miss Lake got desperate. She was a mere girl, and with a girl's audacity she did a thing which an older person would have considered the wildest folly.

"John," she said to the clown, "I'm going to General Wilson to get my horses. I want them and they want me."

Nothing that anybody could say would hold her back, and so away she went to General Wilson's headquarters. She marched in on General Wilson and asked for her horses back. She had a sweet and winning way, and when she cried and told him how heartsick she was for her horses, and how much she knew they missed her, the general let his feelings get the better of his sense of duty, and gave her an order for every horse taken from the circus.

One of Wilson's orderlies afterwards gave a reason for giving the horses back, which, while it is not so romantic, may be partly true. The horses were all trained for ring service and most of them were trained to dance to the music, and to fall upon their knees and sides upon being touched upon the haunches with a spur or the whip.

The whole bunch was turned over to a military band as their mounts, and the orderly said that during the four days that the band was mounted on those beasts there was not an hour when one of them was not dancing around so that he could not keep time, or else horse and man— sometime three or four of them—were rolling on the ground together, the musicians having unwittingly given the horse his lying down cue.

Three years later the now eighteen-year-old Alice Lake, traveling by steamer between Mobile, Alabama, and New Orleans, fell overboard and drowned. Observers speculated that she became dizzy while looking into the water. Others doubted that, since she could twirl on a galloping horse without a problem.

Alice's mother Agnes continued her career as a circus equestrienne, eventually becoming the first American woman to own a circus. In 1876 Agnes suffered a second tragedy when her recently acquired husband Wild Bill Hickok was murdered in Deadwood, Dakota Territory. The avalanche of publicity surrounding Wild Bill's death helped bury the public memory of Alice Lake, who is mostly forgotten today.

11

A RIDE WITH A MAD HORSE IN A FREIGHT-CAR

BY W. H. H. MURRAY

Beyond his religion, clergyman William Henry Harrison Murray loved two things above all: the Adirondack Mountains of New York and horses. Publication of his 1869 book Adventures in the Wilderness, *a collection of essays and stories about events and life in the mountains of Northeastern New York, marked the beginning of outdoor writing in North America. The book's success earned him the nickname of "Adirondack" Murray. His book* The Perfect Horse *followed in 1873. This massive volume on horse selection and training is still used today.*

The two loves of W. H. H. Murray came together in the short story that anchored Adventures in the Wilderness. *"A Ride with a Mad Horse in a Freight-Car" is considered Murray's masterpiece, even though it takes place in circumstances he never experienced himself and features a relationship between a horse and a man that is some-*

what improbable. But it is still a remarkably moving story, one that perfectly expresses the potential for love between a human being and a horse.

~~~~~~

Should the reader ever visit the south inlet of Racquette Lake—one of the loveliest bits of water in the Adirondack wilderness—at the lower end of the pool below the falls, on the left-hand side going up, he will see the charred remnants of a campfire. It was there that the following story was first told—told, too, so graphically, with such vividness, that I found little difficulty, when writing it out from memory two months later, in recalling the exact words of the narrator in almost every instance.

It was in the month of July, 1868, that John and I, having located our permanent camp on Constable's Point, were lying off and on, as sailors say, about the lake, pushing our explorations on all sides out of sheer love of novelty and abhorrence of idleness. We were returning, late one afternoon of a hot, sultry day, from a trip to Shedd Lake, a lonely, out of the way spot which few sportsmen have ever visited, and had reached the falls on South Inlet just after sunset. As we were getting short of venison, we decided to lie by awhile and float down the river on our way to camp, in hope of meeting a deer. To this end we had gone ashore at this point, and, kindling a small fire, were waiting for denser darkness. We had barely started the blaze, when the tap of a carelessly handled paddle against the side of a boat warned us that we should soon have company, and in a moment two boats glided around the curve below and were headed directly toward our bivouac. The boats contained two gentlemen and their guides. We gave them a cordial, hunter-like greeting, and, lighting our pipes, were soon engaged in cheerful conversation, spiced with story-telling. It might have been some twenty minutes or more when another boat, smaller than you ordinarily see even on those waters, containing only the paddler, came noiselessly around the bend below, and stood revealed in the reflection of the firelight. I chanced to be sitting in such a position as to command a full view of the curve in the river, or I should not have known of any approach, for the boat was so sharp and light, and he who urged it along so skilled at the paddle, that not a ripple, no, nor the sound of a drop of water falling from blade or shaft, betrayed the paddler's presence.

If there is anything over which I become enthusiastic, it is such a boat and such paddling. To see a boat of bark or cedar move through the water noiselessly as a shadow drifts across a meadow, no jar or creak above, no gurgling of displaced water below, no whirling and rippling wake astern, is something bordering so nearly on the weird and ghostly, that custom can never make it seem other than marvelous to me.

Thus, as I sat half reclining, and saw that little shell come floating airily out of the darkness into the projection of the firelight, as a feather might come blown by the night-wind, I thought I had never seen a prettier or more fairylike sight. None of the party save myself were so seated as to look down stream, and I wondered which of the three guides would first discover the presence of the approaching boat.

Straight on it came. Light as a piece of finest cork it sat upon and glided over the surface of the river; no dip and roll, no drip of falling water as the paddle shaft gently rose and sank. The paddler, whoever he might be, knew his art thoroughly. He sat erect and motionless. The turn of the wrists, and the easy elevation of his arms as he feathered his paddle, were the only movements visible. But for these the gazer might deem him a statue carved from the material of the boat, a mere inanimate part of it. I have boated much in bark canoe and cedar shell alike, and John and I have stolen on many a camp that never knew our coming or our going, with paddles which touched the water as snowflakes touch the earth; and well I knew, as I sat gazing at this man, that not one boatman, red man or white, in a hundred could handle a paddle like that.

The quick ear of John, when the stranger was within thirty feet of the landing, detected the lightest possible touch of a lily pad against the side of the boat as it just grazed it glancing by, and his "hist" and sudden motion toward the river drew the attention of the whole surprised group thither. The boat glided to the sand so gently as barely to disturb a grain, and the paddler, noiseless in all his movements, stepped ashore and entered our circle.

"Well, stranger," said John, "I don't know how long your fingers have polished a paddle shaft, but it isn't every man who can push a boat up ten rods of open water within twenty feet of my back without my knowing it."

The stranger laughed pleasantly, and, without making any direct reply, lighted his pipe and joined in the conversation. He was tall in stature, wiry, and bronzed. An ugly cicatrice stretched on the left side of his face from temple almost down to chin. His eyes were dark gray, frank, and genial. I concluded at once that he was a gentleman, and had seen service. Before he joined us, we had been whiling away the time by story-telling, and John was at the very crisis of an adventure with a panther, when his quick ear detected the stranger's approach. Explaining this to him, I told John to resume his story, which he did. Thus half an hour passed quickly, all of us relating some experience.

At last I proposed that Mr. Roberts—for so we will call him—should entertain us; "and," continued I, "if I am right in my surmise that you have seen service and been under fire, give us some adventure or incident which may have befallen you during the war."

He complied, and then and there, gentle reader, I heard from his lips the story, which, for the entertainment of friends, I afterward wrote out. It left a deep impression upon all who heard it around our campfire under the pines that night; and from the mind of one I know has never been erased the impression made by the story which I have named "A Ride with a Mad Horse in a Freight-Car."

"Well," said the stranger, as he loosened his belt and stretched himself in an easy, recumbent position, "it is not more than fair that I should throw something into the stock of common entertainment; but the story I am to tell you is a sad one, and I fear will not add to the pleasure of the evening. As you desire it, however, and it comes in the line of the request that I would narrate some personal episode of the war, I will tell it, and trust the impression will not be altogether unpleasant.

"It was at the battle of Malvern Hill—a battle where the carnage was more frightful, as it seems to me, than in any this side of the Alleghenies during the whole war—that my story must begin. I was then serving as major in the ——th Massachusetts Regiment—the old ——th, as we used to call it, and a bloody time the boys had of it too. About 2 P. M. we had been sent out to skirmish along the edge of the wood in which, as our generals suspected, the Rebs lay massing for a charge across the slope, upon the crest of which our army was posted. We had barely entered the underbrush when we met the heavy formations of Magruder in the very act of charging. Of course, our thin line of skirmishers was no impediment to those onrushing masses. They were on us and over us before we could get out of the way. I do not think that half of those running, screaming masses of men ever knew that they had passed over the remnants of as plucky a regiment as ever came out of the old Bay State.

"But many of the boys had good reason to remember that afternoon at the base of Malvern Hill, and I among the number; for when the last line of Rebs had passed over me, I was left among the bushes with the breath nearly trampled and an ugly bayonet gash through my thigh; and mighty little consolation was it for me at that moment to see the fellow who run me through lying stark dead at my side, with a bullet hole in his head, his shock of coarse black hair matted with blood, and his stony eyes looking into mine.

"Well, I bandaged up my limb the best I might, and started to crawl away, for our batteries had opened, and the grape and canister that came hurtling down the slope passed but a few feet over my head. It was slow and painful work, as you can imagine, but at last, by dint of perseverance, I had dragged myself away to the left of the direct range of the batteries, and, creeping to the verge of the wood, looked off over the green slope. I understood by the crash and roar of the guns, the yells and cheers of the men, and that hoarse murmur which those who have been in battle know, but which I cannot describe in words, that there was hot work going on out there; but never have I seen, no, not in that three days' desperate *mêlée* at the Wilderness, nor at that terrific repulse we had at Cold Harbor, such absolute slaughter as I saw that afternoon on the green slope of Malvern Hill.

"The guns of the entire army were massed on the crest, and thirty thousand of our infantry lay, musket in hand, in front. For eight hundred yards the hill sank in easy declension to the wood, and across this smooth expanse the Rebs must charge to reach our lines. It was nothing short of downright insanity to order men to charge that hill; and so his generals told Lee, but he would not listen to reason that day, and so he sent regiment after regiment, and brigade after brigade, and division after division, to certain death. Talk about Grant's disregard of human life, his effort at Cold Harbor—and I ought to know, for I got a minie in my shoulder that day—was hopeful and easy work to what Lee laid on Hill's and Magruder's divisions at Malvern.

"It was at the close of the second charge, when the yelling mass reeled back from before the blaze of those sixty guns and thirty thousand rifles, even as they began to break and fly backward toward the woods, that I saw from the spot where I lay a riderless horse break out of the confused and flying mass, and, with mane and tail erect and spreading nostril, come dashing obliquely down the slope. Over fallen steeds and heaps of the dead she leaped with a motion as airy as that of the flying fox when, fresh and unjaded, he leads away from the hounds, whose sudden cry has broken him off from hunting mice amid the bogs of the meadow. So this riderless horse came vaulting along.

"Now from my earliest boyhood I have had what horsemen call a 'weakness' for horses. Only give me a colt of wild, irregular temper and fierce blood to tame, and I am perfectly happy. Never did lash of mine, singing with cruel sound through the air, fall on such a colt's soft hide. Never did yell or kick send his hot blood from heart to head deluging his sensitive brain with fiery currents, driving him to frenzy or blinding him with fear; but touches, soft and gentle as a woman's, caressing words, and oats given from the open palm, and unfailing kindness, were the means I used to 'subjugate' him. Sweet subjugation, both to him who subdues and to him who yields! The wild, unmannerly, and unmanageable colt, the fear of horsemen the country round, finding in you, not an enemy but a friend, receiving his daily food from you, and all those little 'nothings' which go as far with a horse as a woman, to win and retain affection, grows to look upon you as his protector and friend, and testifies in countless ways his fondness for you.

"So when I saw this horse, with action so free and motion so graceful, amid that storm of bullets, my heart involuntarily went out to her, and my feelings rose higher and higher at every leap she took from amid the whirlwind of fire and lead. And as she plunged at last over a little hillock out of range and came careering toward me as only a riderless horse might come, her head flung wildly from side to side, her nostrils widely spread, her flank and shoulders flecked with foam, her eye dilating, I forgot my wound and all the wild roar of battle, and, lifting myself involuntarily to a sitting posture as she swept grandly by, gave her a ringing cheer.

"Perhaps in the sound of a human voice of happy mood amid the awful din she recognized a resemblance to the voice of him whose blood moistened her shoulders and was even yet dripping from saddle and housings, be that as it may, no sooner had my voice sounded than she flung her head with a proud upward movement into the air, swerved sharply to the left, neighed as she might to a master at morning from her stall, and came trotting directly up to where I lay, and, pausing, looked down upon me as it were in compassion. I spoke again, and stretched out my hand caressingly. She pricked her ears, took a step forward and lowered her nose until it came in contact with my palm. Never did I fondle anything more tenderly, never did I see an animal which seemed to court and appreciate human tenderness as that beautiful mare. I say 'beautiful.' No other word might describe her. Never will her image fade from my memory while memory lasts.

"In weight she might have turned, when well conditioned, nine hundred and fifty pounds. In color she was a dark chestnut, with a velvety depth and soft look about the hair indescribably rich and elegant. Many a time have I heard ladies dispute the shade and hue of her plush-like coat as they ran their white, jeweled fingers through her silken hair. Her body was round in the barrel, and perfectly symmetrical. She was wide in the haunches, without projection of the hipbones, upon which the shorter ribs seemed to lap. High in the withers as she was, the line of her back and neck perfectly curved, while her deep, oblique shoulders and long thick forearm, ridgy with swelling sinews, suggesting the perfection of stride and power. Her knees across the pan were wide, the cannon-bone below them short and thin; the pasterns long and sloping; her hoofs round, dark, shiny, and well set on. Her mane was a shade darker than her coat, fine and thin, as a thoroughbred's always is whose blood is without taint or cross. Her ear was thin, sharply pointed, delicately curved, nearly black around the borders, and as tremulous as the leaves of an aspen. Her neck rose from the withers to the head in perfect curvature, hard, devoid of fat, and well cut up under the chops. Her nostrils were full, very full, and thin almost as parchment. The eyes, from which tears might fall or fire flash, were well brought out, soft as a gazelle's, almost human in their intelligence, while over the small bony head, over neck and shoulders, yea, over the whole body and clean down to the hoofs, the veins stood out as if the skin were but tissue-paper against which the warm blood pressed, and which it might at any moment burst asunder.

"'A perfect animal,' I said to myself, as I lay looking her over—an animal which might have been born from the wind and the sunshine, so cheerful and so swift she seems; an animal which a man would present as his choicest gift to the woman he loved, and yet one which that woman, wife or lady love, would give him to ride when honor and life depended on bottom and speed.

"All that afternoon the beautiful mare stood over me, while away to the right of us the hoarse tide of battle flowed and ebbed. What charm, what delusion of memory, held her there? Was my face to her as the face of her dead master, sleeping a sleep from which not even the wildest roar of battle, no, nor her cheerful neigh at morning, would ever wake him? Or is there in animals some instinct, answering to our intuition, only more potent, which tells them whom to trust and whom to avoid? I know not, and yet some such sense they may have, they must have, or why else should this mare so fearlessly attach herself to me?

"By what process of reason or instinct I know not, but there she chose me for her master; for when some of my men at dusk came searching, and found me, and, laying me on a stretcher, started toward our lines, the mare, uncompelled, of her own free will, followed at my side; and all through that stormy night of wind and rain, as my men struggled along through the mud and mire toward Harrison's Landing, the mare followed, and ever after, until she died, was with me, and was mine, and I, so far as man might be, was hers. I named her Gulnare.

"As quickly as my wound permitted, I was transported to Washington, whither I took the mare with me. Her fondness for me grew daily, and soon became so marked as to cause universal comment. I had her boarded while in Washington at the corner of Street and Avenue. The groom had instructions to lead her around to the window against which was my bed, at the hospital, twice every day, so that by opening the sash I might reach out my hand and pet her. But the second day, no sooner had she reached the street, than she broke suddenly from the groom and dashed away at full speed. I was lying, bolstered up in bed, reading, when I heard the rush of flying feet, and in an instant, with a loud, joyful neigh, she checked herself in front of my window. And when the nurse lifted the sash, the beautiful creature thrust her head through the aperture, and rubbed her nose against my shoulder like a dog. I am not ashamed to say that I put both my arms around her neck, and, burying my face in her silken mane, kissed her again and again. Wounded, weak, and away from home, with only strangers to wait upon me, and scant service at that, the affection of this lovely creature for me, so tender and touching, seemed almost human, and my heart went out to her beyond any power of expression, as to the only being, of all the thousands around me, who thought of me and loved me.

"Shortly after her appearance at my window, the groom, who had divined where he should find her, came into the yard. But she would not allow him to come near her, much less touch her. If he tried to approach she would lash out at him with her heels most spitefully, and then, laying back her ears and opening her mouth savagely, would make a short dash at him, and, as the terrified African disappeared around the corner of the hospital, she would wheel, and, with a face bright as a happy child's, come trotting to the window for me to pet her. I shouted to the groom to go back to the stable, for I had no doubt but that she would return to her stall when I closed the window. Rejoiced at the permission, he departed. After some thirty minutes, the last ten of which she was standing with her slim, delicate head in my lap, while I braided her foretop and combed out her silken mane, I lifted her head, and, patting her softly on either cheek, told her that she must go. I gently pushed her head out of the window and closed it, and then, holding up my hand, with the palm turned toward her, charged her, making the appropriate motion, to 'go away right straight back to her stable.' For a moment she stood looking steadily at me, with an indescribable expression of hesitation and surprise in her clear, liquid eyes, and then, turning lingeringly, walked slowly out of the yard.

"Twice a day for nearly a month, while I lay in the hospital, did Gulnare visit me. At the appointed hour the groom would slip her headstall, and, without a word of command, she would dart out of the stable, and, with her long, leopard-like lope, go sweeping down the street and come dashing into the hospital yard, checking herself with the same glad neigh at my window; nor did she ever once fail, at the closing of the sash, to return directly to her stall. The groom informed me that every morning and evening, when the hour of her visit drew near, she would begin to chafe and worry, and, by pawing and pulling at the halter, advertise him that it was time for her to be released.

"But of all exhibitions of happiness, either by beast or man, hers was the most positive on that afternoon when, racing into the yard, she found me leaning on a crutch outside the hospital building. The whole corps of nurses came to the doors, and all the poor fellows that could move themselves—for Gulnare had become a universal favorite, and the boys looked for her daily visits nearly, if not quite, as ardently as I did—crawled to the windows to see her.

"What gladness was expressed in every movement! She would come prancing toward me, head and tail erect, and, pausing, rub her head against my shoulder, while I patted her glossy neck; then suddenly, with a sidewise spring, she would break away, and with her long tail elevated until her magnificent brush, fine and silken as the golden hair of a blonde, fell in a great spray on either flank, and, her head curved to its proudest arch, pace around me with that high action and springing step peculiar to the thoroughbred. Then like a flash, dropping her brush and laying back her ears and stretching her nose straight out, she would speed away with that quick, nervous, low-lying action which marks the rush of racers, when side by side and nose to nose lapping each other, with the roar of cheers on either hand and along the seats above them, they come straining up the home stretch. Returning from one of these arrowy flights, she would come curveting back, now pacing sidewise as on parade, now dashing her hind feet high into the air, and anon vaulting up and springing through the air, with legs well under her, as if in the act of taking a five-barred gate, and finally would approach and stand happy in her reward—my caress.

"The war, at last, was over. Gulnare and I were in at the death with Sheridan at the Five Forks. Together we had shared the pageant at Richmond and Washington, and never had I seen her in better spirits than on that day at the capital. It was a sight indeed to see her as she came down Pennsylvania Avenue. If the triumphant procession had been all in her honor and mine, she could not have moved with greater grace and pride. With dilating eye and tremulous ear, ceaselessly champing her bit, her heated blood bringing out the magnificent lacework of veins over her entire body, now and then pausing, and with a snort gathering herself back upon her haunches as for a mighty leap, while she shook the froth from her bits, she moved with a high, prancing step down the magnificent street, the admired of all beholders.

"Cheer after cheer was given, huzza after huzza rang out over her head from roofs and balcony, bouquet after bouquet was launched by fair and enthusiastic admirers before her; and yet, amid the crash and swell of music, the cheering and tumult, so gentle and manageable was she, that, though I could feel her frame creep and tremble under me as she moved through that whirlwind of excitement, no check or curb was needed, and the bridle-lines—the same she wore when she came to me at Malvern Hill—lay unlifted on the pommel of the saddle.

"Never before had I seen her so grandly herself. Never before had the fire and energy, the grace and gentleness, of her blood so revealed themselves. This was the day and the event she needed. And all the royalty of her ancestral breed—a race of equine kings—flowing as without taint or cross from him that was the pride and wealth of the whole tribe of desert rangers, expressed itself in her.

"I need not say that I shared her mood. I sympathized in her every step. I entered into all her royal humors. I patted her neck and spoke loving and cheerful words to her. I called her my beauty, my pride, my pet. And did she not understand me? Every word! Else why that listening ear turned back to catch my softest whisper; why the responsive quiver through the frame, and the low, happy neigh?

"'Well,' I exclaimed, as I leaped from her back at the close of the review—alas! that words spoken in lightest mood should portend so much!—'well, Gulnare, if you should die, your life has had its triumph. The nation itself, through its admiring capital, has paid tribute to your beauty, and death can never rob you of your fame.' And I patted her moist neck and foam-flecked shoulders, while the grooms were busy with head and loins.

"That night our brigade made its bivouac just over Long Bridge, almost on the identical spot where four years before I had camped my company of three months' volunteers. With what experiences of march and battle were those four years filled! For three of these years Gulnare had been my constant companion. With me she had shared my tent, and not rarely my rations, for in appetite she was truly human, and my steward always counted her as one of our 'mess.' Twice had she been wounded—once at Fredericksburg, through the thigh; and once at Cold Harbor, where a piece of shell tore away a part of her scalp. So completely did it stun her, that for some moments I thought her dead, but to my great joy she shortly recovered her senses. I had the wound carefully dressed by our brigade surgeon, from whose care she came in a month with the edges of the wound so nicely united that the eye could with difficulty detect the scar.

"This night, as usual, she lay at my side, her head almost touching mine. Never before, unless when on a raid and in face of the enemy, had I seen her so uneasy. Her movements during the night compelled wakefulness on my part. The sky was cloudless, and in the dim light I lay and watched her. Now she would stretch herself at full length, and rub her head on the ground. Then she would start up, and, sitting on her haunches, like a dog, lift one foreleg and paw her neck and ears. Anon she would rise to her feet and shake herself, walk off a few rods, return and lie down again by my side.

"I did not know what to make of it, unless the excitement of the day had been too much for her sensitive nerves. I spoke to her kindly and petted her. In response she would rub her nose against me, and lick my hand with her tongue—a peculiar habit of hers—like a dog. As I was passing my hand over her head, I discovered that it was hot, and the thought of the old wound flashed into my mind, with a momentary fear that something might be wrong about her brain, but after thinking it over I dismissed it as incredible. Still I was alarmed. I knew that something was amiss, and I rejoiced at the thought that I should soon be at home where she could have quiet, and, if need be, the best of nursing.

"At length the morning dawned, and the mare and I took our last meal together on Southern soil—the last we ever took together. The brigade was formed in line for the last time, and as I rode down the front to review the boys she moved with all her old battle grace and power. Only now and then, by a shake of the head, was I reminded of her actions during the night. I said a few words of farewell to the men whom I had led so often to battle, with whom I had shared perils not a few, and by whom, as I had reason to think, I was loved, and then gave, with a voice slightly unsteady, the last order they would ever receive from me: 'Brigade, Attention, Ready to break ranks, *Break Ranks.*'

"The order was obeyed. But ere they scattered, moved by a common impulse, they gave first three cheers for me, and then, with the same heartiness and even more power, three cheers for Gulnare. And she, standing there, looking with her bright, cheerful countenance full at the men, pawing with her forefeet, alternately, the ground, seemed to understand the compliment; for no sooner had the cheering died away than she arched her neck to its proudest curve, lifted her thin, delicate head into the air, and gave a short, joyful neigh.

"My arrangements for transporting her had been made by a friend the day before. A large, roomy car had been secured, its floor strewn with bright, clean straw, a bucket and a bag of oats provided, and everything done for her comfort. The car was to be attached to the through express, in consideration of fifty dollars extra, which I gladly paid, because of the greater rapidity with which it enabled me to make my journey.

"As the brigade broke up into groups, I glanced at my watch and saw that I had barely time to reach the cars before they started. I shook the reins upon her neck, and with a plunge, startled at the energy of my signal, away she flew. What a stride she had! What an elastic spring! She touched and left the earth as if her limbs were of spiral wire. When I reached the car my friend was standing in front of it, the gangplank was ready, I leaped from the saddle and, running up the plank into the car, whistled to her; and she, timid and hesitating, yet unwilling to be separated from me, crept slowly and cautiously up the steep incline and stood beside me.

"Inside I found a complete suit of flannel clothes with a blanket and, better than all, a lunch basket. My friend explained that he had bought the clothes as he came down to the depot, thinking, as he said, "that they would be much better than your regimentals," and suggested that I doff the one and don the other. To this I assented the more readily as I reflected that I would have to pass one night at least in the car, with no better bed than the straw under my feet.

"I had barely time to undress before the cars were coupled and started. I tossed the clothes to my friend with the injunction to pack them in my trunk and express them on to me, and waved him my adieu. I arrayed myself in the nice, cool flannel and looked around. The thoughtfulness of my friend had anticipated every want. An old cane-seated chair stood in one corner. The lunch basket was large and well supplied. Amid the oats I found a dozen oranges, some bananas, and a package of real Havana cigars. How I called down blessings on his thoughtful head as I took the chair and, lighting one of the fine-flavored *figaros*, gazed out on the fields past which we were gliding, yet wet with morning dew. As I sat dreamily admiring the beauty before me, Gulnare came and, resting her head upon my shoulder, seemed to share my mood.

"As I stroked her fine-haired, satin-like nose, recollection quickened and memories of our companionship in perils thronged into my mind. I rode again that midnight ride to Knoxville, when Burnside lay entrenched, desperately holding his own, waiting for news from Chattanooga of which I was the bearer, chosen by Grant himself because of the reputation of my mare. What riding that was! We started, ten riders of us in all, each with the same message. I parted company the first hour out with all save one, an iron-gray stallion of Messenger blood. Jack Murdock rode him, who learned his horsemanship from buffalo and Indian hunting on the plains—not a bad school to graduate from.

"Ten miles out of Knoxville the gray, his flanks dripping with blood, plunged up abreast of the mare's shoulders and fell dead; and Gulnare and I passed through the lines alone. I had ridden the terrible race without whip or spur. With what scenes of blood and flight she would ever be associated!

"And then I thought of home, unvisited for four long years—that home I left a stripling, but to which I was returning a bronzed and brawny man. I thought of Mother and Bob—how they would admire her!—of old Ben, the family groom, and of that one who shall be nameless, whose picture I had so often shown to Gulnare as the likeness of her future mistress; had they not all heard of her, my beautiful mare, she who came to me from the smoke and whirlwind, my battle gift? How they would pat her soft, smooth sides, and tie her mane with ribbons, and feed her with all sweet things from open and caressing palm! And then I thought of one who might come after her to bear her name and repeat at least some portion of her beauty—a horse honored and renowned the country through, because of the transmission of the mother's fame.

"About three o'clock in the afternoon a change came over Gulnare. I had fallen asleep upon the straw, and she had come and awakened me with a touch of her nose. The moment I started up I saw that something was the matter. Her eyes were dull and heavy. Never before had I seen the light go out of them. The rocking of the car as it went jumping and vibrating along seemed to irritate her. She began to rub her head against the side of the car. Touching it, I found that the skin over the brain was hot as fire. Her breathing grew rapidly louder and louder. Each breath was drawn with a kind of gasping effort. The lids with their silken fringe drooped wearily over the lusterless eyes. The head sank lower and lower, until the nose almost touched the floor. The ears, naturally so lively and erect, hung limp and widely apart. The body was cold and senseless. A pinch elicited no motion. Even my voice was at last unheeded. To word and touch there came, for the first time in all our intercourse, no response.

"I knew as the symptoms spread what was the matter. The signs bore all one way. She was in the first stages of phrenitis, or inflammation of the brain. In other words, *my beautiful mare was going mad.*

"I was well versed in the anatomy of the horse. Loving horses from my very childhood, there was little in veterinary practice with which I was not familiar. Instinctively, as soon as the symptoms had developed themselves, and I saw under what frightful disorder Gulnare was laboring, I put my hand into my pocket for my knife, in order to open a vein. There was no knife there. Friends, I have met with many surprises. More than once in battle and scout have I been nigh death; but never did my blood desert my veins and settle so around the heart, never did such a sickening sensation possess me, as when, standing in that car with my beautiful mare before me marked with those horrible symptoms, I made that discovery.

"My knife, my sword, my pistols even, were with my suit in the care of my friend, two hundred miles away. Hastily, and with trembling fingers, I searched my clothes, the lunch basket, my linen; not even a pin could I find. I shoved open the sliding door, and swung my hat and shouted, hoping to attract some brakeman's attention. The train was thundering along at full speed, and none saw or heard me. I knew her stupor would not last long. A slight quivering of the lip, an occasional spasm running through the frame, told me too plainly that the stage of frenzy would soon begin.

"'My God,' I exclaimed in despair, as I shut the door and turned toward her, 'must I see you die, Gulnare, when the opening of a vein would save you? Have you borne me, my pet, through all these years of peril, the icy chill of winter, the heat and torment of summer, and all the thronging dangers of a hundred bloody battles, only to die torn by fierce agonies, when so near a peaceful home?'

"But little time was given me to mourn. My life was soon to be in peril, and I must summon up the utmost power of eye and limb to escape the violence of my frenzied mare. Did you ever see a mad horse when his madness is on him? Take your stand with me in that car, and you shall see what suffering a dumb creature can endure before it dies. In no malady does a horse suffer more than in phrenitis, or inflammation of the brain. Possibly in severe cases of colic, probably in rabies in its fiercest form, the pain is equally intense. These three are the most agonizing of all the diseases to which the noblest of animals is exposed.

"Had my pistols been with me, I should then and there, with whatever strength Heaven granted, have taken my companion's life, that she might be spared the suffering which was so soon to rack and wring her sensitive frame. A horse laboring under an attack of phrenitis is as violent as a horse can be. He is not ferocious as is one in a fit of rabies. He may kill his master, but he does it without design. There is in him no desire of mischief for its own sake, no cruel cunning, no stratagem and malice. A rabid horse is conscious in every act and motion. He recognizes the man he destroys. There is in him an insane *desire to kill*. Not so with the phrenetic horse. He is unconscious in his violence. He sees and recognizes no one. There is no method or purpose in his madness. He kills without knowing it.

"I knew what was coming. I could not jump out, that would be certain death. I must abide in the car, and take my chance of life. The car was fortunately high, long, and roomy. I took my position in front of my horse, watchful, and ready to spring. Suddenly her lids, which had been closed, came open with a snap, as if an electric shock had passed through her, and the eyes, wild in their brightness, stared directly at me. And what eyes they were! The membrane grew red and redder until it was of the color of blood, standing out in frightful contrast with the transparency of the cornea. The pupil gradually dilated until it seemed about to burst out of the socket. The nostrils, which had been sunken and motionless, quivered, swelled, and glowed. The respiration became short, quick and gasping. The limp and dripping ears stiffened and stood erect, pricked sharply forward, as if to catch the slightest sound. Spasms, as the car swerved and vibrated, ran along her frame. More horrid than all, the lips slowly contracted, and the white, sharp-edged teeth stood uncovered, giving an indescribable look of ferocity to the partially opened mouth.

"The car suddenly reeled as it dashed around a curve, swaying her almost off her feet, and, as a contortion shook her, she recovered herself, and rearing upward as high as the car permitted, plunged directly at me. I was expecting the movement, and dodged. Then followed exhibitions of pain, which I pray God I may never see again. Time and again did she dash herself upon the floor, and roll over and over, lashing out with her feet in all directions. Pausing a moment, she would stretch her body to its extreme length, and, lying upon her side, pound the floor with her head as if it were a maul. Then like a flash she would leap to her feet, and whirl round and round until from very giddiness she would stagger and fall. She would lay hold of the straw with her teeth, and shake it as a dog shakes a struggling woodchuck; then dashing it from her mouth, she would seize hold of her own sides, and rend herself. Springing up, she would rush against the end of the car, falling all in a heap from the violence of the concussion.

"For some fifteen minutes without intermission the frenzy lasted. I was nearly exhausted. My efforts to avoid her mad rushes, the terrible tension of my nervous system produced by the spectacle of such exquisite and prolonged suffering, were weakening me beyond what I should have thought it possible an hour before for anything to weaken me. In fact, I felt my strength leaving me. A terror such as I had never yet felt was taking possession of my mind. I sickened at the sight before me, and at the thought of agonies yet to come.

"'My God,' I exclaimed, 'must I be killed by my own horse in this miserable car!' Even as I spoke the end came. The mare raised herself until her shoulders touched the roof, then dashed her body upon the floor with a violence which threatened the stout frame beneath her. I leaned, panting and exhausted, against the side of the car. Gulnare did not stir. She lay motionless, her breath coming and going in lessening respirations. I tottered toward her, and, as I stood above her, my ear detected a low gurgling sound. I cannot describe the feeling that followed. Joy and grief contended within me. I knew the meaning of that sound.

"Gulnare, in her frenzied violence, had broken a blood vessel, and was bleeding internally. Pain and life were passing away together. I knelt down by her side. I laid my head upon her shoulders, and sobbed aloud. Her body moved a little beneath me, as if she would be nearer me, looked once more with her clear eyes into my face, breathed a long breath, straightened her shapely limbs, and died. And there, holding the head of my dead mare in my lap, while the great warm tears fell one after another down my cheeks, I sat until the sun went down, the shadows darkened in the car, and night drew her mantle, colored like my grief, over the world."

12

HOW COMANCHE CAME INTO CAMP

BY ELBRIDGE STREETER BROOKS

As both an editor and writer, Elbridge Streeter Brooks specialized in books for young readers. His works included biographies of famous Americans, from the Founding Fathers to Civil War generals on both sides of the Mason-Dixon Line. Most of Brooks's work was nonfiction, but his handful of novels often involved a teenage boy in the midst of an extraordinary event in American history. Such was Master of the Strong Hearts: A Story of Custer's Last Rally, *published in 1898, twenty-two years after Custer's death on the Little Bighorn River in Montana Territory.*

It's the story of sixteen-year-old Jack Huntingdon, who in 1875 joins his uncle on a government expedition to the Dakota and Wyoming territories. While exploring on his own, Jack is captured by a band of Sioux. He meets a white man named Red Top, an adoptive member of the band, who introduces him to the renowned Sitting Bull.

The legendary Lakota chief sends Jack home to the East to carry the message that the Sioux will never sell their lands.

In Washington Jack meets George Armstrong Custer, who offers him a chance to return to the West. Jack, hoping to meet Red Top again, agrees to go with Custer on a campaign against Sitting Bull. The story reaches its climax in June of 1876 when Custer, after dividing his force into three sections, is soundly defeated by Sitting Bull at the Battle of the Little Bighorn. Custer and more than two hundred soldiers and civilians, everyone in his personal command, die in and around what is now called Last Stand Hill.

Also dead are all the horses of Custer's unit, or so Jack and the survivors in the other sections of the regiment believe. Jack and the soldiers are burying the Seventh Cavalry dead when they discover that there was indeed one living creature left on the battlefield.

~~~~~~

Jack turned sadly away from the spot in which lay his friend the renegade. After that day's crowding experience the light-hearted lad could never more be unfamiliar with death. The Valley of the Little Big Horn had indeed been to him a veritable valley of death.

He found the troopers still at their sad yet brotherly task; but he managed to get the trumpeter apart so that he might tell him what he wished. Briefly he recited Po-to-sha-sha's story and told of the repentant renegade's last wish.

"Wore the flag next to his heart, did he?" said the trumpeter. "Well, by George! such a deserter as that is worth forgiving. I reckon he got more punishment than the service could ever have given him. And turned Indian, too! Well, Jack, drive ahead. You can count me in on this. I reckon we can respect his last wishes, even if he did turn redskin."

And so it came to pass that Red Top the renegade had a Christian burial. For Jack and the trumpeter dug a grave for the squaw man beside that of his faithful Indian wife; over it they planted the stars and stripes, and above it, when all was over, the trumpeter played taps, and Po-to-sha-sha the deserter slept in a soldier's grave.

Jack rode back to the camp in the upper valley that night feeling that, on that day indeed, he had "supped full of horrors." But "out of sight" is very soon "out of mind" with a healthy, happy-go-lucky boy, even if he be strong enough of character and stout enough of heart to never forget, though he may soon stop thinking, about the sights and scenes of so memorable a season as that disastrous campaign of the Little Big Horn in 1876.

Jack found plenty of things to divert his thoughts as he joined the camp; but that night, after mess, as the men sat around the bivouac fire smoking and discussing the events that have now become historic in that fatal incident of Custer's last rally, he found himself listening intently as the troopers talked the matter over and freely gave their opinion for or against the general's conduct, and the apparently needless slaughter of more than two hundred gallant men.

Opinions were widely divided. Some declared that the movement was all wrong from the start.

"The general oughtn't to have divided up," said one critic. "If he'd kept the command together and gone in with us all in a bunch he'd 'a' licked 'em, sure as shootin'!"

"That's so," chimed in another; "that's just the way it came out over yonder"—he jerked his head in the direction of that fatal field still known as Custer's Hill. "Didn't you see how they lay around there in three or four little piles? They were too much divided. I tell you, there's nothing an Indian's so afraid of as massing. He likes to get the outfit separated and go for each part."

"I don't see that," said a corporal, long in the Seventh; "that's just the way the general did the thing before, and it never failed till now. If he could have got at 'em early enough, I know it would have been all right, but you see we were a little too late in the day to give them the surprise party we reckoned on."

"Anyway," said one of the self-constituted critics, "the general was too fresh. He was rash, I say—mighty rash. Why didn't he back out when he saw what he'd got to handle, and wait for the rest of us to come up? I don't suppose he thought he was going to fight all the Indians in Christendom. Ten to one is bigger odds than even Custer ought to face. Seems to me he should have known that and pulled back in time."

"They do say," observed another of the critics—one who counted himself well posted on the news of the day—"they do say that the general and old man Grant had a set-to over somethin' or other, down to Washington, and that the President give it to the general hot and heavy. That set him up to make a record for himself out here in the Indian country, and he was just bound to go in and win—the bigger the victory with the smallest outfit, so much the better. And that's how comes it he's layin' out there where he is, and two hundred good fellows alongside of him, instead of legging it after the Indians with us at his heels. Sounds kind of likely now, doesn't it?"

"No, sir, I'll be hanged if it does," exclaimed Jack's friend, the trumpeter. "Say, did you see who was out there on that field? There was the general, and Cap'n Tom, his brother, and Mr. Boston Custer, his other brother, and Cap'n Calhoun, his brother-in-law, and that young Autie Reed, his nephew, to say nothing of those officers who were his closest friends, Keogh and Yates and Cook. Does it stan' to reason that the general would 'a' gone in, selfish-like and just out o' spite, and used up his whole family and his friends, only to make a show? No, sir, it don't. You fellows know such a lot, you make me just sick with your ideas."

But the critics were not silenced by this outburst.

"Well, p'r'aps that ain't so," was the response from one of the most pronounced of them; "but I tell you, the general's tactics were wrong. Why didn't he go slow when he struck that trail that brought us over here? How do we know that he followed orders in hurrying up his fight? General Terry's got a cool head, and just as like as not he told Custer to hold on and wait for him and Gibbon's column as soon as he'd struck the trail."

"Lot you know," said the trumpeter. "Why, I was right by the general's horse ready to sound the advance when General Terry was bidding him good-bye—up there on the Rosebud, you know. And General Terry said to him—I heard him—says he, 'Use your own judgment, Custer; if you do strike a big trail, just you do what you think best.' All he cautioned him was to hold on to his wounded. 'Whatever you do, Custer,' he says, 'hold on to your wounded.' I heard him say that."

"Well, he held on to 'em, sure enough, didn't he?" remarked one of the troopers. "I reckon none of 'em got away. They were all there."

"Right you are, Jimmy," responded a chorus of comrades, and one remarked, "Say, boys, did you see old Butler—sergeant of Cap'n Tom Custer's troop? Did you see where he was? I tell you, he put in his best licks 'fore he threw up the sponge. There he lay, all by his lonesome, down toward the ford, and I'll bet I picked up a pint o' empty ca'tridge shells under him. How he must have laid them Indians out! He was always a rattling good shot, the sergeant was."

"Empty shells!" growled another trooper. "H'm! that don't say much. I tell you, boys, it was the ca'tridges that whipped us. Nine out of ten of them were defective. They were dirty, and they corroded the ejectors so's you couldn't get the empty shells out of the chambers without using your knife to pick 'em out. That's what ailed our guns t' other day. And I tell you it just killed the general's men. How much you going to do when you've got to stop between shots to dig the shells out 'n the ejectors—'specially when the Indians have got better and newer guns than you have? And where did they get them? At the agencies. Government guns, too. What do you say to that? I call it manslaughter, I do. What redress have poor chaps like us got when the government sends us out here to lick the Indians, and then turns round and sells the Indians guns to kill us with—better guns than ours, too?"

"It's all dirty politics and favoritism and lettin' the Indian agents have a chance to make some money, no matter who's hurt, that does that business," remarked an indignant comrade. "And we get the worst end of the shoddy contracts and the no-account guns—and that does our business."

Whereupon the discussion drifted off into a general arraignment of all in authority over them, as is always the case with all subordinates in warlike or peaceful surroundings, and always has been the case since ever the first man in the world hired another to serve him. Grumbling is the subordinate's privilege, even if it is not his prerogative.

But even criticism and grumbling must end in time, and good humor return, as it did in this case around the glimmering bivouac fires on the bluffs of the Little Big Horn. For, notwithstanding the somber nature of their surroundings, their duties of that ghastly day— the same duties for which they would be detailed on the morrow—the troopers must have their relaxation as certainly as their fault-finding. So before long—before taps were sounded and the weary troopers tumbled into bed—they were all skylarking about their quarters; or, dropping into an absurd step, paraded about the fire, singing that good-humored travesty upon themselves just then a favorite in New York music-halls:

"There was Sergeant John McCafferty and Capt'n Donahue,
They made us march and toe the mark in gallant Company Q.
Oh, the drums did roll, upon me soul, and this is the way we go:
Forty miles a day on beans and hay, in the regular army, O!"

You can't long keep soldiers or sailors in a somber mood, even though death lies behind them, before them, or all about them! They say there was joking in the ranks even when the six hundred of the Light Brigade—"all that was left of them"—rode out of the death-trap at Balaclava! Dewey's men went skylarking to breakfast in the lull of Manila's fight, and Hobson's comrades put up a bit of "funning" as they rowed into the Spanish clutches at Santiago.

But the trumpeter said to Jack, "It makes me sick, Jack, so it does, to hear those freshies from St. Paul—why, they joined the command after you did, Jack—giving their opinion over the general's tactics, and what he ought to have done! A battle had to come, didn't it? That's what we're here for. If the general hadn't come here, but had struck south to find Crook, or had waited for Terry, why, the Indians wouldn't have hung around till he picked out the time to lick 'em. They'd have just up and got. That's their way. If they'd done so, who'd have got the blame? Custer. He came here; he found 'em; he sailed in to whip 'em. He struck the whole Sioux nation, and got the worst of it. Well, what of it? Isn't it better to stand up and take your medicine like a man, even if it does kill you, than hold back and be afraid to stick your nose out for fear some one'll pull it? General Custer died like a hero; and so did his men; and this country'll never forget 'em, you mark my words."

From all of which Jack Huntingdon was led to infer that the trumpeter thought more of Custer's dash than of Reno's timidity—although no names were mentioned, for the trumpeter was too good a soldier to go against the rules of discipline. And still the never-answered questions stayed with both of them: "Why did not Benteen go with those packs? Why didn't Reno go, too?"

Next day the work of clearing and temporarily marking the battlefield that was a burying ground was concluded, and at once preparations began for a speedy withdrawal. For General Terry, who was, like Reno, no seasoned Indian fighter, felt himself on dangerous and uncertain ground, and decided to fall back at once to the supply camp on the Yellowstone. He had no inclination to go off "playing tag" with the whole Sioux nation, and wisely deemed discretion the better part of valor. His column, as well as that of General Crook, had been defeated by the well-generalled and warlike Sioux. He wanted reinforcements before he advanced.

So preparations for withdrawal were made. But in the afternoon of the day before departure Jack accompanied a detail sent to make one last survey of the two hundred and sixty graves on and about Custer's Hill. And as they waited there Jack sought once more the twin graves under the cottonwoods, and said a boyish adieu to the good Mi-mi, who had made him the corn-dumplings, and the odd squaw man who had been his friend in time of need. The rent flag still fluttered above the renegade's last resting-place, and Jack with a sigh turned away, going, as he knew, to that civilization which this poor exile longed for, yet would not seek because of his faithfulness to her who had been faithful to him. As he left, Jack somehow found himself saying over and over a scrap that he had heard somewhere, but which he could neither place nor patch out—"in their deaths they were not divided."

"It suits them, anyhow," he declared, "whoever said it."

The dusk was closing in upon the bleak and bluff-like cliffs, the scarred and scarped heights that rampart the fair and now fertile valley of the Little Big Horn, as the detail rode campward across the valley.

They were to ascend by the ravine-like coulee up which Reno's men had scrambled in their panic-like flight; but, from their trail, the sharp ridges of the bluffs, touched with the twilight, stood dim and ghostly in the dusk.

As Jack looked his last upon the ridge along which Custer's men had galloped to their death, and where he had taken the long leap that gave him life, he caught every now and then a glimpse of a moving form outlined on the edge of the bluff. At last he pointed it out to his friend the trumpeter.

"It looks like a riderless horse," he said. "But, of course, it can't be."

"The ghost of Custer's troop, I reckon," the trumpeter said, half in fun and half in fear. For superstition touches more people in this world than we are ready to admit. "Looks that way, don't it, Jack? though, of course, that's all foolishness. Hark! hear that! By George! it is a horse— or the ghost of the troop."

They all started as, down from the bluff, came the quavering notes of a neigh.

"The last call of the outpost!" the trumpeter declared, and the whole detail breathed a bit easier as they toiled up the ascent and at last dismounted beside the newly lighted bivouac fire.

But, even as they flung themselves down at mess, once again that quavering neigh of the ghostly troop horse fell upon their ears, and in the distance sounded the approaching tramp of a warhorse. More than one man started to his feet, while the detail that had seen the phantom charger on the bluffs looked at each other in query.

"It's the ghost of the troop horse, Jack," the trumpeter declared. "I wonder is it a warning—or what?"

The trampling sounded nearer; another neigh, quavering, pitiful, almost appealing in its tones, as if begging companionship or welcome, came to their ears, and then, past the challenging outposts and the startled sentries, the ghost of the troop horse came within the lines, and stood trembling before the bivouac fire.

"It's one of ours!" cried Captain McDougall, who stood by. "Stir up that fire, Jack, won't you? Let's see if we know it."

The flare shot up, and in its light the newcomer stood revealed. Bleeding from severe wounds, weak and weary, and with a desire for pity and comfort that was deeply pathetic shining in his eyes, the scarred but beautiful sorrel laid its head against the captain's shoulder as if to claim protection.

Jack sprang forward. "Why! it's Comanche!" he said.

"You're right, Jack. By Jove! it is," cried the captain, flinging his arms about the neck of the sorrel. "Poor Myles Keogh! It's his Comanche. And I believe, boys, he's the only living thing we shall ever see from our side of that battlefield. Let's give him a rousing welcome, boys. Come! three cheers for Comanche!"

And about the bivouac fire the cheers of welcome rang out so lustily that, from all the camp, came officers and men anxious to know the cause and to join again in a salvo of welcome to the noble charger Comanche, sole survivor of the fight, gallant Captain Keogh's splendid Kentucky sorrel.

Next day the shattered command took the backward way, retiring to the supply-camp on the Yellowstone. There Terry was heavily reinforced. Men were hurried also to the strengthening of Crook at the south; and the two commands, uniting in August, 1876, entered upon the protracted search for the Sioux that ended, not in capture, as hoped, but only when Crazy Horse disappeared in the fastnesses of the Dakota Mountains, and Sitting Bull had escaped across the border into British possessions. Once again had the Master of the Strong Hearts proved himself a match for the Long-Swords, against whom he still made bad medicine.

In the end, however, the white man of course triumphed. It was not, in the nature of things, possible for the starving and divided hostiles long to resist the marshaled forces of the United States.

Colonel Miles and Colonel Merritt, both of whom, as general of the army and commander of the Manila expedition, were later to win renown in the war with Spain, pursued the Sioux with energy and determination; the union of the separated Indian bands was prevented and when Lame Deer, the Minniconjou chief, with the last of the resisting hostiles, was surprised and routed on the Rosebud in May, 1877, Crazy Horse, the valiant Ogallala, driven to surrender himself, ran "amuck" on his way to the guard-house at Camp Robinson, and died as a true hostile wished to die—defying the white man.

Three years later, in July, 1881, Sitting Bull himself, pining for his loved home land, crossed the border and, at Standing Rock, surrendered with all his following.

The greatest of all the Sioux wars was over. The prowess of the Long-Swords had overcome the skill, as it had broken the spirit, of the medicine chief, and Custer was avenged.

As for Jack, long before the ending of that summer campaign of 1876, he was speeding to the eastward toward civilization and home. His own "campaign" had not been a success; and yet, in its way, it had been a more surprising success than even his wildest fancy imagined. For he had taken part in the most famous of Indian campaigns, and had a share in the most notable tragedy of all our Indian warfare.

~~~~~~

In reality, Comanche was not the only equine survivor of Last Stand Hill. Several grievously wounded horses were found on the battlefield, still living but too badly injured to save. Other Seventh Cavalry mounts were captured and ended their lives as Indian ponies. But Comanche was the ultimate survivor, living a life of ease and honor at Ft. Riley, Kansas, until his death. He was believed to be twenty-nine years old at the time of his death in 1891.

~~~~~~

13

A HORSE'S TALE

BY MARK TWAIN

The great American humorist and novelist Samuel Clemens, who used the pen name Mark Twain, was a campaigner against cruelty to animals, particularly during the last few years of his life. His greatest weapon was his pen, and his 1904 book A Dog's Tale *told a popular and sentimental story that made the point to a wide audience. In 1907 he followed that book with* A Horse's Tale, *which was supposed to do the same thing for horses.*

It was less successful than the dog book, possibly because of an excess of narrators and possibly because of an equal excess of melodrama. But Mark Twain's brilliant prose and innate humor meant that even a minor book of his was far superior to books written by almost anyone else. The story of Soldier Boy, an army mount, was truly moving, in spite of its sentimentality. Here are the chapters narrated by Soldier Boy and other horses.

SOLDIER BOY—PRIVATELY TO HIMSELF

I am Buffalo Bill's horse. I have spent my life under his saddle—with him in it, too, and he is good for two hundred pounds, without his clothes; and there is no telling how much he does weigh when he is out on the warpath and has his batteries belted on. He is over six feet, is young, hasn't an ounce of waste flesh, is straight, graceful, springy in his motions, quick as a cat, and has a handsome face, and black hair dangling down on his shoulders, and is beautiful to look at; and nobody is braver than he is, and nobody is stronger, except myself. Yes, a person that doubts that he is fine to see should see him in his beaded buckskins, on my back and his rifle peeping above his shoulder, chasing a hostile trail, with me going like the wind and his hair streaming out behind from the shelter of his broad slouch. Yes, he is a sight to look at then—and I'm part of it myself.

I am his favorite horse, out of dozens. Big as he is, I have carried him eighty-one miles between nightfall and sunrise on the scout; and I am good for fifty, day in and day out, and all the time. I am not large, but I am built on a business basis. I have carried him thousands and thousands of miles on scout duty for the army, and there's not a gorge, nor a pass, nor a valley, nor a fort, nor a trading post, nor a buffalo range in the whole sweep of the Rocky Mountains and the Great Plains that we don't know as well as we know the bugle calls.

He is Chief of Scouts to the Army of the Frontier, and it makes us very important. In such a position as I hold in the military service one needs to be of good family and possess an education much above the common to be worthy of the place. I am the best-educated horse outside of the hippodrome, everybody says, and the best mannered. It may be so, it is not for me to say; modesty is the best policy, I think. Buffalo Bill taught me the most of what I know, my mother taught me much, and I taught myself the rest. Lay a row of moccasins before me—Pawnee, Sioux, Shoshone, Cheyenne, Blackfoot, and as many other tribes as you please—and I can name the tribe every moccasin belongs to by the make of it. Name it in horse-talk, and could do it in American if I had speech.

I know some of the Indian signs—the signs they make with their hands, and by signal fires at night and columns of smoke by day. Buffalo Bill taught me how to drag wounded soldiers out of the line of fire with my teeth; and I've done it, too; at least I've dragged *him* out of the battle when he was wounded. And not just once, but twice. Yes, I know a lot of things. I remember forms, and gaits, and faces; and you can't disguise a person that's done me a kindness so that I won't know him thereafter wherever I find him. I know the art of searching for a trail, and I know the stale track from the fresh. I can keep a trail all by myself, with Buffalo Bill asleep in the saddle; ask him—he will tell you so. Many a time, when he has ridden all night, he has said to me at dawn, "Take the watch, Boy; if the trail freshens, call me." Then he goes to sleep. He knows he can trust me, because I have a reputation. A scout horse that has a reputation does not play with it.

My mother was all American—no alkali-spider about *her*, I can tell you; she was of the best blood of Kentucky, the bluest Blue-grass aristocracy, very proud and acrimonious—or maybe it is ceremonious. I don't know which it is. But it is no matter; size is the main thing about a word, and that one's up to standard. She spent her military life as colonel of the Tenth Dragoons, and saw a deal of rough service—distinguished service it was, too. I mean, she *carried* the Colonel; but it's all the same. Where would he be without his horse? He wouldn't arrive. It takes two to make a colonel of dragoons. She was a fine dragoon horse, but never got above that. She was strong enough for the scout service, and had the endurance, too, but she couldn't quite come up to the speed required; a scout horse has to have steel in his muscle and lightning in his blood.

My father was a bronco. Nothing as to lineage—that is, nothing as to recent lineage—but plenty good enough when you go a good way back. When Professor Marsh was out here hunting bones for the chapel of Yale University he found skeletons of horses no bigger than a fox, bedded in the rocks, and he said they were ancestors of my father. My mother heard him say it; and he said those skeletons were two million years old, which astonished her and made her Kentucky pretensions look small and pretty antiphonal, not to say oblique. Let me see. . . . I used to know the meaning of those words, but . . . well, it was years ago, and 'tisn't as vivid now as it was when they were fresh. That sort of words doesn't keep, in the kind of climate we have out here. Professor Marsh said those skeletons were fossils. So that makes me part blue grass and part fossil; if there is any older or better stock, you will have to look for it among the Four Hundred, I reckon. I am satisfied with it. And am a happy horse, too, though born out of wedlock.

And now we are back at Fort Paxton once more, after a forty-day scout, away up as far as the Big Horn. Everything quiet. Crows and Blackfeet squabbling—as usual—but no outbreaks, and settlers feeling fairly easy.

The Seventh Cavalry still in garrison here; also the Ninth Dragoons, two artillery companies, and some infantry. All glad to see me, including General Alison, commandant. The officers' ladies and children well, and called upon me—with sugar. Colonel Drake, Seventh Cavalry, said some pleasant things; Mrs. Drake was very complimentary; also Captain and Mrs. Marsh, Company B, Seventh Cavalry; also the Chaplain, who is always kind and pleasant to me, because I kicked the lungs out of a trader once. It was Tommy Drake and Fanny Marsh that furnished the sugar—nice children, the nicest at the post, I think.

That poor orphan child is on her way from France—everybody is full of the subject. Her father was General Alison's brother; married a beautiful young Spanish lady ten years ago, and has never been in America since. They lived in Spain a year or two, then went to France. Both died some months ago. This little girl that is coming is the only child. General Alison is glad to have her. He has never seen her. He is a very nice old bachelor, but is an old bachelor just the same and isn't more than about a year this side of retirement by age limit; and so what does he know about taking care of a little maid nine years old? If I could have her it would be another matter, for I know all about children, and they adore me. Buffalo Bill will tell you so himself.

I have some of this news from overhearing the garrison gossip, the rest of it I got from Potter, the General's dog. Potter is the Great Dane. He is privileged, all over the post, like Shekels, the Seventh Cavalry's dog, and visits everybody's quarters and picks up everything that is going in the way of news. Potter has no imagination, and no great deal of culture, perhaps, but he has a historical mind and a good memory, and so he is the person I depend upon mainly to post me up when I get back from a scout. That is, if Shekels is out on depredation and I can't get hold of him.

Little Cathy Alison, the general's niece, soon arrives and becomes a favorite of Buffalo Bill and the rest of the garrison. Soldier Boy becomes both her teacher and her companion. Cathy becomes a skilled rider on his back and is made an honorary officer. Soldier Boy's status increases among the animals of the garrison and his reputation spreads outside its walls, a fact he discovers when a new horse arrives. Soldier Boy speaks first in chapter 6.

SOLDIER BOY AND THE MEXICAN PLUG

"When did you come?"

"Arrived at sundown."

"Where from?"

"Salt Lake."

"Are you in the service?"

"No. Trade."

"Pirate trade, I reckon."

"What do you know about it?"

"I saw you when you came. I recognized your master. He is a bad sort. Trap-robber, horse-thief, squaw-man, renegado—Hank Butters—I know him very well. Stole you, didn't he?"

"Well, it amounted to that."

"I thought so. Where is his pard?"

"He stopped at White Cloud's camp."

"He is another of the same stripe, is Blake Haskins." (*Aside.*) They are laying for Buffalo Bill again, I guess. (*Aloud.*) "What is your name?"

"Which one?"

"Have you got more than one?"

"I get a new one every time I'm stolen. I used to have an honest name, but that was early; I've forgotten it. Since then I've had thirteen *aliases*."

"Aliases? What is alias?"

"A false name."

"Alias. It's a fine large word, and is in my line; it has quite a learned and cerebrospinal incandescent sound. Are you educated?"

"Well, no, I can't claim it. I can take down bars, I can distinguish oats from shoe-pegs, I can blaspheme a saddle boil with the college-bred, and I know a few other things—not many; I have had no chance, I have always had to work; besides, I am of low birth and no family. You speak my dialect like a native, but you are not a Mexican Plug, you are a gentleman, I can see that; and educated, of course."

"Yes, I am of old family, and not illiterate. I am a fossil."

"A which?"

"Fossil. The first horses were fossils. They date back two million years."

"Great sand and sage-brush! Do you mean it?"

"Yes, it is true. The bones of my ancestors are held in reverence and worship, even by men. They do not leave them exposed to the weather when they find them, but carry them three thousand miles and enshrine them in their temples of learning, and worship them."

"It is wonderful! I knew you must be a person of distinction, by your fine presence and courtly address, and by the fact that you are not subjected to the indignity of hobbles, like myself and the rest. Would you tell me your name?"

"You have probably heard of it—Soldier Boy."

"What!—the renowned, the illustrious?"

"Even so."

"It takes my breath! Little did I dream that ever I should stand face to face with the possessor of that great name. Buffalo Bill's horse! Known from the Canadian border to the deserts of Arizona, and from the eastern marches of the Great Plains to the foothills of the Sierra! Truly this is a memorable day. You still serve the celebrated Chief of Scouts?"

"I am still his property, but he has lent me, for a time, to the most noble, the most gracious, the most excellent, her Excellency Catherine, Corporal-General Seventh Cavalry and Flag-Lieutenant Ninth Dragoons, U.S.A.,—on whom be peace!"

"Amen. Did you say *her* Excellency?"

"The same. A Spanish lady, sweet blossom of a ducal house. And truly a wonder; knowing everything, capable of everything; speaking all the languages, master of all sciences, a mind without horizons, a heart of gold, the glory of her race! On whom be peace!"

"Amen. It is marvelous!"

"Verily. I knew many things, she has taught me others. I am educated. I will tell you about her."

"I listen—I am enchanted."

"I will tell a plain tale, calmly, without excitement, without eloquence. When she had been here four or five weeks she was already erudite in military things, and they made her an officer—a double officer. She rode the drill every day, like any soldier; and she could take the bugle and direct the evolutions herself. Then, on a day, there was a grand race, for prizes—none to enter but the children. Seventeen children entered, and she was the youngest. Three girls, fourteen boys— good riders all. It was a steeplechase, with four hurdles, all pretty high. The first prize was a most cunning half-grown silver bugle, and mighty pretty, with red silk cord and tassels. Buffalo Bill was very anxious; for he had taught her to ride, and he did most dearly want her to win that race, for the glory of it. So he wanted her to ride me, but she wouldn't; and she reproached him, and said it was unfair and unright, and taking advantage; for what horse in this post or any other could stand a chance against me? and she was very severe with him, and said, 'You ought to be ashamed—you are proposing to me conduct unbecoming an officer and a gentleman.' So he just tossed her up in the air about thirty feet and caught her as she came down, and said he *was* ashamed; and put up his handkerchief and pretended to cry, which nearly broke her heart, and she petted him, and begged him to forgive her, and said she would do anything in the world he could ask but that; but he said he ought to go hang himself, and he *must*, if he could get a rope;

it was nothing but right he should, for he never, never could forgive himself; and then *she* began to cry, and they both sobbed, the way you could hear him a mile, and she clinging around his neck and pleading, till at last he was comforted a little, and gave his solemn promise he wouldn't hang himself till after the race; and wouldn't do it at all if she won it, which made her happy, and she said she would win it or die in the saddle; so then everything was pleasant again and both of them content. He can't help playing jokes on her, he is so fond of her and she is so innocent and unsuspecting; and when she finds it out she cuffs him and is in a fury, but presently forgives him because it's him; and maybe the very next day she's caught with another joke; you see she can't learn any better, because she hasn't any deceit in her, and that kind aren't ever expecting it in another person.

"It was a grand race. The whole post was there, and there was such another whooping and shouting when the seventeen kids came flying down the turf and sailing over the hurdles—oh, beautiful to see! Halfway down, it was kind of neck and neck, and anybody's race and nobody's. Then, what should happen but a cow steps out and puts her head down to munch grass, with her broadside to the battalion, and they a-coming like the wind; they split apart to flank her, but she?— why, she drove the spurs home and soared over that cow like a bird! and on she went, and cleared the last hurdle solitary and alone, the army letting loose the grand yell, and she skipped from the horse the same as if he had been standing still, and made her bow, and everybody crowded around to congratulate, and they gave her the bugle, and she put it to her lips and blew 'boots and saddles' to see how it would go, and BB was as proud as you can't think! And he said, 'Take Soldier Boy, and don't pass him back till I ask for him!' and I can tell you he wouldn't have said that to any other person on this planet. That was two months and more ago, and nobody has been on my back since but the Corporal-General Seventh Cavalry and Flag-Lieutenant of the Ninth Dragoons, U.S.A.,—on whom be peace!"

"Amen. I listen—tell me more."

"She set to work and organized the Sixteen, and called it the First Battalion Rocky Mountain Rangers, U.S.A., and she wanted to be bugler, but they elected her Lieutenant-General *and* Bugler. So she ranks her uncle the commandant, who is only a Brigadier. And doesn't she train those little people! Ask the Indians, ask the traders, ask the soldiers; they'll tell you. She has been at it from the first day. Every morning they go clattering down into the plain, and there she sits on my back with her bugle at her mouth and sounds the orders and puts them through the evolutions for an hour or more; and it is too beautiful for anything to see those ponies dissolve from one formation into another, and waltz about, and break, and scatter, and form again, always moving, always graceful, now trotting, now galloping, and so on, sometimes near by, sometimes in the distance, all just like a state ball, you know, and sometimes she can't hold herself any longer, but sounds the 'charge,' and turns me loose! and you can take my word for it, if the battalion hasn't too much of a start we catch up and go over the breastworks with the front line.

"Yes, they are soldiers, those little people; and healthy, too, not ailing any more, the way they used to be sometimes. It's because of her drill. She's got a fort, now—Fort Fanny Marsh. Major-General Tommy Drake planned it out, and the Seventh and Dragoons built it. Tommy is the Colonel's son, and is fifteen and the oldest in the Battalion; Fanny Marsh is Brigadier-General, and is next oldest—over thirteen. She is daughter of Captain Marsh, Company B, Seventh Cavalry. Lieutenant-General Alison is the youngest by considerable; I think she is about nine and a half or three-quarters. Her military rig, as Lieutenant-General, isn't for business, it's for dress parade, because the ladies made it. They say they got it out of the Middle Ages—out of a book—and it is all red and blue and white silks and satins and velvets; tights, trunks, sword, doublet with slashed sleeves, short cape, cap with just one feather in it; I've heard them name these things; they got them out of the book; she's dressed like a page, of old times, they say. It's the daintiest outfit that ever was—you will say so, when you see it. She's lovely in it—oh, just a dream! In some ways she is just her age, but in others she's as old as her uncle, I think. She is very learned. She teaches her uncle his book. I have seen her sitting by with the book and reciting to him what is in it, so that he can learn to do it himself.

"Every Saturday she hires little Indians to garrison her fort; then she lays siege to it, and makes military approaches by make-believe trenches in make-believe night, and finally at make-believe dawn she draws her sword and sounds the assault and takes it by storm. It is for practice. And she has invented a bugle call all by herself, out of her own head, and it's a stirring one, and the prettiest in the service. It's to call *me*—it's never used for anything else. She taught it to me, and told me what it says: '*It is I, Soldier—come!*' and when those thrilling notes come floating down the distance I hear them without fail, even if I am two miles away; and then—oh, then you should see my heels get down to business!

"And she has taught me how to say good morning and good night to her, which is by lifting my right hoof for her to shake; and also how to say goodbye; I do that with my left foot—but only for practice, because there hasn't been any but make-believe goodbyeing yet, and I hope there won't ever be. It would make me cry if I ever had to put up my left foot in earnest. She has taught me how to salute, and I can do it as well as a soldier. I bow my head low, and lay my right hoof against my cheek. She taught me that because I got into disgrace once, through ignorance. I am privileged, because I am known to be honorable and trustworthy, and because I have a distinguished record in the service; so they don't hobble me nor tie me to stakes or shut me tight in stables, but let me wander around to suit myself. Well, trooping the colors is a very solemn ceremony, and everybody must stand uncovered when the flag goes by, the commandant and all; and once I was there, and ignorantly walked across right in front of the band, which was an awful disgrace: Ah, the Lieutenant-General was so ashamed, and so distressed that I should have done such a thing before all the world, that she couldn't keep the tears back; and then she taught me the salute, so that if I ever did any other unmilitary act through ignorance I could do my salute and she believed everybody would think it was apology enough and would not press the matter. It is very nice and distinguished; no other horse can do it; often the men salute me, and I return it. I am privileged to be present when the Rocky Mountain Rangers troop the colors and I stand solemn, like the children, and I salute when the flag goes by. Of course when she goes to her fort her sentries sing out 'Turn out the guard!' and then . . . do you catch that refreshing early morning whiff from the mountain pines and the wild flowers? The night is far spent; we'll hear the bugles before long. Dorcas, the black woman, is very good and nice; she takes care of the Lieutenant-General, and is Brigadier-General Alison's mother, which makes her mother-in-law to the Lieutenant-General. That is what Shekels says. At least it is what I think he says, though I never can understand him quite clearly. He—"

"Who is Shekels?"

"The Seventh Cavalry dog. I mean, if he *is* a dog. His father was a coyote and his mother was a wildcat. It doesn't really make a dog out of him, does it?"

"Not a real dog, I should think. Only a kind of a general dog, at most, I reckon. Though this is a matter of ichthyology, I suppose; and if it is, it is out of my depth, and so my opinion is not valuable, and I don't claim much consideration for it."

"It isn't ichthyology; it is dogmatics, which is still more difficult and tangled up. Dogmatics always are."

"Dogmatics is quite beyond me, quite; so I am not competing. But on general principles it is my opinion that a colt out of a coyote and a wildcat is no square dog, but doubtful. That is my hand, and I stand pat."

"Well, it is as far as I can go myself, and be fair and conscientious. I have always regarded him as a doubtful dog, and so has Potter. Potter is the Great Dane. Potter says he is no dog, and not even poultry—though I do not go quite so far as that."

"And I wouldn't, myself. Poultry is one of those things which no person can get to the bottom of, there is so much of it and such variety. It is just wings, and wings, and wings, till you are weary: turkeys, and geese, and bats, and butterflies, and angels, and grasshoppers, and flying fish, and—well, there is really no end to the tribe; it gives me the heaves just to think of it. But this one hasn't any wings, has he?"

"No."

"Well, then, in my belief he is more likely to be dog than poultry. I have not heard of poultry that hadn't wings. Wings is the *sign* of poultry; it is what you tell poultry by. Look at the mosquito."

"What do you reckon he is, then? He must be something."

"Why, he could be a reptile; anything that hasn't wings is a reptile."

"Who told you that?"

"Nobody told me, but I overheard it."

"Where did you overhear it?"

"Years ago. I was with the Philadelphia Institute expedition in the Badlands under Professor Cope, hunting mastodon bones, and I overheard him say, his own self, that any plantigrade circumflex vertebrate bacterium that hadn't wings and was uncertain was a reptile. Well, then, has this dog any wings? No. Is he a plantigrade circumflex verte-brate bacterium? Maybe so, maybe not; but without ever having seen him, and judging only by his illegal and spectacular parentage, I will bet the odds of a bale of hay to a bran mash that he looks it. Finally, is he uncertain? That is the point—is he uncertain? I will leave it to you if you have ever heard of a more uncertainer dog than what this one is?"

"No, I never have."

"Well, then, he's a reptile. That's settled."

"Why, look here, whatsyourname—"

"Last alias, Mongrel."

"A good one, too. I was going to say, you are better educated than you have been pretending to be. I like cultured society, and I shall cul-tivate your acquaintance. Now as to Shekels, whenever you want to know about any private thing that is going on at this post or in White Cloud's camp or Thunder-Bird's, he can tell you; and if you make friends with him he'll be glad to, for he is a born gossip, and picks up all the tittle-tattle. Being the whole Seventh Cavalry's reptile, he doesn't belong to anybody in particular, and hasn't any military duties; so he comes and goes as he pleases, and is popular with all the house cats and other authentic sources of private information. He understands all the languages, and talks them all, too. With an accent like gritting your teeth, it is true, and with a grammar that is no improvement on blasphemy—still, with practice you get at the meat of what he says, and it serves. . . . Hark! That's the reveille. . . .

"Faint and far, but isn't it clear, isn't it sweet? There's no music like the bugle to stir the blood, in the still solemnity of the morning twi-light, with the dim plain stretching away to nothing and the spectral mountains slumbering against the sky. You'll hear another note in a minute—faint and far and clear, like the other one, and sweeter still, you'll notice. Wait . . . listen. There it goes! It says, '*It is I, Soldier—come!*' . . .

". . . Now then, watch me leave a blue streak behind!"

SOLDIER BOY AND SHEKELS

"Did you do as I told you? Did you look up the Mexican Plug?"

"Yes, I made his acquaintance before night and got his friendship."

"I liked him. Did you?"

"Not at first. He took me for a reptile, and it troubled me, because I didn't know whether it was a compliment or not. I couldn't ask him, because it would look ignorant. So I didn't say anything, and soon liked him very well indeed. Was it a compliment, do you think?"

"Yes, that is what it was. They are very rare, the reptiles; very few left, now-a-days."

"Is that so? What is a reptile?"

"It is a plantigrade circumflex vertebrate bacterium that hasn't any wings and is uncertain."

"Well, it—it sounds fine, it surely does."

"And it is fine. You may be thankful you are one."

"I am. It seems wonderfully grand and elegant for a person that is so humble as I am; but I am thankful, I am indeed, and will try to live up to it. It is hard to remember. Will you say it again, please, and say it slow?"

"Plantigrade circumflex vertebrate bacterium that hasn't any wings and is uncertain."

"It *is* beautiful, anybody must grant it; beautiful, and of a noble sound. I hope it will not make me proud and stuck-up—I should not like to be that. It is much more distinguished and honorable to be a reptile than a dog, don't you think, Soldier?"

"Why, there's no comparison. It is awfully aristocratic. Often a duke is called a reptile; it is set down so, in history."

"Isn't that grand! Potter wouldn't ever associate with me, but I reckon he'll be glad to when he finds out what I am."

"You can depend upon it."

"I will thank Mongrel for this. He is a very good sort, for a Mexican Plug. Don't you think he is?"

"It is my opinion of him; and as for his birth, he cannot help that. We cannot all be reptiles, we cannot all be fossils; we have to take what comes and be thankful it is no worse. It is the true philosophy."

"For those others?"

"Stick to the subject, please. Did it turn out that my suspicions were right?"

"Yes, perfectly right. Mongrel has heard them planning. They are after BB's life, for running them out of Medicine Bow and taking their stolen horses away from them."

"Well, they'll get him yet, for sure."

"Not if he keeps a sharp lookout."

"*He* keep a sharp lookout! He never does; he despises them, and all their kind. His life is always being threatened, and so it has come to be monotonous."

"Does he know they are here?"

"Oh yes, he knows it. He is always the earliest to know who comes and who goes. But he cares nothing for them and their threats; he only laughs when people warn him. They'll shoot him from behind a tree the first he knows. Did Mongrel tell you their plans?"

"Yes. They have found out that he starts for Fort Clayton day after tomorrow, with one of his scouts; so they will leave tomorrow, letting on to go south, but they will fetch around north all in good time."

"Shekels, I don't like the look of it."

Cathy is so proud of her unit that she offers to escort Buffalo Bill to Fort Clayton. Soldier Boy picks up the story in the next chapter.

SOLDIER BOY AND SHEKELS AGAIN

"Well, this is the way it happened. We did the escort duty; then we came back and struck for the plain and put the Rangers through a rousing drill—oh, for hours! Then we sent them home under Brigadier-General Fanny Marsh; then the Lieutenant-General and I went off on a gallop over the plains for about three hours, and were lazying along home in the middle of the afternoon, when we met Jimmy Slade, the drummer-boy, and he saluted and asked the Lieutenant-General if she had heard the news, and she said no, and he said:

"'Buffalo Bill has been ambushed and badly shot this side of Clayton, and Thorndike the scout, too; Bill couldn't travel, but Thorndike could, and he brought the news, and Sergeant Wilkes and six men of Company B are gone, two hours ago, hotfoot, to get Bill. And they say—'

"'Go!' she shouts to me—and I went."

"Fast?"

"Don't ask foolish questions. It was an awful pace. For four hours nothing happened, and not a word said, except that now and then she said, 'Keep it up, Boy, keep it up, sweetheart; we'll save him!' I kept it up. Well, when the dark shut down, in the rugged hills, that poor little chap had been tearing around in the saddle all day, and I noticed by the slack knee-pressure that she was tired and tottery, and I got dreadfully afraid; but every time I tried to slow down and let her go to sleep, so I could stop, she hurried me up again; and so, sure enough, at last over she went!

"Ah, that was a fix to be in I for she lay there and didn't stir, and what was I to do? I couldn't leave her to fetch help, on account of the wolves. There was nothing to do but stand by. It was dreadful. I was afraid she was killed, poor little thing! But she wasn't. She came to, by-and-by, and said, 'Kiss me, Soldier,' and those were blessed words. I kissed her—often; I am used to that, and we like it. But she didn't get up, and I was worried. She fondled my nose with her hand, and talked to me, and called me endearing names—which is her way—but she caressed with the same hand all the time. The other arm was broken, you see, but I didn't know it, and she didn't mention it. She didn't want to distress me, you know.

"Soon the big gray wolves came and hung around, and you could hear them snarl and snap at each other, but you couldn't see anything of them except their eyes, which shone in the dark like sparks and stars. The Lieutenant-General said, 'If I had the Rocky Mountain Rangers here, we would make those creatures climb a tree.' Then she made believe that the Rangers were in hearing, and put up her bugle and blew the 'assembly'; and then, 'boots and saddles'; then the 'trot'; 'gallop'; '*charge!*' Then she blew the 'retreat,' and said, 'That's for you, you rebels; the Rangers don't ever retreat!'

"The music frightened them away, but they were hungry, and kept coming back. And of course they got bolder and bolder, which is their way. It went on for an hour, then the tired child went to sleep, and it was pitiful to hear her moan and nestle, and I couldn't do anything for her. All the time I was laying for the wolves. They are in my line; I have had experience. At last the boldest one ventured within my lines, and I landed him among his friends with some of his skull still on him, and they did the rest. In the next hour I got a couple more, and they went the way of the first one, down the throats of the detachment. That satisfied the survivors, and they went away and left us in peace.

"We hadn't any more adventures, though I kept awake all night and was ready. From midnight on the child got very restless, and out of her head, and moaned, and said, 'Water, water—thirsty'; and now and then, 'Kiss me, Soldier'; and sometimes she was in her fort and giving orders to her garrison; and once she was in Spain, and thought her mother was with her. People say a horse can't cry; but they don't know, because we cry inside.

"It was an hour after sunup that I heard the boys coming, and recognized the hoof-beats of Pomp and Cæsar and Jerry, old mates of mine; and a welcomer sound there couldn't ever be. Buffalo Bill was in a horse litter, with his leg broken by a bullet, and Mongrel and Blake Haskins's horse were doing the work. Buffalo Bill and Thorndike had killed both of those toughs.

"When they got to us, and Buffalo Bill saw the child lying there so white, he said, 'My God!' and the sound of his voice brought her to herself, and she gave a little cry of pleasure and struggled to get up, but couldn't, and the soldiers gathered her up like the tenderest women, and their eyes were wet and they were not ashamed, when they saw her arm dangling; and so were Buffalo Bill's, and when they laid her in his arms he said, 'My darling, how does this come?' and she said, 'We came to save you, but I was tired, and couldn't keep awake, and fell off and hurt myself, and couldn't get on again.' 'You came to save me, you dear little rat? It was too lovely of you!' 'Yes, and Soldier stood by me, which you know he would, and protected me from the wolves; and if he got a chance he kicked the life out of some of them—for you know he would, BB.' The sergeant said, 'He laid out three of them, sir, and here's the bones to show for it.' 'He's a grand horse,' said BB; 'he's the grandest horse that ever was! and has saved your life, Lieutenant-General Alison, and shall protect it the rest of his life—he's yours for a kiss!' He got it, along with a passion of delight, and he said, 'You are feeling better now, little Spaniard—do you think you could blow the advance?' She put up the bugle to do it, but he said wait a minute first. Then he and the sergeant set her arm and put it in splints, she wincing but not whimpering; then we took up the march for home, and that's the end of the tale; and I'm her horse. Isn't she a brick, Shekels?"

"Brick? She's more than a brick, more than a thousand bricks—she's a reptile!"

"It's a compliment out of your heart, Shekels. God bless you for it!"

~~~~~~

After the horses overhear officers talking about the joys of bullfighting, they try to figure out what is so special about the sport. Here the Mexican Plug Mongrel tries to figure it out with the help of another horse.

~~~~~~

MONGREL AND THE OTHER HORSE

"Sage-brush, have you have been listening?"

"Yes."

"Isn't it strange?"

"Well, no, Mongrel, I don't know that it is."

"Why don't you?"

"I've seen a good many human beings in my time. They are created as they are; they cannot help it. They are only brutal because that is their make; brutes would be brutal if it was *their* make."

"To me, Sage-brush, man is most strange and unaccountable. Why should he treat dumb animals that way when they are not doing any harm?"

"Man is not always like that, Mongrel; he is kind enough when he is not excited by religion."

"Is the bullfight a religious service?"

"I think so. I have heard so. It is held on Sunday."

(*A reflective pause, lasting some moments.*) Then: "When we die, Sagebrush, do we go to heaven and dwell with man?"

"My father thought not. He believed we do not have to go there unless we deserve it."

General Alison decides to take Cathy to visit her Spanish homeland and gives in to her pleas to bring Soldier Boy along. But Cathy's beloved horse is stolen shortly after their arrival. He picks up his story several months later.

SOLDIER BOY—TO HIMSELF

It is five months. Or is it six? My troubles have clouded my memory. I have been all over this land, from end to end, and now I am back again since day before yesterday, to that city which we passed through, that last day of our long journey, and which is near her country home. I am a tottering ruin and my eyes are dim, but I recognized it. If she could see me she would know me and sound my call. I wish I could hear it once more; it would revive me, it would bring back her face and the mountains and the free life, and I would come—if I were dying I would come! She would not know *me*, looking as I do, but she would know me by my star. But she will never see me, for they do not let me out of this shabby stable—a foul and miserable place, with two wrecks like myself for company.

How many times have I changed hands? I think it is twelve times—I cannot remember; and each time it was down a step lower, and each time I got a harder master. They have been cruel, every one; they have worked me night and day in degraded employments, and beaten me; they have fed me ill, and some days not at all. And so I am but bones, now, with a rough and frowsy skin humped and cornered upon my shrunken body—that skin which was once so glossy, that skin which she loved to stroke with her hand. I was the pride of the mountains and the Great Plains; now I am a scarecrow and despised. These piteous wrecks that are my comrades here say we have reached the bottom of the scale, the final humiliation; they say that when a horse is no longer worth the weeds and discarded rubbish they feed to him, they sell him to the bullring for a glass of brandy, to make sport for the people and perish for their pleasure.

To die—that does not disturb me; we of the service never care for death. But if I could see her once more! If I could hear her bugle sing again and say, "It is I, Soldier—come!"

Cathy Alison searches for Soldier Boy, finally tracing him to a bullring. She arrives just in time to realize that Soldier Boy has had his abdomen ripped open by a bull. She rushes into the ring toward him. Soldier Boy staggers toward her and falls at her feet, dying before he realizes that Cathy has also been gored. She lives long enough to be carried away, and before she dies she asks that "Taps" be played for Soldier Boy.

14

THE AMERICAN CAVALRY HORSE

BY CAPTAIN WILMOT E. ELLIS

In retrospect 1905 seems late to be writing about the importance of the cavalry horse, but mounted soldiers still had value to an army for a few more years. Captain Wilmot E. Ellis was able to describe the kind of horses needed by the cavalry during the last decades of the nineteenth century, when they offered the only means of battlefield transportation. Ellis was a perfect candidate to provide a look backward. Later in his career junior officers complained to the army's Office of the Inspector General that the then-Colonel Ellis was "an old army fossil." He retired soon after, tired of what the army had become—an organization where horses had only ceremonial duties. These are his ideas about the making of a good cavalry horse.

A nation's strength in war depends not only upon its men, but also upon its horses. Every army needs cavalry and the efficiency of cavalry hinges, to a great extent, upon the quality and quantity of the supply of horses.

The United States has more horses than any other country except Russia, owning about sixteen millions to Russia's twenty-five millions. The animal was first carried to America by the Spaniards early in the sixteenth century. The wild herds which abounded in the Southwest until quite recently were probably the direct descendants of horses abandoned in that region by De Soto and other explorers.

Later colonists brought animals from several European countries. Wherever the settler went, the horse went with him and helped him to subdue the soil, to fight his enemies, and to face the hardships of life in a new world. Naturally, the pioneers' stock was usually poor; but before the Revolution, as the wealth of the colonists increased, the importation of English thoroughbreds had effected a marked improvement in the prevailing types.

Since those days, horse-breeding as an industry has grown with the growth of the country, though like any other industry it has had its ups and downs. At the present time it is prosperous, after surviving some particularly hard knocks.

More than once the prophets have shaken their heads and declared that the days of the horse were numbered. The electric car has driven him from the street railway service—surely a welcome release from an intolerable slavery. The bicycle and the automobile have disputed his possession of the roads, and the traction engine is doing some of his work on the farm. And a few years ago certain military experts, real or pretended, were loudly asserting that even his usefulness in warfare was practically over, for the development of the long-range rifle and the machine gun had rendered cavalry obsolete.

This last prediction was completely falsified during the recent war in South Africa, when the British government found itself compelled to spend several million dollars in buying horses abroad. Its agents found their best and most satisfactory market in the United States. They organized a great depot at Lathrop, Missouri, and their large purchases did much to stimulate the breeding of saddle horses in that and neighboring states.

The demand was increased by the expansion of our own cavalry establishment from ten to fifteen regiments in 1901. Many of the Western breeders are now making a specialty of supplying the cavalry with mounts, and it is gratifying to note that a distinct type of animal, specially adapted to the use of mounted soldiers, is beginning to appear.

Hitherto the United States army has usually purchased its horses by contract made through the quartermaster's department, but the results have not proved entirely satisfactory. The system has proved extravagant, as several middlemen are involved, and the government frequently pays as much as a hundred and twenty-five dollars for a sixty-dollar horse. The last army appropriation bill provides for purchase in open market, and cavalry officers feel that this policy will result in economy to Uncle Sam and an improvement in the quality of mounts. Some foreign war offices, notably that of Austria, conduct their own stock farms. This scheme has been advocated for the United States by prominent cavalry officers, but the experiment has never been tried, principally because it contravenes the time-honored policy that the government should not come into competition with private enterprise.

The horses presented for sale are passed upon by a board, ordinarily composed of an officer of the quartermaster's department, a cavalry officer, and an army veterinarian. The officers pass upon the horses with particular reference to "form," and the animals that they accept are minutely inspected by the veterinarian for soundness. Each horse—technically referred to as a "remount"—successfully passing the scrutiny of the inspectors is branded "U. S." on the left fore shoulder. Later it is branded on the hoof of the near fore foot with the designation of the company to which it is assigned.

The regulation cavalry horse must be a gelding of hardy color, sound and well-bred, gentle under the saddle, free from vicious habits, with free and prompt action at the walk, trot, and gallop, without blemish or defect, of a kind disposition, and with easy mouth and gait. Its height must be between fifteen hands and a quarter and sixteen hands; his weight between nine hundred and fifty and eleven hundred and fifty pounds.

The prescribed age is from four to eight years, but animals under five years are seldom accepted, and the best authorities recommend a minimum age of six years when hard field service is anticipated. There are other more or less technical requirements as to the points of a well-built, hardy, and active saddle horse. These specifications have been summed up in the following maxim: "Many good, few indifferent, no bad points."

It is manifestly out of the question to furnish thoroughbreds for cavalry service, for the supply of suitable ones is limited, the expense would be much greater, and these high-strung, mettlesome animals demand an amount of care quite inconsistent with the exigencies of active field work. Officers—who in our service are required to purchase their own mounts—usually provide themselves with thoroughbred chargers, or at least with very well-bred ones. Just now, however, most cavalry officers of moderate means do not feel disposed to purchase expensive animals, on account of the risk incurred in the Philippine service.

Our government does not reimburse its officers for losses of mounts in time of war, and only under very limited conditions does it repay them in time of peace. The equine mortality in the Philippines has been large. The enervating climate affects horses as well as men, and a disease called *surra* has caused serious loss.

Our two great official centers of instruction in military horsemanship—besides the cavalry regiments, each of which, of course, is in itself a school of training—are West Point, for cadets, and the Fort Riley Cavalry School, for the younger officers. At both places the instructors are senior officers. In the United States service, civilians have never been employed as riding masters.

There is nothing unduly conservative about the American cavalry instruction, and our officers are keen to avail themselves of all useful novelties. For instance, the West Point cadets have taken up the use of the double-reined bridle and the typical hunting and polo saddle. Not long ago, in quest of new ideas, an officer was detailed for a two years' course at the great French cavalry school at Saumur.

There is an analogy, not altogether fanciful, between the experiences of the equine recruit and the soldier recruit, or the "plebe" at West Point. The horse, fresh from the freedom of the ranch, finds himself among strange surroundings. The troop herd to which he is admitted receives him with calm indifference, but to himself it is a matter of such serious import that he is apt to grow feverish and excited in his new environment.

All the horses of a particular troop, as far as practicable, are of the same color, and the newcomer is assigned according to the shade of his coat. He is allowed to run freely with the troop herd in the corral and on the range. During this period he is "sized up" by the old troop horses, and often receives an admonitory kick or bite if inclined to be too frisky.

In order to steady him, he is picketed and stalled with old and gentle troop horses as neighbors. He is gradually introduced to the stir and activity of military life, being led by a soldier mounted on a quiet animal through those parts of the post where drills and ceremonies are being held.

The training in the riding school is begun by teaching the horse to take the snaffle bit properly, and to respond to the pressure of the rein on his neck, and to that of his rider's legs. He is next fixed in the regulation gaits of the walk, trot, and gallop, and taught to jump ditches and hurdles. Simultaneously with these exercises he is gradually accustomed to the saber and to the discharge of firearms.

Freedom from fear is not as difficult to acquire as it might seem, for the ordinary horse, if he has not been abused, readily learns to fear nothing except what his memory associates with physical pain. As soon as the horse responds satisfactorily to the snaffle, he is fitted with a curb bit. The curb is the regulation bit of the service, principally because by its use the trooper can manage the horse at all times, employing the left hand alone, with the pressure of the legs as an aid. Bitting is a science in itself, to which the efficient cavalry officer attaches the utmost importance.

The Rarey system plays an important part in the training of the American cavalry horse. It is an elaborate and detailed system formulated before the Civil War by John S. Rarey, a famous American horsebreaker of his day. With slight modifications, it has been embodied in the United States Cavalry Drill Regulations, and is employed to subdue stubborn animals. It is also brought into general use in the latter stages of training, to complete a cavalry charger's education, and to impress upon him once for all that man is master.

One of the most useful of these advanced exercises is the throwing of the horse. The animal is first equipped with the surcingle and watering-bridle. The trooper attaches one end of a long strap to the pastern of the off foreleg, and passes the other end through a ring on the top of the surcingle. The horse's near foreleg is then tied up by means of a short strap. Taking the free end of the long strap in his hand, the soldier places himself opposite the animal's croup on the near side, and urges his mount to step forward. As it does so, the trooper pulls on the long strap, which brings it to its knees. When it ceases to plunge, the trooper leans back on the strap, and the horse will gradually lie down on the near side.

The horse is prevented from rising by passing the reins under the surcingle and pulling his head to the right if he makes any attempt to change his position. Before allowing him to rise, the straps should be removed from his legs. After several repetitions of this exercise, the horse will usually lie down without making it necessary to use the straps.

As a rule, each trooper has his own horse to care for and to ride—an arrangement which leads the soldier to take pride in his charge and to establish that understanding between horse and man which is so essential to cavalry efficiency. It is this mutual confidence which enables our gritty, active cavalrymen to furnish such fine exhibitions of horsemanship and daredevil riding.

These showy exercises, however, are but a small part of cavalry routine. The trooper has to think of discipline and drill, of carbine and revolver practice, of saber exercises; of such practical details as bitting, saddling, packing, feeding, shoeing, and stable management, of the duties of mounted reconnaissance, and of the maintenance of men and horses in the hardy form that has made our records for forced marches unsurpassed in the history of the world. So manifold is his service, and so indispensable is he to an army in the field, that it is easy to understand why all the leading nations of Europe are increasing their mounted forces, and why the American military student views with alarm any proposed reduction of our own modest-sized cavalry establishment.

V
WORKING HORSES

15

ANECDOTES OF
AMERICAN HORSES

AUTHOR UNKNOWN

This affectionate tale of two working horses in western New York during the time of the Erie Canal appeared in one of the publications known as "the knowledge magazines." These were extremely low-priced compilations of fact-based articles aimed at middle-class readers, products of the expanding public education system. The variety of topics in the knowledge magazines was breathtaking. The volume that includes the story of ferry horse Grizzle and farm horse Charlie also includes a biography of the British spy John Andre, a treatise on the botany of bogs, an explanation of how to milk a cow, and a reflection on babyhood. This horse story is typical of the magazines: easy to read, brief, and intriguing.

A short distance below Fort Erie, and about a mile from where the river Niagara escapes over a barrier of rock from the depths of Lake Erie, a ferry has long been established across that broad and there exceedingly rapid river, the distance from shore to shore being a little over one-third of a mile. On the Canada side of the river is the small village of Waterloo, and opposite thereto on the United States side is the large village of Blackrock—distant from the young and flourishing city of Buffalo two miles.

In completing the Erie Canal, a pier or dam was erected up and down the river and opposite to Blackrock at no great distance from the shore, for the purpose of raising the waters of the Niagara to such a height that they might be made to supply an adjoining section of the Erie Canal. This pier was (and is) a great obstruction to the ferryboats; for previous to its erection passengers embarked from *terra-firma* on one side of the river and were landed without any difficulty on the other; but after this dam was constructed it became necessary to employ two sets of boats—one to navigate the river, and the other the basin—so that all passengers, as well as goods or luggage, had to be landed upon this narrow wall or pier, and re-shipped.

Shortly after the erection of the pier-dam, a boat propelled by horses was established between this pier and the Canada shore. The horses moved upon a circular platform which consequently was put in motion, to which other machinery was connected, that acted upon the paddle wheels attached to the sides of the boat. The boat belonged to persons connected with the ferry on the American side of the river; but, owing to the barrier formed by the pier, the horses employed on the boat were stabled at night in the village of Waterloo. I well recollect the first day this boat began to ply, for the introduction of a boat of that description, in those days, and in such a situation, was considered an event of some magnitude.

The two horses (for that boat had but two) worked admirably, considering the very few lessons they had had (upon the treadmill, as it was called) previous to their introduction upon the main river. One of the horses employed on the new ferryboat had once been a dapple gray, but at the period I am speaking of he had become white. He was still hale and hearty, for he had a kind and indulgent master. The first evening after the horses had been a short time in the stable, to which they were strangers, they were brought out for the purpose of being watered at the river, the common custom at this place. The attendant was mounted upon the bay horse,—the white one was known to be so gentle and docile that he was allowed to drink where he pleased.

I happened to be standing close by in company with my friend W——n, the ferry contractor on the Canada side, and thus had an opportunity of witnessing the whole proceedings of old Grizzle, the name that the white horse still went by. The moment he got round the corner of the building, so as to have a view of his home on the opposite side, he stopped and gazed intently.

He then advanced to the brink of the river, then he again stopped and looked earnestly across for a short time, then waded into the water until it had reached his chest, drank a little, lifted his head and, with his lips closed, and his eyes fixed upon some object on the farther shore, remained for a short time perfectly motionless.

Apparently having made up his mind to the task, he then waded farther into the river until the water reached his ribs, when off he shot into deep water without a moment's more hesitation. The current being so strong and rapid, the river boiling and turmoiling over a rocky bed at the rate of six miles the hour, it was impossible for the courageous and attached animal to keep a direct course across, although he breasted the waves heroically, and swam with remarkable vigor.

Had he been able to steer his way directly across, the pier wall would have proved an insurmountable barrier. As it was, the strength of the current forced him down to below where the lower extremity of this long pier abuts upon an island, the shore of which being low and shelving, he was enabled to effect a landing with comparative ease. Having regained *terra-firma*, he shook the water from his dripping flanks, but he did not halt over a few minutes, when he plunged into the basin and soon regained his native shore.

The distance from where Grizzle took the water to where he effected a landing on the island was about seven hundred yards; but the efforts made to swim directly across, against the powerful current, must have rendered the undertaking a much more laborious one. At the commencement of his voyage, his arched neck and withers were above the surface, but before he reached the island nothing but his head was visible to us.

He reached his own stable door, that home for which he had risked so much, to the no small astonishment of his owner. This unexpected visit evidently made a favorable impression upon his master, for he was heard to vow that if old Grizzle performed the same feat a second time, for the future he should remain on his own side of the river and never be sent to the mill again. Grizzle was sent back to work the boat on the following day, but he embraced the very first opportunity that occurred of escaping, swam back in the way he had done before, and his owner, not being a person to break the promise he had once made, never afterwards dispossessed him of the stall he had long been accustomed to, but treated him with marked kindness and attention.

During my residence on the headwaters of the Susquehanna, I owned a small American horse of the name of Charlie that was very remarkable for his attachment to my own person, as well as for his general good qualities. He was a great favorite with all the family; and being a favorite, he was frequently indulged with less work and more to eat than any of the other horses on the farm.

At a short distance from the dwelling-house was a small but luxuriant pasture, where, during the summer, Charlie was often permitted to graze. When this pasture had been originally reclaimed from its wild forest state, about ten years previous to the period of which I am speaking, four or five large trees of the sugar maple species had been left standing when the rest were cut down, and means had afterwards been found to prevent their being scorched by the fire at the time the rest of the timber had been consumed. Though remarkably fine trees of their kind, they were, however, no great ornament, their stems being long and bare, their heads small and by no means full of leaves, the case generally with trees that have grown up in close contact with each other in the American forests. But if they were no ornament, they might serve as shade-trees.

Beneath one of these trees Charlie used to seek shelter, as well from the heat of the meridian sun, as from the severe thunder gusts that occasionally ravage that part of the country. On an occasion of this sort Charlie had taken his stand close to his favorite tree, his tail actually pressing against it, his head and body in an exact line with the course of the wind; apparently understanding the most advantageous position to escape the violence of the storm, and quite at home, as it were, for he had stood in the same place some scores of times.

The storm came on and raged with such violence that the tree under which the horse had taken shelter was literally torn up by the roots. I happened to be standing at a window from whence I witnessed the whole scene. The moment Charlie heard the roots giving way behind him, that is, on the contrary side of the tree from where he stood, and probably feeling the uprooted tree pressing against his tail, he sprang forward and barely cleared the ground upon which, at the next moment, the top of the huge forest tree fell with such a force that the crash was tremendous, for every limb and branch were actually riven asunder.

I have many a time seen horses alarmed, nay, exceedingly frightened; but never in my life did I witness any thing of the sort that bore the slightest comparison to Charlie's extreme terror; and yet Charlie, on ordinary occasions, was by no means a coward. He galloped, he reared his mane and tossed his head, he stopped short and snorted wildly, and then he darted off at the top of his speed in a contrary direction, and then as suddenly stopped and set off in another, until long after the storm had considerably abated, and it was not until after the lapse of some hours that he ventured to reconnoiter—but that at a considerable distance—the scene of his narrow escape.

For that day at least his appetite had been completely spoiled, for he never offered to stoop his head to the ground while daylight continued. The next day his apprehension seemed somewhat abated, but his curiosity had been excited to such a pitch that he kept pacing from place to place, never sailing to halt as he passed within a moderate distance of the prostrate tree, gazing thereat in utter bewilderment, as if wholly unable to comprehend the scene he had witnessed the preceding day.

After this occurrence took place I kept this favorite horse several years, and during the summer months he usually enjoyed the benefit of his old pasture. But it was quite clear that he never forgot, on any occasion, the narrow escape he had had; for neither the burning rays of the noontide summer sun, nor the furious raging of the thunderstorm, could compel Charlie to seek shelter under one of the trees that still remained standing in his small pasture.

16

THE CUMBERSOME HORSE

BY H. C. BUNNER

Henry Cuyler Bunner was probably best known as an editor of Puck Magazine, *a publication that managed to find humor in politics. But he was also a poet, a novelist, and an author of short stories.*

Bunner specialized in ironic takes on life in Manhattan, a world in which horses rarely figured. But one of his best-known works was the story of an old farm horse who insisted that a promise be kept, no matter how inconvenient.

It is not to be denied that a sense of disappointment pervaded Mr. Brimmington's being in the hour of his first acquaintance with the isolated farmhouse which he had just purchased, sight unseen, after long epistolary negotiations with Mr. Hiram Skinner, postmaster, carpenter, teamster, and real estate agent of Bethel Corners, who was now driving him to his new domain.

Perhaps the feeling was of a mixed origin. Indian Summer was much colder up in the Pennsylvania hills than he had expected to find it; and the hills themselves were much larger and bleaker and barer, and far more indifferent in their demeanor toward him, than he had expected to find them. Then Mr. Skinner had been something of a disappointment, himself. He was too familiar with his big, knobby, red hands; too furtive with his small, close-set eyes; too profuse of tobacco-juice, and too raspingly loquacious. And certainly the house itself did not meet his expectations when he first saw it, standing lonely and desolate in its ragged meadows of stubble and wild grass on the unpleasantly steep mountainside.

And yet Mr. Skinner had accomplished for him the desire of his heart. He had always said that when he should come into his money—forty thousand dollars from a maiden aunt—he would quit forever his toilsome job of preparing Young Gentlemen for admission to the Larger Colleges and Universities, and would devote the next few years to writing his long-projected "History of Prehistoric Man." And to go about this task he had always said that he would go and live in perfect solitude—that is, all by himself and a chore-woman—in a secluded farmhouse, situated upon the southerly slope of some high hill—an old farmhouse—a Revolutionary farmhouse, if possible—a delightful, long, low, rambling farmhouse—a farmhouse with floors of various levels—a farmhouse with crooked stairs, and with nooks and corners and quaint cupboards—this—this had been the desire of Mr. Brimmington's heart.

Mr. Brimmington, when he came into his money at the age of forty-five, fixed on Pike County, Pennsylvania, as a mountainous country of good report. A postal guide informed him that Mr. Skinner was the postmaster of Bethel Corners; so Mr. Brimmington wrote to Mr. Skinner.

The correspondence between Mr. Brimmington and Mr. Skinner was long enough and full enough to have settled a treaty between two nations. It ended by a discovery of a house lonely enough and aged enough to fill the bill. Several hundred dollars' worth of repairs were needed to make it habitable, and Mr. Skinner was employed to make them. Toward the close of a cold November day, Mr. Brimmington saw his purchase for the first time.

In spite of his disappointment, he had to admit, as he walked around the place in the early twilight, that it was just what he had bargained for. The situation, the dimensions, the exposure, were all exactly what had been stipulated. About its age there could be no question. Internally, its irregularity—indeed, its utter failure to conform to any known rules of domestic architecture—surpassed Mr. Brimmington's wildest expectations. It had stairs eighteen inches wide; it had rooms of strange shapes and sizes; it had strange, shallow cupboards in strange places; it had no hallways; its windows were of odd design, and whoso wanted variety in floors could find it there. And along the main wall of Mr. Brimmington's study there ran a structure some three feet and a half high and nearly as deep, which Mr. Skinner confidently assured him was used in old times as a wall bench or a dresser, indifferently.

"You might think," said Mr. Skinner, "that all that space inside there was jest wasted; but it ain't so. Them seats is jest filled up inside with braces so's that you can set on them good and solid." And then Mr. Skinner proudly called attention to the two coats of gray paint spread over the entire side of the house, walls, ceilings and woodwork, blending the original portions and the Skinner restorations in one harmonious, homogeneous whole.

Mr. Skinner might have told him that this variety of gray paint is highly popular in some rural districts, and is made by mixing lamp-black and ball-blue with a low grade of white lead. But he did not say it; and he drove away as soon as he conveniently could, after formally introducing him to Mrs. Sparhawk, a gaunt, stern-faced, silent, elderly woman. Mrs. Sparhawk was to take charge of his bachelor establishment during the daytime. Mrs. Sparhawk cooked him a meal for which she very properly apologized. Then she returned to her kitchen to "clean up." Mr. Brimmington went to the front door, partly to look out upon his property, and partly to turn his back on the gray paint. There were no steps before the front door, but a newly graded mound or earthwork about the size of a half-hogshead. He looked out upon his apple-orchard, which was further away than he had expected to find it. It had been out of bearing for ten years, but this Mr. Brimmington did not know. He did know, however, that the whole outlook was distinctly dreary.

As he stood there and gazed out into the twilight, two forms suddenly approached him. Around one corner of the house came Mrs. Sparhawk on her way home. Around the other came an immensely tall, whitish shape, lumbering forward with a heavy tread. Before he knew it, it had scrambled up the side of his mound with a clumsy, ponderous rush, and was thrusting itself directly upon him when he uttered so lusty a cry of dismay that it fell back startled; and, wheeling about a great long body that swayed on four misshapen legs, it pounded off in the direction it had come from, and disappeared around the corner. Mr. Brimmington turned to Mrs. Sparhawk in disquiet and indignation.

"Mrs. Sparhawk," he demanded; "what is that?"

"It's a horse," said Mrs. Sparhawk, not at all surprised, for she knew that Mr. Brimmington was from the city. "They hitch 'em to wagons here."

"I know it is a horse, Mrs. Sparhawk," Mr. Brimmington rejoined with some asperity, "but whose horse is it, and what is it doing on my premises?"

"I don't rightly know whose horse it *is*," replied Mrs. Sparhawk; "the man that used to own it, he's dead now."

"But what," inquired Mr. Brimmington sternly, "is the animal doing here?"

"I guess he b'longs here," Mrs. Sparhawk said. She had a cold, even, impersonal way of speaking, as though she felt that her safest course in life was to confine herself strictly to such statements of fact as might be absolutely required of her.

"But, my good woman," replied Mr. Brimmington, in bewilderment, "how can that be? The animal can't certainly belong on my property unless he belongs to me, and that animal certainly is not mine."

Seeing him so much at a loss and so greatly disturbed in mind, Mrs. Sparhawk relented a little from her strict rule of life, and made an attempt at explanation. "He b'longed to the man who owned this place first off; and I don' know for sure, but I've heard tell that he fixed it some way so's that the horse would sort of go with the place."

Mr. Brimmington felt irritation rising within him. "But," he said, "it's preposterous! There was no such consideration in the deed. No such thing can be done, Mrs. Sparhawk, without my acquiescence!"

"I don't know nothin' about that," said Mrs. Sparhawk; "what I do know is, the place has changed hands often enough since, and the horse has always went with the place."

There was an unsettled suggestion in the first part of this statement of Mrs. Sparhawk that gave a shock to Mr. Brimmington's nerves. He laughed uneasily.

"Oh, er, yes! I see. Very probably there's been some understanding. I suppose I am to regard the horse as a sort of lien upon the place—a— what do they call it?—an encumbrance. Yes," he repeated, more to himself than to Mrs. Sparhawk, "an encumbrance. I've got a gentleman's country place with a horse encumbrant."

Mrs. Sparhawk heard him, however. "It *is* a sorter cumbersome horse," she said. And without another word she gathered her shawl about her shoulders, and strode off into the darkness.

Mr. Brimmington turned back into the house, and busied himself with a vain attempt to make his long-cherished furniture look at home in his new leaden-hued rooms. The ungrateful task gave him the blues and, after an hour of it, he went to bed.

He was dreaming leaden-hued dreams, oppressed, uncomfortable dreams, when a peculiarly weird and uncanny series of thumps on the front of the house awoke him with a start. The thumps might have been made by a giant with a weaver's beam, but he must have been a very drunken giant to group his thumps in such a disorderly parody of time and sequence.

Mr. Brimmington had too guileless and clean a heart to be the prey of undefined terrors. He rose, ran to the window and opened it. The moonlight lit up the raw, frosty landscape with a cold, pale, diffused radiance, and Mr. Brimmington could plainly see right below him the cumbersome horse, cumbersomely trying to maintain a footing on the top of the little mound before the front door. When, for a fleeting instant, he seemed to think that he had succeeded in this feat, he tried to bolt through the door. As soon, however, as one of his huge knees smote the panel, his hind feet lost their grip on the soft earth, and he wobbled back down the incline, where he stood shaking and quivering, until he could muster wind enough for another attempt to make a catapult of himself. The veil-like illumination of the night, which turned all things else to a dim, silvery gray, could not hide the scars and bruises and worn places that spotted the animal's great, gaunt, distorted frame. His knees were as big as a man's head. His feet were enormous. His joints stood out from his shriveled carcass like so many pine knots. Mr. Brimmington gazed at him, fascinated, horrified, until a rush more desperate and uncertain than the rest threatened to break his front door in.

"Hi!" shrieked Mr. Brimmington; "go away!"

It was the horse's turn to get frightened. He lifted his long, coffin-shaped head toward Mr. Brimmington's window, cast a sort of blind, cross-eyed, ineffectual glance at him, and with a long-drawn, wheezing, cough-choked whinny he backed down the mound, got himself about, end for end, with such extreme awkwardness that he hurt one poor knee on a hitching post that looked to be ten feet out of his way, and limped off to the rear of the house.

The sound of that awful, rusty, wind-broken whinny haunted Mr. Brimmington all the rest of that night. It was like the sound of an orchestra run down, or of a man who is utterly tired of the whooping cough and doesn't care who knows it.

The next morning was bright and sunshiny, and Mr. Brimmington awoke in a more cheerful frame of mind than he would naturally have expected to find himself in after his perturbed night. He found himself inclined to make the best of his purchase and to view it in as favorable a light as possible. He went outside and looked at it from various points of view, trying to find and if possible to dispose of the reason for the vague sense of disappointment which he felt, having come into possession of the rambling old farmhouse, which he had so much desired.

He decided, after a long and careful inspection, that it was the *proportions* of the house that were wrong. They were certainly peculiar.

It was singularly high between joints in the first story, and singularly low in the second. In spite of its irregularity within, it was uncompromisingly square on the outside. There was something queer about the pitch of its roof, and it seemed strange that so modest a structure with no hallway whatever should have vestibule windows on each side of its doors, both front and rear.

But here an idea flashed into Mr. Brimmington's mind that in an instant changed him from a carping critic to a delighted discoverer. He was living in a Block House! Yes; that explained—that accounted for all the strangeness of its architecture. In an instant he found his purchase invested with a beautiful glamour of adventurous association. Here was the stout and well-planned refuge to which the grave settlers of an earlier day had fled to guard themselves against the attack of the vindictive redskins. He saw it all. A moat, crossed no doubt by draw-bridges, had surrounded the building. In the main room below, the women and children had huddled while their courageous defenders had poured a leaden hail upon the foe through loopholes in the upper story. He walked around the house for some time, looking for loop-holes.

So pleased was Mr. Brimmington at his theory that the morning passed rapidly away, and when he looked at his watch he was surprised to find that it was nearly noon. Then he remembered that Mr. Skinner had promised to call on him at eleven, to make anything right that was not right. Glancing over the landscape he saw Mr. Skinner approaching by a circuitous track. He was apparently following the course of a snake fence, which he could readily have climbed. This seemed strange, as his way across the pastureland was seemingly unimpeded. Thinking of the pastureland made Mr. Brimmington think of the white horse, and casting his eyes a little further down the hill he saw that animal slowly and painfully steering a parallel course to Mr. Skinner, on the other side of the fence. Mr. Skinner went out of sight behind a clump of trees, and when he arrived it was not upon the side of the house where Mr. Brimmington had expected to see him appear.

As they were about to enter the house Mr. Brimmington noticed the marks of last night's attack upon his front door, and he spoke to Mr. Skinner about the horse.

"Oh, yes," said Mr. Skinner, with much ingenuousness; "that horse. I was meaning to speak to you about that horse. Fact is, I've kinder got that horse on my hands, and if it's no inconvenience to you, I'd like to leave him where he is for a little while."

"But it would be very inconvenient, indeed, Mr. Skinner," said the new owner of the house. "The animal is a very unpleasant object; and, moreover, it attempted to break into my front door last night."

Mr. Skinner's face darkened. "Sho!" he said; "you don't mean to tell me that?"

But Mr. Brimmington did mean to tell him that, and Mr. Skinner listened with a scowl of unconcealed perplexity and annoyance. He bit his lip reflectively for a minute or two before he spoke.

"Too bad you was disturbed," he said at length. "You'll have to keep the bars up to that meadow and then it won't happen again."

"But, indeed, it must not happen again," said Mr. Brimmington. "The horse must be taken away."

"Well, you see it's this way, friend," returned Mr. Skinner, with a rather ugly air of decision. "I really ain't got no choice in the matter. I'd like to oblige you, and if I'd known as far back that you would have objected to the animal I'd have had him took somewheres. But, as it is, there ain't no such a thing as getting that there horse off this here place till the frost's out of the ground. You can see for yourself that that horse, the condition he's in now, couldn't no more go up nor down this hill than he could fly. Why, I came over here a-foot this morning on purpose not to take them horses of mine over this road again. It can't be done, sir."

"Very well," suggested Mr. Brimmington. "Kill the horse."

"I ain't killin' no horses," said Mr. Skinner. "You may if you like; but I'd advise you not to. There's them as mightn't like it."

"Well, let them come and take their horse away, then," said Mr. Brimmington.

"Just so," assented Mr. Skinner. "It's they who are concerned in the horse, and they have a right to take him away. I would if I was any ways concerned, but I ain't." Here he turned suddenly upon Mr. Brimmington.

"Why, look here," he said, "you ain't got the heart to turn that there horse out of that there pasture where he's been for fifteen years! It won't do you no sorter hurt to have him stay there till spring. Put the bars up, and he won't trouble you no more."

"But," objected Mr. Brimmington, weakly, "even if the poor creature were not so unsightly, he could not be left alone all winter in that pasture without shelter."

"That's just where you're mistaken," Mr. Skinner replied, tapping his interlocutor heavily upon the shoulder. "He don't mind it not one mite. See that shed there?" And he pointed to a few wind-racked boards in the corner of the lot. "There's hoss-shelter; and as for feed, why there's feed enough in that meadow for two such as him."

In the end, Mr. Brimmington, being utterly ignorant of the nature and needs of horseflesh, was over-persuaded, and he consented to let the unfortunate white horse remain in his pasture lot to be the sport of the winter's chill and bitter cruelty. Then he and Mr. Skinner talked about some new paint.

It was the dead vast and middle of Mr. Brimmington's third night in his new house, when he was absolutely knocked out of a calm and peaceful slumber by a crash so appalling that he at first thought that the side of the mountain had slid down upon his dwelling. This was followed by other crashes, thumps, the tearing of woodwork and various strange and gruesome noises. Whatever it might be, Mr. Brimmington felt certain that it was no secret midnight marauder, and he hastened to the eighteen-inch stairway without even waiting to put on a dressing gown. A rush of cold air came up from below, and he had no choice but to scuttle back for a bathrobe and a candle while the noises continued, and the cold air floated all over the house.

There was no difficulty in locating the sounds. Mr. Brimmington presented himself at the door of the little kitchen, pulled it open, and, raising the light above his head, looked in. The rush of wind blew out his light, but not before he had had time to see that it was the white horse that was in the kitchen, and that he had gone through the floor.

Subsequent investigation proved that the horse had come in through the back door, carrying that and its two vestibule windows with him, and that he had first trampled and then churned the thin floor into match-wood. He was now reposing on his stomach, with his legs hanging down between the joists into the hollow under the house—for there was no cellar. He looked over his shoulder at his host and emitted his bloodcurdling wail.

"My gracious!" said Mr. Brimmington.

That night Mr. Brimmington sat up with the horse, both of them wrapped, as well as Mr. Brimmington could do it, in bedclothes. There is not much you can do with a horse when you have to sit up with him under such circumstances. The thought crossed Mr. Brimmington's mind of reading to him, but he dismissed it.

In the interview the next day, between Mr. Brimmington and Mr. Skinner, the aggressiveness was all on Mr. Brimmington's side, and Mr. Skinner was meek and wore an anxious expression. Mr. Brimmington had, however, changed his point of view. He now realized that sleeping out of winter nights might be unpleasant, even painful to an aged and rheumatic horse. And, although he had cause of legitimate complaint against the creature, he could no longer bear to think of killing the animal with whom he had shared that cold and silent vigil.

He commissioned Mr. Skinner to build for the brute a small but commodious lodging, and to provide a proper stock of provender—commissions which Mr. Skinner gladly and humbly accepted. As to the undertaking to get the horse out of his immediate predicament, however, Mr. Skinner absolutely refused to touch the job.

"That horse don't like me," said Mr. Skinner; "I know he don't; I seen it in his eyes long ago. If you like, I'll send you two or three men and a block-and-tackle, and they can get him out; but not me; no, sir!"

Mr. Skinner devoted that day to repairing damages, and promised on the morrow to begin the building of the little barn. Mr. Brimmington was glad there was going to be no greater delay, when, early in the evening, the sociable white horse tried to put his front feet through the study window.

But of all the noises that startled Mr. Brimmington, in the first week of his sojourn in the farmhouse, the most alarming awakened him about eight o'clock of the following morning. Hurrying to his study, he gazed in wonder upon a scene unparalleled even in the History of Prehistoric Man. The boards had been ripped off the curious structure which was supposed to have served the hardy settlers for a wall bench and a dresser, indifferently.

This revealed another structure in the form of a long crib or bin, within which, apparently trying to back out through the wall, stood Mr. Skinner, holding his toolbox in front of him as if to shield himself, and fairly yelping with terror. The front door was off its hinges, and there stood Mrs. Sparhawk wielding a broom to keep out the white horse, who was viciously trying to force an entrance. Mr. Brimmington asked what it all meant; and Mrs. Sparhawk, turning a desperate face upon him, spoke with the vigor of a woman who has kept silence too long.

"It means," she said, "that this here house of yours is this here horse's stable; *and the horse knows it*; and that there was the horse's manger. This here horse was old Colonel Josh Pincus's regimental horse, and so provided for in his will; and this here man Skinner was to have the caring of him until he should die a natural death, and then he was to have this stable; and till then the stable was left to the horse. And now he's taken the stable away from the horse, and patched it up into a dwelling-house for a fool from New York City; and the horse don't like it; and the horse don't like Skinner. And when he come back to git that manger for your barn, the horse sot onto him. And that's what's the matter, Mr. Skimmerton."

"Mrs. Sparhawk," began Mr. Brimmington—

"I *ain't* no Sparhawk!" fairly shouted the enraged woman, as with a furious shove she sent the Cumbersome Horse staggering down the doorway mound; "this here's Hiram Skinner, the meanest man in Pike County, and I'm his wife, let out to do day's work. You've had one week of him—how would you have liked twenty years?"

17

A DRUMMER'S HORSE

BY R. M. LOCKHART

FROM *OUR DUMB ANIMALS*, 1912

Our Dumb Animals *was probably the first, and certainly the most important, of the publications devoted to animal welfare. Debuting in 1868, it was produced by the Massachusetts Society for the Prevention of Cruelty to Animals and was distributed throughout the United States. On the masthead of each issue the magazine declared, "We Speak for Those Who Cannot Speak for Themselves." Almost all animals, wild and domestic, have been covered at one time or another during the life of the magazine, which exists today in the form of the MSPCA newsletter "Companion."*

Horses were a particular focus for the first fifty years of the publication, until they disappeared from city streets and rural roads. Some of the articles described the horrors of life for mistreated working horses, but others, like this one, painted a much happier picture.

As a traveling salesman in the Southern states, several years ago, with a route covering a wide stretch of country territory, it became necessary for me to have a horse and buggy to reach my customers. I purchased my outfit at Thomasville, Georgia, and prepared to start upon a long trip. From remarks which were made in my hearing, I must confess that I had some misgiving as to whether my horse would meet the requirements and prove a trusty roadster. I was informed that this horse was so wild and vicious that no one could drive him; that the owner had been anxious to sell him at any price on account of damages he had already done; that he had a predilection for smashing buggies and the unruly habit of madly running away under the least provocation.

The first thing I did was to cut off the blinders from the bridle so that my horse could see me and assure himself, whenever he liked, that I was with him, no matter where our business took us or what strange scenes or obstacles we encountered. I took pains to see that his harness fitted him and started off and for the next two months almost waited for him to run away.

He had shown no inclination to bolt through fear or sudden fright or any other cause up to this time; he had grown so affectionate and been so gentle that I began to travel with the lines fastened to a hook in the top of my vehicle to allow him to go as he pleased. He quickly learned to be guided by the motions of my hands and I thought at times I saw him turn his eyes towards me as if inquiring the right direction.

When I made my calls I left him standing untied and it mattered not how long I was away, he awaited patiently my return and greeted me with a joyous whinny and a rub of his head against my body. I taught him to obey the sound of a whistle. When I blew once, he stopped; twice, he started, and he never failed to respond.

His fondness for candy and fruit was like that of a child and wherever "sweets" were obtainable he reminded me of his expectation that I would buy. I had made a little agreement to give him such things for good behavior and kept my promise, but somehow I always felt that it was he who was rewarding me for my kindness.

I drove him for three years without a mishap, without a whip, and with that confidence that is born of a mutual understanding. When the nights were so dark that I could not see the road nor my horse, I gave him the reins and he brought me safely to my journey's end.

No man ever traveled with a more faithful animal or a more agreeable companion. I have never driven a horse that so well fulfilled my requirements. When we had to part, and I must add that it brought me real sorrow, I put him in the hands of a friend who promised me that he would look well to his care. Wherever the faithful finally go, there will my good horse be.

18

WHITE DANDY: MASTER AND I— A HORSE'S STORY

BY VELMA CALDWELL MELVILLE

Another advocate of animal rights was a Wisconsin woman named Velma Caldwell Melville, who was widely published in women's magazines of the late nineteenth century. Melville was an active supporter of Henry Bergh, a wealthy New Yorker who founded the Society for the Prevention of Cruelty to Animals in 1866. Twelve years later Melville was struck by the worldwide success of Black Beauty. *Anna Sewell, the book's English author, intended it as a morality tale for people who worked with horses, but its message of the horrors of mistreatment for working horses struck a chord with a much wider audience.*

Melville decided that North America needed its own version of Black Beauty. *Her book featured a horse named White Dandy and was written entirely in his voice. As in the original, other horse characters tell their stories of abuse.*

From his earliest days, White Dandy knows nothing but kind-ness. His job as a riding and driving horse for Dr. Richard Wallace suits him perfectly and he's an enthusiastic worker as the doctor goes about his rounds. While Dr. Wallace demands much, he is equally demanding that the hostlers who care for his beloved horse do their jobs kindly.

Dr. Wallace's brother Fred, also a doctor, is less careful and White Dandy notices how the horses used by the doctor and his sons can be treated with thoughtlessness and occasional cruelty. The memories of these incidents frighten White Dandy when his master makes a momentous decision.

CHAPTER 11

One autumn Master determined to "go West." Why he went I do not know, but he was to stay "some months," they said. How I did hope he would take me along, but he did not.

"Be kind to Dandy," was his parting injunction, as usual, to Herman, the man who had succeeded Park Winters as hostler. Of course, I did not know what going West means, and could not think that "some months" were longer than the time he had spent in Chicago. The morning he started he came into my stall and talked to me a long while. Among other things he said: "Be a good boy, Dandy, and when I come home we'll go and live at the farm—you and I."

I did miss him so! The days were all dreary, and I dreaded to go to sleep at night, because I would be obliged to awake to a fresh sense of my loss. I cannot begin to give all my experience during his absence, but will note a few instances. Of a truth, I realized as never before what it is to be a horse.

Dr. and Mrs. Wallace were not a happy couple. The latter was less outspoken than in the early days of her married life, but she was equally as self-willed, only more cunning and underhanded about it. Fred drank all the time, but people could not ordinarily tell when he was intoxicated. The barn boys said he could "carry a good deal." The two boys, Chet and Carm, were wild and lawless. The former was smart and a great student, though. Poor Carm, better but weaker, was always in disgrace. His teacher and father called him a "numbskull," and gradually the latter came to indulge Chet in everything and deny Carm just as prodigally.

There were two other children in the house now—Tommy and Elizabeth, or "Bobby," as the little girl called herself, and others fell into the habit. I liked Bobby from the time Master first held the little yellow-haired creature on my back for a ride; and she always clapped her little hands on seeing me, and cried, "Dandy! Dandy!" I liked her for herself, and also because Dr. Dick loved her. It did me good to know that he had this little child to pet and think about.

Things went well enough for a week or so after Master left, then Chet began to drive me. Sometimes when the doctor would use me for a long drive in the day, soon after dark, while I was yet eating my supper, the boy, with some companion, would come into the barn and put my harness on. Herman would object, and there would be a fuss between them, always ending in my being hitched in a buggy or road cart and driven out. It was the second time that this occurred that I discovered that Chet was under the influence of liquor, as was also his companion, and they carried bottles with them. Chet used the whip freely and I went as fast as I could, but the oftener they touched those bottles the harder they drove.

After what seemed to me hours of agony, they pulled up before a brilliantly lighted old building out in the country, hitched me, and staggered in. The wind was raw and cold, and the sweat pouring off me. I surely thought Chet would remember my blanket, but he didn't, and there I had to stand one, two, three, four, or more dreadful hours. Long before they came out I was alternately chilling and burning. I ached and trembled.

They drove home as fast as they came, whipping nearly all the way, though I was doing my best. Herman swore profusely (people did not do that around the barn when Master was home) as he rubbed me down rapidly with a coarse cloth before blanketing me closely. How I felt!

And thirsty—it did seem I must have water or choke, but he gave me none for some reason. By morning I was so stiff I could scarcely move, my breath was short and came hard, and my skin was hot. Dr. Fred ordered me early.

"I don't think Dandy is able to go out, sir, to-day," Herman replied. "The young gentlemen had him out all night almost, and he is all stiffened up."

Dr. Fred muttered something and ordered out the bays, calling out to Herman, as he drove off, to get Dr. Dick's box of horse medicine and give me aconite—two-drop doses of the tincture every two hours—until the fever was gone; then to alternate bryonia, and thus according to directions given in the book with the box.

I noticed that I began to feel better pretty soon, and by afternoon Mrs. Wallace said she wanted me hitched up. Herman demurred, but had to finally give in. I was as stiff as ever when I got home again.

That very night Chet harnessed me again, despite Herman's angry protest, and drove me ten miles. If only he had taken the trouble to look in my eyes, I am sure he must have seen how wretched I felt. This time he carelessly threw a blanket over me, but did not buckle it over my chest, and in a little while the wind had blown it half off me. It would have been entirely off—and it might as well have been—but for a corner catching on the top of the collar.

That time gray was showing in the east before he started for home. With vile, profane words he bade me "Get up," emphasizing by stinging blows of the whip, saying to his companion that he must make the ten miles before his father was up. I suppose no man was ever compelled to stand tied to a post all night; if there had, he would surely be going up and down the earth preaching mercy and justice to those who have the power over horses. Another thing made that night especially wearing was the fact that I was tied short, and my front feet were much lower than my back ones. Such a strain as I was on!

It does seem that horses deserve the little consideration necessary to tie them in a decent spot. I have heard many of my kind speak of this matter. In some villages the hitching places along the sidewalks are most uncomfortable, the animals being obliged to stand on a twist, ofttimes with the front feet lower and in a mud puddle. Is it any wonder we sometimes protest by vigorously pawing the sidewalks, if we can reach them? Give us fair play.

Well, I was too lame to get out at all, after that night, for a week. I had rheumatism. Had Master been there to treat me, I might have recovered, but Herman knew nothing about horse doctoring, and so it ran on. If I did get a little better, it was only to be overdriven and exposed. Another time there was to be a horse race five miles off, and Chet drove Prince and I in the buggy.

Then I found out how it hurts a heavy-bodied, short-legged horse to be driven with a light-bodied, long-limbed one. He drove, as usual, just as fast as he could make us go, uphill and down the same. More than once I thought I should fall, and by the time he stopped I was whiter than even nature intended me to be, being covered with foam.

Prince was not nearly so tired, but he said it irritated and fretted him to be driven with a horse of my build.

It was only a little country horse race, and the animals were chiefly working ones with neither inclination, strength, nor training for the racetrack. The men were wild with excitement, and betting was going on all around. After a while three men got on their horses' backs and started. The crowd yelled and clapped their hands; the riders buried the cruel spurs in the horses' sides, and leaned as far forward as possible.

Of course, some one had to beat, and it was a long-legged, bony creature that won the first heat. Three times the same ones run, and twice the long-legged one won, but the others had done their best; yes, more than that, I may say.

Poor things! There they stood, sweat and blood covering their sides, every nerve and muscle overstrained, and their masters cursing them for their defeat. The entire afternoon was consumed in this manner. Among others Prince was taken on the track. I knew by his eye, and the poise of his head he did not like it, but he behaved nicely until a cruel-looking fellow got on his back and dug the rowels in; with one bound he was off, and the rider had hard work to keep his seat. He won the heat, and I was scarcely enjoying his victory when, quick as a flash, he reached out and catching the fellow by the shoulder flung him headlong some feet away.

Someone caught the bridle strap, and, as soon as the fellow could pick himself up, he flew at the offender, dealing him a blow between the eyes with a club chancing to be handy. "Hold on!" Chet cried, but another, and another blow followed. My noble gray friend staggered, gathered up, staggered again, then fell. A half-dozen convulsive shivers passed over his frame and he was dead.

In a fury of anger and terror the young master sprang upon Prince's slayer. They grappled, but strong hands separated them, and Chet had only to put my harness in the buggy, get on my back, and ride sorrowfully homeward. Dr. Fred was in a temper, to be sure, and immediately had an officer after the man who had killed his horse.

All night and, for many nights, I could not close my eyes without seeming to see poor Prince in the death throes, and all because he dared to resent unfair treatment. I heard Herman say that the fellow had paid for the horse, that Chet and his father had had a quarrel, and that Mrs. Wallace insisted on the former leaving home.

"Yes, she's mighty keen fer the first woman's boys to leave home," remarked an old man who worked around the barn. "She's wantin' 'em out of the way so her young uns 'll git the property."

"Guess there won't be enough to fight over if Dr. Dick stays away long," Herman replied.

Speaking of horse races reminds me to say that if all racehorses, or those that are made to run, could tell their stories they would fill volumes with tales of injustice and suffering. All animals will, if humanely treated, do their best for their masters; but a kind word and reassuring pat will go much further toward winning a race than all the spurs and curses in the world. Many a race has been lost through the very efforts made to win it.

Coolness and self-possession are indispensable in both horse and rider. I remember being at a state fair with my master some years later, and witnessing a race. Among the competitors was a handsome little black horse, all grit and goodness, but, owing to its owner being partly intoxicated, it lost the stake, in consequence incurring his wrath. And how he did pound the noble little beast! A number of disapprovals arose from the multitude, but no one ventured to interfere. The animal was his, you know.

CHAPTER 12

I had no idea before that year's experience that little things—at least what men call little things—could so affect the health and spirits of a horse. I had even felt a little scornful sometimes when I saw strong-looking animals go along with drooping heads, and noticed how dull and stupid they looked. But when I came to endure hardships and have no petting (though Herman was better to me than most men are to their own horses) I felt differently about it. We need encouragement.

Chet did not take me out after Prince's tragic death for some time, but Dr. Fred drove me a great deal, as there was only the bays and myself then. Topsy had had no regular breaking yet, but Chet declared his intention of attending to the matter at once. When he did undertake it he frightened the poor thing almost to death, and what the outcome would have been I can only surmise, had not a humane man noticed him one day and chided him for his method, or rather lack of method.

"Let me show you my way," he said.

I suppose Chet was getting tired of the job, so surrendered. From being always handled, Topsy was all right, so long as no harness was introduced, or any unusual noise made near her; but at the first unfamiliar sight or sound she was a bunch of terrified, prancing nerves, expecting the worst, and usually getting it, in the form of a whipping.

"She's got to learn that I'm boss," was a favorite expression of Chet's.

"Well, my boy," said the gentleman, "I suppose it is necessary for a horse to know it has a master, but it is equally necessary for us to recognize that they have rights, and also that bullying an animal is not being, in a manly sense, its master. Now I have broken scores of horses, and never yet whipped but one, and I have always hated myself for doing that."

Then he began to gently rub Topsy's head and neck with his hands, and later with a brush. She seemed to enjoy this, and when he let the latter gradually pass over her shoulders and back, she offered no resistance. He worked with her fifteen minutes or longer, then turned her into the little enclosure she occupied during the day.

I think I neglected to say I was resting out at the farm for a day or two when this occurred. In two or three hours the man came again, and repeated the handling and brushing, only this time he touched the whole body, talking kindly and reassuring all the while.

"She is going to be an uncommonly easy subject, I predict," he announced.

"But who'd have patience for such slow getting on?" Chet scornfully asked.

"I should imagine a little time apparently wasted in the beginning less loss than a fine horse ruined in the end," the old man quietly answered.

When he let the young mare go that time she seemed slow to leave him, though he had brushed her even to her heels. The next time he handled her with greater freedom, brushing and talking and finally showing her a little sack of straw. She eyed it a while, smelled it, and then seemed not to care for it.

The man now began to rub her with this, gradually increasing the noise it made. Of course, she was a little shy of this, and inclined to go away. A few gentle touches of the brush reassured her. Then he put a halter on her. She had often worn one before. After this he applied the straw again, stopping every little while to brush and smooth her. In a little time she paid no attention either to the noise or the touch of the sack.

The next day he gave her four lessons of similar character. Later he rattled tin cans and the like about her from head to heels, and had small boys blow tin horns in all directions. Topsy told me afterwards that so long as she could hear that man's voice or feel his touch, she was not afraid of anything.

Afterward he gradually introduced the bridle and harness. Like all horses, she objected to the bit, and I fancy people would make more fuss than we do, if they had to wear it. It was the first night that Topsy was at the livery barn after her "breaking," and she was saying she minded the bit worst of all. An old horse replied that well she might hate it.

"For years," she said, "my tongue has been in a measure paralyzed. It always hangs out of my mouth when the bit is in, and I can't help it. Sometimes it is more helpless than others and I almost starve. I get better at times where some one owns me who puts a bit in my mouth that don't hurt; but I am getting used up anyway, and change hands often, and the majority of bits makes the trouble worse."

"I was once troubled that way," spoke up another horse, "and my master kept changing bits until he got one that was all right and then I got over it."

"I, too, had a paralyzed tongue," said another, "but it was not the bit, it was genuine paralysis—might have been caused by that in the first place, though I never thought of it. Anyway they applied electricity to the nerves and gave me some medicine three times a day—'strychnia,' they called it, one-hundredth of a grain at a dose. I soon got well."

"My tongue was all torn to pieces once with a frosty bit," put in another. "And how I did suffer! No one noticed it until it was all ulcerated, and I could not eat and scarcely drink. My master was one of those careless fellows who never examines his horse, and seems to forget that, however much they suffer, they can't speak for themselves. He did not know what to do for me and so sent for a neighbor, who told him to use alum wash until the ulcers were all gone, and leave the bit out until my mouth got well, meanwhile feeding me soft food."

And still another spoke of her teeth becoming long and rough, and lacerating her tongue badly. She said they filed the teeth and wet her tongue and mouth with a lotion made of calendula and water.

Topsy was a beauty in harness, and Chet was proud of her in his way, but from the first I feared hers would be a hard life, but my darkest forebodings came short of the dread reality. Among other experiences that winter was one in horseshoeing. Master had been exceedingly particular always about my feet, but Herman was like a majority of other men; knew nothing of the business himself and trusted entirely to the smith, who chanced to be a new one.

I had often heard Master and the good blacksmith in the old home denounce the fashion of trimming the frog and thinning the sole until it yielded to the pressure of the thumb, and that was just what this smith did. And then he put on great, heavy shoes, driving in spikes rather than nails. I admit that I kicked and plunged, but it was all wrong, and I knew it; then the last spike went through into the foot. This made me rear and plunge worse than ever, and the blacksmith struck me with the hammer.

"See here, Dr. Dick Wallace won't stand that," cried Herman. "He allows no man to strike Dandy."

"Don't reckon he's better than other horses," he answered.

"Folks might differ on that," said Herman.

Well, I got out of there at last, but my foot hurt intolerably, and I limped. Herman spoke of it to Dr. Fred, but the latter was in one of his gruff moods, and only answered: "It most always lames 'em at first."

That night a man came for a doctor in great haste; some one had taken poison by mistake. Dandy was ordered. If I could have spoken, how soon I would have convinced Herman that, with that terrible torture in my foot, I could not go, but I could only mutely look at him, and he, half asleep, paid no attention. It was a good many miles we went, and the doctor drove like mad. It seemed to me that running through fire would have been easy compared with the pain in my foot, aggravated by the ceaseless concussion of the hard roads.

With a blanket thrown over me, I was left tied in a shed. How I longed to lie down on something! All I could do was to hold up that leg. The pains extended clear into my shoulders, and the cords of my neck were growing stiff.

After a long time, a man came out and unhitched me from the road cart. The moment I was free I lay down. Directly the man ran and brought Dr. Fred. They bade me get up, and, rather than to disobey, I tried it, but the moment I threw any weight on that foot had to immediately lay down again. Presently the man noticed me holding that foot, and asked if I was not newly shod. Then Dr. Fred remembered.

"Well, Dandy," he said, "we must get home. Try it once more." I got on my feet, but had to hold that one up for awhile. Gradually I compelled myself to put it down, for I knew we must go, as he had said. That was long years ago, but even now I can feel some of the agony of that slow journey.

He went with Herman and me to the shop, and fiercely ordered that shoe removed. The smith was not nearly so independent then. When the doctor saw the heavy thing he raved more than ever.

"Do you put such shoes as those on a horse like this?" he cried. The result was that all the shoes came off, and I was put in my stall till my feet got well.

"An ounce at the toe means a pound at the withers," quoted the old stable man. "And there's truth in it; glad the doctor had sense enough to refuse them."

It was four weeks before I could be shod again, and in the meantime I had a very sore foot. They gave me aconite to keep down my fever, and used arnica on my foot after paring away the horn and poulticing until suppuration ceased. My one thought was: "Will Master never come home?"

And so the winter and spring passed. "Several months," I thought as much! My experience was pretty much the same right through, but I felt years older when once again I rested my head on my beloved Master's shoulder.

There was a new stable boy when he came back; Paddy, they called him. Dr. Fred and Herman had quarreled some time before. There was a new span of horses, too; John and Jean. The old stable man privately told Master of some of my hardships, and with tears in his eyes, the latter whispered: "Forgive me, Dandy."

VI

RACEHORSES

19

THE GREAT MATCH RACE BETWEEN ECLIPSE AND SIR HENRY

BY AN OLD TURFMAN

Working horses made up the great majority of the three million or so horses who lived in the United States during the first half of the nineteenth century. But the relatively small number of sporting horses drew a disproportionate amount of attention and money. Horse racing, for both sporting and gambling purposes, was almost universally popular. The sport found itself standing in for the regional conflict between North and South several times during the decades leading up to the Civil War, never more so than in the Great Match Race of 1823.

This is how the match was proposed by newspaper advertisements to horsemen North and South during the early months of 1823:

Great match race . . . over the Union Course, Long Island, May 27th, 1823. Heats four miles, for $20,000. The Southern gentlemen to be allowed to name their horse at the starting post.

A writer who described himself as "An Old Turfman," actually Cadwallader R. Colden, manager of the Union Course itself, told the story of the race a few years later.

~~~~~~

Doubts were entertained by some of the New York sportsmen to the last moment whether this great match would be contested by the Virginia gentlemen. They, it was perfectly understood, had left Virginia, with five horses, selected from the best racers which North Carolina and Virginia could boast of, and proceeded to the estate of Mr. Bela Badger, adjacent to Bristol, in Pennsylvania, distant from the Union Course, about ninety miles, where, having a fine course upon which to exercise and try their horses, they had made a halt.

The horses selected for this great occasion, as also to contend for the three purse races to be run for, on the three days subsequent to the match, heats of four, three, and two miles, were Betsey Richards, five years old; her full brother, John Richards, four years; Sir Henry, four years; Flying Childers, five years; all by Sir Archy; and Washington, four years old, by Timoleon, a son of Sir Archy. With one of the three first named, it was the intention of Mr. William R. Johnston to run the match. Of these, at the time he left home, John Richards was his favorite; his next choice was Sir Henry, and thirdly, the mare; although some of the Southern gentlemen (and amongst others Gen. Wynn) gave their opinion in favor of running the mare, fearing lest Henry might get frightened by so large a crowd of people and swerve from the track.

Unfortunately for the Virginians, their favorite, John Richards, in a trial race, while at Mr. Badger's, met with an accident, by receiving a cut in the heel or frog of one of his forefeet, which rendered it necessary to throw him out of train; Washington also fell amiss, and he and Richards were left behind at Mr. Badger's. With the other three the Southern sportsmen proceeded to the Union Course, where they arrived five or six days previous to that fixed upon for the match.

The ill-fortune which befell the Virginians by laming their best horse in the onset seemed to pursue them, for scarcely had they arrived at Long Island and become fixed in their new quarters, when Mr. Johnston, the principal on their part, upon whose management and attention their success in a great measure depended, was seized with indisposition, so sudden and violent, as to confine him not only to his room, but to his bed, which he was unable to leave on the day of the race. Thus the Southrons, deprived of their leader, whose skill and judgment, whether in the way of stable preparation, or generalship in the field, could be supplied by none other, had to face their opponents under circumstances thus far disadvantageous and discouraging. Notwithstanding these unexpected and untoward events, they met the coming contest manfully, having full and unimpaired confidence in their two remaining horses, Sir Henry and Betsey Richards, and backed their opinion to the moment of starting.

At length the rising sun gave promise that the eventful day would prove fine and unclouded. I was in the field at the peep of dawn and observed that the Southern horse and mare, led by Harry Curtis in their walk, were both plated, treated alike, and both in readiness for the approaching contest. It was yet unknown to the Northern sportsmen which was to be their competitor.

The road from New York to the course, a distance of eight miles, was covered by horsemen and a triple line of carriages in an unbroken chain, from the dawn of day until one o'clock, the appointed hour of starting. The stands on the ground for the reception of spectators were crowded to excess at an early hour, and the club house, and balcony extending along its whole front, was filled by ladies; the whole track, or nearly so, for a mile distance in circuit, was lined on the inside by carriages and horsemen, and the throng of pedestrians surpassed all belief—*not less than sixty thousand spectators were computed to be in the field.*

About half past twelve o'clock Sir Henry made his appearance on the course as the champion of the South and was soon confronted by his antagonist. I shall now endeavor to give a brief description of these noted racers. Sir Henry is a dark sorrel or chestnut color, with one hind foot white, and a small star in the forehead; his mane and tail about two shades lighter than that of his body; he has been represented as being fifteen hands and one inch high, but having taken his measure, his exact height is only fourteen hands three and a half inches. His form is compact, bordering upon what is termed pony-built, with a good shoulder, fine clean head, and all those points which constitute a fine forehand; his barrel is strong, and well ribbed up towards the hip; waist rather short; chinbone strong, rising or arched a little over the loin, indicative of ability to carry weight; sway short; the loin full and strong; haunches strong and well let down; hindquarters somewhat high and sloping off from the coupling to the croup; thighs full and muscular, without being fleshy; hocks, or houghs, strong, wide, and pretty well let down; legs remarkably fine, with a full proportion of bone; back sinew, or Achilles tendon, large, and well detached from the canon bone; stands firm, clear, and even, moves remarkably well, with his feet in line; possesses great action and muscular power, and although rather under size, the exquisite symmetry of his form indicates uncommon strength and hardihood. He was bred by Mr. Lemuel

Long, near Halifax, in the state of North Carolina, and foaled on the 17th day of June, 1819. He was sired by Sir Archy (son of imported chestnut Diomed), his dam by Diomed, . . .

Eclipse is a dark sorrel horse with a star, the near hind foot white, said to be fifteen hands three inches in height, but in fact measures, by the standard, only fifteen hands and two inches. He possesses great power and substance, being well spread and full made throughout his whole frame, his general mould being much heavier than what is commonly met with in the thoroughbred blood-horse; he is, however, right in the cardinal points, very deep in the girth, with a good length of waist; loin wide and strong; shoulder by no means fine, being somewhat thick and heavy, yet strong and deep; breast wide, and apparently too full, and too much spread for a horse of great speed; arms long, strong, and muscular; head by no means fine; neck somewhat defective, the junction with the head having an awkward appearance, and too fleshy, and bagging too much upon the underside, near the throttle; his forelegs, from the knee downwards, are short and strong, with a large share of bone and sinew; upon the whole his forehand is too heavy.

To counterbalance this, his hindquarters are as near perfection as it is possible to imagine. From the hooks, or hip bone, to the extremity of the hindquarter, including the whole sweep from the hip to the hough, he has not an equal; with long and full muscular thighs, let down almost to the houghs, which are also particularly long, and well let down upon the cannon bone; legs short, with large bone and strong tendon, well detached, upon which he stands clear and even. Although his form throughout denotes uncommon strength, yet to the extraordinary fine construction of his hindquarters, I conceive him indebted for his great racing powers, continuance, and ability, equal to any weight. I have closely observed him in his gallops; if he has a fault, it is that of falling a little too heavy on his forefeet, and dwelling a little too long on the ground; but then the style and regularity with which he brings up his haunches, and throws his gaskins forward, overbalance other defects.

He was sired by Duroc, a Virginia horse, bred by Wade Moseby, Esq., and got by imported chestnut Diomed, out of Amanda, by Grey Diomed, a son of old Medley. His (Eclipse's) dam was the noted gray mare Miller's Damsel, got by imported Messenger. He was bred by Gen. Nathaniel Coles, of Queens County, Long Island, and foaled on the 25th of May, 1814.

All horses date their age from the 1st of May. Thus a horse foaled any time in the year 1819, would be considered four years old on the 1st day of May, 1828. Consequently, Sir Henry, although not four years old complete until the 17th day of June, had, on the 27th of May, to carry the regulated weight (agreeably to the then rules of the course) for a four year old, viz. 108 pounds. Eclipse, being nine years old, carried weight for an aged horse, 126 pounds.

At length the appointed hour arrived, the word was given to saddle, and immediately afterwards to mount. Eclipse was rode by William Crafts, dressed in a crimson jacket and cap, and Sir Henry by a Virginia boy, of the name of John Walden, dressed in a sky blue jacket, with cap of the same color. The custom on the Union Course is to run to the left about, or with the left hand next to the poles; Eclipse, by lot, had the left, or inside station at the start. Sir Henry took his ground about twenty-five feet wide of him, to the right, with the evident intention of making a run in a straight line for the lead. The preconcerted signal was a single tap of the drum. All was now breathless anxiety; the horses came up evenly; the eventful signal was heard, they went off handsomely together; Henry, apparently quickest, made play from the score, obtained the lead, and then took a hard pull. By the time they had gone the first quarter of a mile, which brought them round the first turn, to the commencement of what is termed the back side of the course, which is a straight run, comprising the second quarter of a mile, he was full three lengths ahead; this distance he with little variation maintained, running steadily with a hard pull during the first, second, third, and for about three-fourths of the fourth round or mile, the pace, all this time, a killing one.

It may be proper to note that the course is nearly an oval of one mile, with this small variation, that the back and front are straight lines of about a quarter of a mile each, connected at each extremity by semicircles of also a quarter of a mile each. When the horses were going the last round, being myself well mounted, I took my station at the commencement of the stretch or last quarter, where I expected a violent exertion would be made at this last straight run in, when they left the straight part on the back of the course and entered upon the last turn.

Henry was, as heretofore, not less than three lengths in the clear ahead. They had not proceeded more than twenty rods upon the first part of the sweep when Eclipse made play, and the spur and whip were both applied freely; when they were at the extreme point or center of the sweep, I observed the right hand of Crafts disengaged from his bridle, making free use of his whip; when they had swept about three-fourths of the way round the turn and had advanced within twenty-five rods of my station, I clearly saw that Crafts was making every exertion with both spur and whip to get Eclipse forward, and scored him sorely, both before and behind the girths; at this moment Eclipse threw his tail into the air, and flirted it up and down, after the manner of a tired horse or one in distress and great pain; and John Buckley, the jockey (and present trainer), who I kept stationed by my side, observed, "Eclipse is done."

When they passed me about the commencement of the stretch, seventy to eighty rods from home, the space between them was about sixteen feet, or a full length and a half in the clear. Here the rider of Henry turned his head round and took a view for an instant of his adversary; Walden used neither whip nor spur, but maintained a hard and steady pull, under which his horse appeared accustomed to run. Craft continued to make free use of the whip; his right hand in so doing was necessarily disengaged from the bridle, his arm often raised high in air, his body thrown abroad, and his seat loose and unsteady; not having strength to hold and gather his horse with one hand, and at the same time keep his proper position; in order to acquire a greater purchase, he had thrown his body quite back to the cantle of the saddle, stuck his feet forward by way of bracing himself with the aid of the stirrups, and in this style, he was belaboring his horse, going in the last quarter.

Buckley exclaimed, (and well he might) "Good G——d, look at Billy." From this place to the winning post, Eclipse gained but a few feet, Henry coming ahead about a length in the clear. The shortest time of this heat, as returned by the judges on the stand, was 7 minutes 37½ seconds. Many watches, and mine (which was held by a gentleman on the stand) among others, made it 7 minutes 40 seconds; and this time the Southern gentlemen reported.

I pushed immediately up to the winning post, in order to view the situation of the respective horses after this very trying and severe heat; for it was in fact running the whole four miles. Sir Henry was less distressed than I expected to find him; Eclipse also bore it well, but of the two, he appeared the most jaded; the injudicious manner in which he had been rode, had certainly annoyed, and unnecessarily distressed him; the cause of his throwing out his tail, and flirting it up and down, as already observed, was now apparent; Craft, in using his whip wildly, had struck him too far back, and had cut him not only upon his sheath, but had made a deep incision upon his testicles, and it was no doubt the violent pain occasioned thereby, that caused the noble animal to complain, and motion with his tail, indicative of the torture he suffered. The blood flowed profusely from one or both of these foul cuts, and trickling down the inside of his hind legs, appeared conspicuously upon the white hind foot, and gave a more doleful appearance to the discouraging scene of a lost heat.

The incapacity of Crafts to manage Eclipse (who required much urging, and at the same time to be pulled hard) was apparent to all; he being a slender made lad, in body weight about 100 lbs. only. A person interested in the event, seeing Buckley, who had rode the horse on a former occasion, with me, requested that I would keep him within call, and ready to ride in case of an emergency. It was, however, soon settled and announced that Mr. Purdy would ride him the second heat, upon which, long faces grew shorter, and Northern hope revived—six to four was, nevertheless, offered on the Southern horse, but no takers.

The horses, after a lapse of 30 minutes, were called up for a second heat. I attentively viewed Eclipse while saddling, and was surprised to find that to appearance he had not only entirely recovered, but seemed full of mettle, lashing and reaching out with his hind feet, anxious and impatient to renew the contest. Mr. Purdy having mounted his favorite was perfectly at home and self-confident. The signal being again given, he went off rapidly from the start; Sir Henry being now entitled to the inside, took the track, and kept the lead, followed closely by Eclipse, whom Mr. Purdy at once brought to his work, knowing that game and stoutness was his play, and his only chance of success, that of driving his speedy adversary, up to the top of his rate, without giving him the least respite.

Henry went steadily on, nearly at the top of his speed, keeping a gap open between himself and Eclipse of about twenty feet without much variation for about two miles and seven-eighths, or until towards the conclusion of the third mile they had arrived nearly opposite the four-mile distance post. Here Purdy made his run, and when they had advanced forty rods further, which brought them to the end of the third mile, was close up, say nose and tail. They now entered upon the fourth and last mile, which commences with a turn or sweep the moment you leave the starting post. Here the crowd was immense; I was at this moment on horseback, stationed down the stretch or straight run, a short distance below the winning post, in company with a friend, and Buckley the jockey, who kept close to me during the whole race. We pushed out into the center, or open space of the ground, in order to obtain a more distinct view of the struggle, which we saw making for the lead; every thing depended upon this effort of Purdy; well he knew it; his case was a desperate one, and required a desperate attempt; it was to risk all, for all; he did not hesitate.

When the horses had got about one third of the way round the sweep, they had so far cleared the crowd as to afford us a distinct view of them a little before they reached the center of the turn; Eclipse had lapped Henry about head and girth and appeared evidently in the act of passing. Here Buckley vociferated, see Eclipse! Look at Purdy! By heaven on the inside! I was all attention.

Purdy was on the left hand or inside of Henry. I felt alarmed for the consequence, satisfied that he had thus hazarded all; I feared that Walden would take advantage of his position, and by reining in, force him against or inside one of the poles; when they had proceeded a little more than half way round the sweep, the horses were a dead lap; when about three-fourths round, Eclipse's quarter covered Henry's head and neck, and just as they had finished the bend, and were entering upon the straight run, which extends along the back part of the course, Eclipse for the first time was fairly clear, and ahead.

He now with the help of the persuaders, which were freely bestowed, kept up his run, and continued gradually, though slowly, to gain during the remaining three quarters of a mile and came in about two lengths ahead. As they passed up the stretch or last quarter of a mile, the shouting, clapping of hands, waving of handkerchiefs, long and loud applause sent forth by the Eclipse party, exceeded all description; it seemed to roll along the track as the horses advanced, resembling the loud and reiterated shout of contending armies.

I have been thus particular in stating that Mr. Purdy made his pass on the inside, understanding that many gentlemen and particularly Mr. Stevens, the principal in the match on the part of Eclipse (and for aught I know Mr. Purdy himself), insist that the *go by* was given on the outside. After the heat was over, I found that my friend Mr. M. Buckley and myself were far from the only persons that had observed the mode in which Mr. Purdy ran up and took the inside track from his adversary.

The circumstance was in the mouths of hundreds. In corroboration of which, I will quote a passage from the *New York Evening Post*, of May 28th, 1823, giving a description of this second heat:

Henry took the lead as in the first heat until about two-thirds around on the third mile, when Purdy seized with a quickness and dexterity peculiar to himself, the favorable moment that presented, when appearing to aim at the outside, he might gain the inside, made a dash at him accordingly, and *passed him on the left.*

Here, then, the observations of many independent of my friend Mr. M. Buckley, or myself, added to the instantaneous and striking remark of B., which did not fail to rivet my peculiar attention, form a wonderful coincidence. Thus circumstanced, and long conversant with turf matters, rules, and practices, and familiar with sights of this kind, it was impossible I could be mistaken. I was not mistaken, the honest belief of some gentlemen to the contrary notwithstanding. Time, this second heat, 7 minutes, 49 seconds.

It was now given out, that in place of the boy Walden, who had rode Sir Henry the two preceding heats, that Arthur Taylor, a trainer of great experience, and long a rider, equaled by few, and surpassed by none, would ride him this last and decisive heat. At the expiration of 30 minutes the horses were once more summoned to the starting post, and Purdy and Taylor mounted; the word being given, they went off at a quick rate; Purdy now taking the lead, and pushing Eclipse from the score; and indeed, the whole four miles, applying the whip and spur incessantly; evidently resolved to give Sir Henry no respite but to cause him, if determined to trail, to employ all his speed and strength without keeping any thing in reserve for the run in.

Sir Henry continued to trail, apparently under a pull, never attempting to come up, until they had both fairly entered the straight run towards the termination of the last mile and had advanced within about sixty rods from home. Here Sir Henry being about five yards behind, made a dash, and ran up to Eclipse so far as to cover his quarter or haunch with his head, and for a moment had the appearance of going past; he made a severe struggle for about two hundred yards, when he again fell in the rear, and gave up the contest.

Thus terminated the most interesting race ever run in the United States. Besides the original stake of $20,000 each, it was judged that upwards of $900,000 changed hands. In this last heat Sir Henry carried 110 lbs. being two pounds over his proper weight; it not being possible to bring Arthur Taylor to ride less, and although a small horse and wanting twenty days of being four years old, he made the greatest run ever witnessed in America. Time, this heat, 8 minutes, 24 seconds.

Thus the three heats, or twelve miles, were run in 528 minutes, 50 seconds, or an average of 7 minutes, 57 seconds each heat; or 1 minute, 59 seconds per mile.

20

THE STORY OF A JOCKEY

BY RICHARD HARDING DAVIS

Horse racing remained at the forefront of public imagination during the first decades of the twentieth century in spite of roadblocks put up by anti-gambling crusaders. The drama of the sport attracted the attention of some of the best and best-known writers in the country, including Richard Harding Davis, who rose to fame as an intrepid war correspondent during the Spanish-American War. Davis enjoyed producing stories for young readers in which a moral message was wrapped around an exciting tale, but his reputation as a hard-hitting journalist drew adult readers to these stories as well.

Among the best of his short stories is this one. A young lover of horses rejects the chance of an alluring payoff, preferring to protect his own honor and that of a horse he loves.

Young Charley Chadwick had been brought up on his father's farm in New Jersey. The farm had been his father's before his father died and was still called Chadwick's Meadows in his memory. It was a very small farm and for the most part covered with clover and long, rich grass that were good for pasturing and nothing else. Charley was too young, and Mrs. Chadwick was too much of a housekeeper and not enough of a farmer's wife to make the most out of the farm, and so she let the meadows to the manager of the Cloverdale Stock Farm. This farm is only half a mile back from the Monmouth Park racetrack at Long Branch.

The manager put a number of young colts in it to pasture and took what grass they did not eat to the farm. Charley used to ride these colts back to the big stables at night, and soon grew to ride very well, and to know a great deal about horses and horse breeding and horse racing. Sometimes they gave him a mount at the stables, and he was permitted to ride one of the racehorses around the private track, while the owner took the time from the judges' stand.

There was nothing in his life that he enjoyed like this. He had had very few pleasures, and the excitement and delight of tearing through the air on the back of a great animal, was something he thought must amount to more than anything else in the world. His mother did not approve of his spending his time at the stables, but she found it very hard to refuse him, and he seemed to have a happy faculty of picking up only what was good, and letting what was evil pass by him and leave him unhurt. The good that he picked up was his love for animals, his thoughtfulness for them, and the forbearance and gentleness it taught him to use, with even the higher class of animals who walk on two legs.

He was fond of all the horses, because they were horses; but the one he liked best was Heroine, a big black mare that ran like an express train. He and Heroine were the two greatest friends in the stable. The horse loved him as a horse does love its master sometimes, and though

Charley was not her owner, he was in reality her master, for Heroine would have left her stall and carried Charley off to the ends of the continent if he had asked her to run away.

When a man named Oscar Behren bought Heroine, Charley thought he would never be contented again. He cried about it all along the country road from the stables to his home, and cried about it again that night in bed. He knew Heroine would feel just as badly about it as he did, if she could know they were to be separated. Heroine went off to run in the races for which her new master had entered her, and Charley heard of her only through the newspapers.

She won often and became a great favorite, and Charley was afraid she would forget the master of her earlier days before she became so famous. And when he found that Heroine was entered to run at the Monmouth Park racetrack, he became as excited over the prospect of seeing his old friend again as though he were going to meet his promised bride, or a long-lost brother who had accumulated several millions in South America.

He was at the station to meet the Behren horses, and Heroine knew him at once and he knew Heroine, although she was all blanketed up and had grown so much more beautiful to look at that it seemed like a second and improved edition of the horse he had known. Heroine won several races at Long Branch, and though her owner was an unpopular one, and one of whom many queer stories were told, still Heroine was always ridden to win, and win she generally did.

The race for the July Stakes was the big race of the meeting, and Heroine was the favorite. Behren was known to be backing her with thousands of dollars, and it was almost impossible to get anything but even money on her. The day before the race McCallen, the jockey who was to ride her, was taken ill, and Behren was in great anxiety and greatly disturbed as to where he could get a good substitute. Several people told him it made no difference, for the mare was as sure as sure could be, no matter who rode her. Then some one told him of Charley, who had taken out a license when the racing season began, and who had ridden a few unimportant mounts.

Behren looked for Charley and told him he would want him to ride for the July Stakes, and Charley went home to tell his mother about it, in a state of wild delight. To ride the favorite, and that favorite in such a great race, was as much to him as to own and steer the winning yacht in the transatlantic match for the cup.

He told Heroine all about it, and Heroine seemed very well pleased. But while he was standing hidden in Heroine's box stall, he heard something outside that made him wonder.

It was Behren's voice, and he said in a low tone, "Oh, McCallen's well enough, but I didn't want him for this race. He knows too much. The lad I've got now, this country boy, wouldn't know if the mare had the blind staggers."

Charley thought over this a great deal, and all that he had learned on the tracks and around the stables came to assist him in judging what it was that Behren meant, and that afternoon he found out.

The racetrack with the great green enclosures and the grandstand as high as a hill were as empty as a college campus in vacation time, but for a few of the stable boys and some of the owners, and a waiter or two. It was interesting to think what it would be like a few hours later when the trains had arrived from New York with eleven cars each and the passengers hanging from the steps, and the carriages stretched all the way from Long Branch. Then there would not be a vacant seat on the grandstand or a blade of grass untrampled.

Charley was not nervous when he thought of this, but he was very much excited. Howland S. Maitland, who owned a stable of horses and a great many other expensive things, and who was one of those gentlemen who make the racing of horses possible, and Curtis, the secretary of the meeting, came walking towards Charley, looking in at the different horses in the stalls.

"Heroine," said Mr. Maitland, as he read the name over the door. "Can we have a look at her?" he said.

Charley got up and took off his hat. "I am sorry, Mr. Maitland," he said, "but my orders from Mr. Behren are not to allow any one inside. I am sure if Mr. Behren were here he would be very glad to show you the horse; but you see, I'm responsible, sir, and—"

"Oh, that's all right!" said Mr. Maitland pleasantly, as he moved on.

"There's Mr. Behren now," Charley called after him, as Behren turned the corner. "I'll run and ask him."

"No, no, thank you," said Mr. Maitland hurriedly, and Charley heard him add to Mr. Curtis, "I don't want to know the man." It hurt Charley to find that the owner of Heroine and the man for whom he was to ride was held in such bad repute that a gentleman like Mr. Maitland would not know him, and he tried to console himself by thinking that it was better he rode Heroine than some less conscientious jockey whom Behren might order to play tricks with the horse and the public.

Mr. Behren came up with a friend, a red-faced man with a white derby hat. He pointed at Charley with his cane.

"My new jockey," he said. "How's the mare?" he asked.

"Very fit, sir," Charley answered.

"Had her feed yet?"

"No," Charley said.

The feed was in a trough, which the stable boy had lifted outside into the sun. They were mixing it under Charley's supervision, for as a rider he did not stoop to such menial work as carrying the water and feed, but he always overlooked the others when they did it. Behren scooped up a handful and examined it carefully.

"It's not as fresh as it ought to be for the price they ask," he said to the friend with him. Then he threw the handful of feed back into the trough and ran his hand through it again, rubbing it between his thumb and fingers and tasting it critically. Then they passed on up the row.

Charley sat down again on an overturned bucket and looked at the feed trough, then he said to the stable boys, "You fellows can go now and get something to eat if you want to." They did not wait to be urged. Charley carried the trough inside the stable and took up a handful of the feed and looked and sniffed at it. It was fresh from his own barn; he had brought it over himself in a cart that morning.

Then he tasted it with the end of his tongue and his face changed. He glanced around him quickly to see if any one had noticed, and then, with the feed still clenched in his hand, ran out and looked anxiously up and down the length of the stable. Mr. Maitland and Curtis were returning from the other end of the road.

"Can I speak to you a moment, sir?" said Charley anxiously. "Will you come in here just a minute? It's most important, sir. I have something to show you."

The two men looked at the boy curiously and halted in front of the door. Charley added nothing further to what he had said but spread a newspaper over the floor of the stable and turned the feed trough over on it. Then he stood up over the pile and said, "Would you both please taste that?"

There was something in his manner which made questions unnecessary. The two gentlemen did as he asked. Then Mr. Curtis looked into Mr. Maitland's face, which was full of doubt and perplexity, with one of angry suspicion.

"Cooked," he said.

"It does taste strangely," commented the horse owner gravely.

"Look at it; you can see if you look close enough," urged Curtis excitedly. "Do you see that green powder on my finger? Do you know what that is? An ounce of that would turn a horse's stomach as dry as a limekiln. Where did you get this feed?" he demanded of Charley.

"Out of our barn," said the boy. "And no one has touched it except myself, the stable boys, and the owner."

"Who are the stable boys?" demanded Mr. Curtis.

"Who's the owner?" asked Charley.

"Do you know what you are saying?" warned Mr. Maitland sharply. "You had better be careful."

"Careful!" said Charley indignantly. "I will be careful enough." He went over to Heroine, and threw his arm up over her neck. He was terribly excited and trembling all over. The mare turned her head towards him and rubbed her nose against his face.

"That's all right," said Charley. "Don't you be afraid. I'll take care of *you*."

The two men were whispering together. "I don't know anything about you," said Mr. Maitland to Charley. "I don't know what your idea was in dragging me into this. I'm sure I wish I was out of it. But this I do know, if Heroine isn't herself today, and doesn't run as she has run before, and I say it though my own horses are in against her, I'll have you and your owner before the Racing Board, and you'll lose your license and be ruled off every track in the country."

"One of us will," said Charley stubbornly. "All I want you to do, Mr. Maitland, is to put some of that stuff in your pocket. If anything is wrong they will believe what you say, when they wouldn't listen to me. That's why I called you in. I haven't charged any one with anything. I only asked you and Mr. Curtis to taste the feed that this horse was to have eaten. That's all. And I'm not afraid of the Racing Board, either, if the men on it are honest."

Mr. Curtis took some letters out of his pocket and filled the envelopes with the feed, and then put them back in his pocket, and Charley gathered up the feed in a bucket and emptied it out of the window at the back of the stable.

"I think Behren should be told of this," said Mr. Maitland.

Charley laughed; he was still excited and angry. "You had better find out which way Mr. Behren is betting first," he said, "if you can."

"Don't mind the boy. Come away," said Mr. Curtis. "We must look into this."

The Fourth of July holidaymakers had begun to arrive; and there were thousands of them, and they had a great deal of money, and they wanted to bet it all on Heroine. Everybody wanted to bet on Heroine; and the men in the betting ring obliged them.

But there were three men from Boston who were betting on the field against the favorite. They distributed their bets in small sums of money among a great many different bookmakers; even the oldest of the racing men did not know them.

But Mr. Behren seemed to know them. He met one of them openly in front of the grandstand, and the stranger from Boston asked politely if he could trouble him for a light. Mr. Behren handed him his cigar, and while the man puffed at it he said, "We've got $50,000 of it up. It's too much to risk on that powder. Something might go wrong; you mightn't have mixed it properly, or there mayn't be enough. I've known it miss before this. Minerva, she won once with an ounce of it inside her. You'd better fix that jockey."

Mr. Behren's face was troubled, and he puffed quickly at his cigar as the man walked away. Then he turned and moved slowly towards the stables.

A gentleman with a field glass across his shoulder stopped him and asked, "How's Heroine?" and Mr. Behren answered, "Never better; I've $10,000 on her," and passed on with a confident smile.

Charley saw Mr. Behren coming, and bit his lip and tried to make his face look less conscious. He was not used to deception. He felt much more like plunging a pitchfork into Mr. Behren's legs, but he restrained that impulse, and chewed gravely on a straw. Mr. Behren looked carefully around the stable, and wiped the perspiration from his fat red face. The day was warm, and he was excited.

"Well, my boy," he said in a friendly, familiar tone as he seated himself, "it's almost time. I hope you are not rattled."

Charley said "No." He felt confident enough.

"It would be a big surprise if she went back on us, wouldn't it?" suggested the owner gloomily.

"It would, indeed," said Charley.

"Still," said Mr. Behren, "such things have been. Racin' is full of surprises, and horses are full of tricks. I've known a horse, now, get pocketed behind two or three others and never show to the front at all. Though she was the best of the field, too. And I've known horses go wild and jump over the rail and run away with the jock, and sometimes they fall. And sometimes I've had a jockey pull a horse on me and make me drop every cent I had up. You wouldn't do that, would you?" he asked. He looked up at Charley with a smile that might mean anything.

Charley looked at the floor and shrugged his shoulders. "I ride to orders, I do," he said. "I guess the owner knows his own business best. When I ride for a man and take his money I believe he should have his say. Some jockeys ride to win. I ride according to orders."

He did not look up after this, and he felt thankful that Heroine could not understand the language of human beings. Mr. Behren's face rippled with smiles. This was a jockey after his own heart.

"If Heroine should lose," he said, "I say, if she should, for no one knows what might happen, I'd have to abuse you fearful right before all the people. I'd swear at you and say you lost me all my money, and that you should never ride for me again. And they might suspend you for a month or two, which would be very hard on you," he added reflectively.

"But then," he said more cheerfully, "if you had a little money to live on while you were suspended it wouldn't be so hard, would it?" He took a large roll of bank bills from his pocket and counted them, smoothing them out on his fat knee and smiling up at the boy. "It wouldn't be so bad, would it?" he repeated. Then he counted aloud, "Eight hundred, nine hundred, one thousand."

He rose and placed the bills under a loose plank of the floor, and stamped it down on them. "I guess we understand each other, eh?" he said.

"I guess we do," said Charley.

"I'll have to swear at you, you know," said Behren, smiling.

"I can stand that," Charley answered.

~~~~~~

As the horses paraded past for the July Stakes, the people rushed forward down the inclined enclosure and crushed against the rail and cheered whichever horse they best fancied.

"Say, you," called one of the crowd to Charley, "you want to win, you do. I've got $5 on that horse you're a-riding."

Charley ran his eyes over the crowd that were applauding and cheering him and Heroine, and calculated coolly that if every one had only $5 on Heroine there would be at least $100,000 on the horse in all.

The man from Boston stepped up beside Mr. Behren as he sat on his dogcart alone.

"The mare looks very fit," he said anxiously. "Her eyes are like diamonds. I don't believe that stuff affected her at all."

"It's all right," whispered Behren calmly. "I've fixed the boy."

The man dropped back off the wheel of the cart with a sigh of relief, and disappeared in the crowd. Mr. Maitland and Mr. Curtis sat together on the top of the former's coach. Mr. Curtis had his hand over the packages of feed in his pockets.

"If the mare don't win," he said, "there will be the worst scandal this track has ever known." The perspiration was rolling down his face. "It will be the death of honest racing."

"I cannot understand it," said Mr. Maitland. "The boy seemed honest, too."

The horses got off together. There were eleven of them. Heroine was amongst the last, but no one minded that because the race was a long one. And within three-quarters of a mile of home Heroine began to shake off the others and came up slowly through the crowd, and her thousands of admirers yelled. And then Maitland's Good Morning and Reilly swerved in front of her, or else Heroine fell behind them, it was hard to tell which, and Lady Betty closed in on her from the right. Her jockey seemed to be trying his best to get her out of the triangular pocket into which she had run. The great crowd simultaneously gave an anxious questioning gasp. Then two more horses pushed to the front, closing the favorite in and shutting her off altogether.

"The horse is pocketed," cried Mr. Curtis, "and not one man out of a thousand would know that it was done on purpose."

"Wait!" said Mr. Maitland.

"Bless that boy!" murmured Behren, trying his best to look anxious. "She can never pull out of that."

They were within half a mile of home. The crowd was panic-stricken and jumping up and down.

"Heroine!" they cried, as wildly as though they were calling for help, or the police. "Heroine!" Charley heard them above the noise of the pounding hoofs, and smiled in spite of the mud and dirt that the great horses in front flung in his face and eyes.

"Heroine," he said, "I think we've scared that crowd about long enough. Now, punish Behren." He sank his spurs into the horse's sides and jerked her head towards a little opening between Lady Betty and Chubb. Heroine sprang at it like a tiger and came neck to neck with the leader. And then, as she saw the wide track empty before her, and no longer felt the hard backward pull on her mouth, she tossed her head with a snort, and flew down the stretch like an express, with her jockey whispering fiercely in her ear.

Heroine won with a grand rush, by three lengths, but Charley's face was filled with anxiety as he tossed up his arm in front of the judges' stand. He was covered with mud and perspiration, and panting with exertion and excitement. He distinguished Mr. Curtis's face in the middle of the wild crowd around him, then patted his legs and hugged and kissed Heroine's head, and danced up and down in the ecstasy of delight.

"Mr. Curtis," he cried, raising his voice above the tumult of the crowd, and forgetting, or not caring, that they could hear, "send some one to the stable, quick. There's a thousand dollars there Behren offered me to pull the horse. It's under a plank near the back door. Get it before he does. That's evidence the Racing Board can't—"

But before he could finish, or before Mr. Curtis could push his way towards him, a dozen stable boys and betting men had sprung away with a yell towards the stable, and the mob dashed after them. It gathered in volume as a landslide does when it goes down hill; and the people in the grandstand and on the coaches stood up and asked what was the matter; and some cried "Stop thief!" and others cried "Fight!"

and others said that a bookmaker had given big odds against Heroine, and was "doing a welsh." The mob swept around the corner of the long line of stables like a charge of cavalry, and dashed at Heroine's lodgings.

The door was open, and on his knees at the other end was Behren, digging at the planks with his fingernails. He had seen that the boy had intentionally deceived him, and his first thought, even before that of his great losses, was to get possession of the thousand dollars that might be used against him. He turned his fat face, now white with terror, over his shoulder, as the crowd rushed into the stable, and tried to rise from his knees; but before he could get up, the first man struck him between the eyes, and others fell on him, pummeling him and kicking him and beating him down.

If they had lost their money, instead of having won, they could not have handled him more brutally. Two policemen and a couple of men with pitchforks drove them back; and one of the officers lifted up the plank, and counted the thousand dollars before the crowd.

Either Mr. Maitland felt badly at having doubted Charley, or else he admired his riding, for he bought Heroine when Behren was ruled off the racetracks and had to sell his horses, and Charley became his head jockey. And just as soon as Heroine began to lose, Mr. Maitland refused to have her suffer such degradation, and said she should stop while she could still win. And then he presented her to Charley, who had won so much and so often with her, and Charley gave up his license and went back to the farm to take care of his mother, and Heroine played all day in the clover fields.

21

WORLD RECORD IS SET BY MAN O' WAR

FROM THE *NEW YORK TIMES*,
JUNE 13, 1920

*Riddle's Speed Miracle Shatters All Previous Marks for Mile
and Three Furlongs*

Wins Belmont by a Block

Finishes Half-Furlong before Donnacona

Great Throng Is Amazed

Horse racing found itself in a struggle for its life as the 1920s approached. The sport had survived the anti-gambling fervor of ten years earlier (reformers had moved on to alcoholic beverages) but the World War had badly damaged the international breeding and racing industries.

By June 13, 1920, when the story of Man o' War's victory in the previous day's Belmont Stakes appeared in the New York Times, *the sport had already begun to climb out of the doldrums, thanks at least*

partially to the charismatic red colt. Thousands crowded the grand-
stands when he raced. Millions of dollars were bet on him during his
sixteen-month racing career. His Belmont Stakes was fully represen-
tative of his career: a great throng was indeed amazed by his accom-
plishment.

The Times *article displays the combination of straightforward*
reporting and adulation that was typical of news coverage of the
remarkable horse. It appeared without a byline, customary at the time
in racing journalism.

Samuel D. Riddle's great race horse, Man o' War, gave at Belmont
Park yesterday what was beyond a doubt the greatest exhibition of
speed ever witnessed on any racetrack when he shattered the world's
record for a mile and three furlongs in winning the $10,000 Belmont
Stakes, while a crowd of 25,000 sat stunned by the almost unbelievably
brilliant performance. The champion did not just clip the mark, but
literally shattered it, for he ran the distance in 2:14 1-5, which is two
and three-fifths seconds faster than any horse had ever run it before.

The world's record was previously held by Dean Swift, which ran
the mile and three furlongs in 2:16 4-5 at Liverpool, England, in 1908.
The next lowest mark was made in the running of the Belmont last
year when Sir Barton set a new American record for the distance of
2:17 2-5. The Canadian and Australian records do not even closely
approach the English and American marks, which stood until yesterday afternoon.

When the figures were posted there was a hum of amazement in
the packed stands. Every one had been expecting Man o' War to lower
the record made by Sir Barton last year, but no one was quite ready to
believe it would be lowered to the extent of several seconds and take

the world's mark with it. Not even his owner had thought he would stage such a performance, for he had not sent his colt out with the expectation of making such wonderful time.

BEST OF ALL TIMES AND CLIMES

The race left no doubt in the minds of all turfmen present that they had seen the greatest horse of this or any other age. Up to this time they had been content to say that he was America's finest product, but after he had crossed the line in the Belmont and his time was flashed there were none among the veterans of the turf who could think of a horse who compared with him. It is safe to say that Man o' War is the superhorse of the ages as far as records go back; a horse the likes of which will probably never be seen by the present generation of horsemen. Man o' War would seem to typify the final goal of breeders, the perfect racehorse, gifted with all the essentials of greatness. The son of Fair Play has set a mark which all horses save himself are likely to shoot at vainly for many years to come.

The Belmont Stakes did not, of course, present a real contest. No one in the great throng had expected that it would. The public as well as horsemen have given up any idea that any three-year-old in the country can make Man o' War get out of a gallop. It was not a race but an exhibition by a great horse and as such it more than satisfied everyone who saw the colt in action. There is pleasure enough for those present in the thought that they have seen the world's greatest racehorse and moreover have been witnesses of his record-making performance. Man o' War finds himself in the position of Alexander of yore, seeking new worlds to conquer, and as there are no horses of his age to race with him he has only the reduction of records for various distances as a stimulus.

DAVID HARUM IS WITHDRAWN

It was the original intention to send two horses against the Fair Play colt in the Belmont Stakes, but W. R. Coe's David Harum was withdrawn and only G. W. Loft's Donnacona was left to act as a running mate. Donnacona is a high class colt, one of the best of his age and it is something of a measure of the greatness of Man o' War that Donnacona finished a sixteenth of a mile back of the winner although doing his best to the end.

There was scarcely any speculation on the race. Man o' War was quoted at the prohibitive odds of 1 to 20 as against 12 to 1 for the Loft colt. Practically the only wagers made were by persons who wanted, for the sake of sentiment, to say that they had made a bet on Man o' War.

The start for the Belmont is made from a chute which leads across the straightaway track into the training track. From this latter the horses turn into the main track at the turn, which leads to the stretch.

As the barrier went up Man o' War popped to the front and jockey Clarence Kummer, wearing his gold stirrups again, let the Fair Play colt run with a fair flight of speed from the beginning. Man o' War never waits for a pacemaker. His habit of running races is to go to the front and bid his rival to come on and catch him.

Through the training track course Man o' War maintained a lead of about two lengths, and was still under restraint, while Donnacona was moving along at a fast clip and apparently had something left. As the horses reached that point where they turned into the main track Donnacona moved up resolutely until he closed the gap of daylight which had appeared between the horses since the start. From the stands it appeared that he was right at the heels of the champion, and the Loft horse was moving with fine speed.

FLASHES AWAY FROM RIVAL

Kummer looked back and, seeing Donnacona, gave Man o' War his head. The son of Fair Play developed a new rate of speed in half a dozen strides. He began to move away from his rival as though the latter was anchored. At the turn into the stretch Man o' War was four lengths in front, and he had not yet been permitted to run as it was quite evident he wished to.

As Man o' War reached the stretch the crowd began to yell to Kummer to let him run, for it was the desire of everyone to see a new record made. Kummer did as they desired. Instead of taking a pull on his mount, as he had done in his previous race, he let Man o' War step along all through the stretch, although at no time urging him. He simply let the colt run freely, and then it became evident how he outclasses the others of his age. He not only left a wide margin between him and Donnacona, but he made a joke of the race as such. He gained a length with every two strides and, although his head was still held high in the air, he increased his lead by a sixteenth of a mile in the distance of the stretch. Man o' War was around the turn and being pulled up as Donnacona crossed the finish line.

There was great cheering for the champion when he came back to the stands and general congratulations for Mr. Riddle for the establishment of the new world's record. Horsemen who watched the race thought the Fair Play colt could have reduced the mark by at least another fraction of a second had he been in the least extended. Though he was fairly flying through the stretch, he was not running at his top speed. Kummer sat perfectly still on him, neither urging nor restraining him, and perhaps one touch of the whip would have taken another two-fifths from the time. This was the first time that Man o' War had ever raced at such a distance, but when he pulled up he was not even breathing hard.

VII

LEGENDARY HORSES

22

HOW I BOUGHT AND TRAINED CAPTAIN

BY HIS OWNER, W. A. SIGSBEE

When George Wharton James and W. A. Sigsbee met at the Panama-Pacific Exposition in San Francisco in 1915, it was the coming together of two accomplished showmen, an encounter that proved profitable to each of them. James was a respected writer of travelogues and nature books. Sigsbee was an admired trainer of horses. But each made his fortune by presenting himself to the public, James with dramatic readings to audiences and Sigsbee by demonstrating the accomplishments of the horses he had trained.

James was fascinated with what he saw in San Francisco: a horse named Captain who appeared to be able to count, differentiate between colors, make change, and play "Nearer My God to Thee" on the chimes. James believed there was no fraud involved, although he acknowledged that the horse probably didn't understand the words to the hymn. He also thought it was possible that Captain was taking unwitting cues from Sigsbee, even if they weren't visible.

But James was sufficiently impressed to produce a book two years later that told the story of Captain, whom he called "The Horse with the Human Brain." Part of the book was his own analysis, part was a first-person (or first-horse) account of Captain's take on the situation, and part was Sigsbee's story of how he found and trained his famous horse. Here is Sigsbee's contribution.

~~~~~~

I was brought up in the horse business. My father and uncles were horsemen before I was born. They lived in Dane County, Wisconsin, twelve miles from Madison, and there I first saw the light. One of my uncles had trotting horses, and almost as soon as I could do anything I used to go and help him. When I was fourteen years old I was regularly employed by him during my vacations, to help on the farm, in the stables, and to accompany him to the trotting track.

I soon learned to ride as a jockey, and up to the time I was eighteen years old that was my occupation. Then I began to work for myself. I bought, educated or trained, and then sold horses and dogs. I was much interested in them and always seemed to have fair success in their management.

As I grew older I used to go with my own horses to the County and State Fairs, the latter being held at Madison. When I was twenty-four years old I married, settled down on a farm, and as horse-trading seemed to be the business I was especially adapted for, naturally I followed it. Whenever my neighbors wanted a horse that was extra well trained they would come to me, and if I showed them one that could do a few tricks, they liked it nonetheless, and were not unwilling to pay a little extra for the pains I had taken.

The year after I was married I moved to Humboldt, Iowa, where I bought another farm and for four more years continued my work as farmer and horse-trader. Then I bought the Park Hotel, in the town of Humboldt, which I ran for eleven years, never, however, for one moment losing my interest in horses. In fact, it was one of the most profitable parts of my business.

Many farmers, show-men, circus-men, and others came to the town and stopped at my hotel, so I was never away from the atmosphere of the horse ring. Many a time, when they were in a tight place, the show or circus men would come and ask me to help them out, for my reputation as a trainer had spread, and it was pretty generally understood that I was an exceptional hand for teaching horses and dogs rather unusual and interesting tricks.

In time the great circus masters, like Barnum and Bailey, Al Ringling, and others, came to me and asked me to train horses for them, so that my horse business grew, and with it my reputation. Naturally I was always on the lookout for colts that promised well, or horses that seemed extra intelligent, and my eyes were keen for mares that showed a superior order of intelligence that were soon to have colts.

About this time my eyes were attracted to a beautiful mare, evidently with foal. No sooner did I see her than I wanted her. I found on inquiry that she had been bred to a spotted Arabian, as fine and beautiful a creature as she herself was. Satisfied that she was what I wanted, I purchased her. Already I had begun to speculate as to what I should do with her colt. If it was a prettily shaped animal, was as intelligent as the father and mother, I decided it should receive the best education I was capable of giving.

As the days of the mare's time passed I grew more and more anxious. My hopes were raised high, and I was correspondingly expectant and at the same time afraid. What if the colt should prove stupid? I awaited the birth of that colt as eagerly as a royal family awaits the birth of the child of a king, hence you can understand my delight and satisfaction, when the little lady came, that I found her faultless in appearance, neat, trim, dainty, and beautiful, with intelligent eyes and face and every indication of being a most superior animal.

From the hour of her birth I watched her far more closely than many a child is watched. I was in and out of the stable a score of times a day. While she appeared intelligent, I wanted to know with certainty as soon as I could. I was not long in discovering, and this was how it was done. My barn had double doors—one on each side. As it was warm weather I had both doors open to allow a current of air through the building. When the colt was four or five days old, I wished to hitch up the mare and drive her but did not think it wise to let so small and young a colt go along. So I closed the doors and left her inside. She became much excited at being separated from her mother; ran around wildly, whinnied, and generally fretted. But I felt she would have to learn to lose her mother, so I drove away and left her to fight it out as best she could.

The next day I went into the barn and groomed down the mare, the colt apparently paying no attention, but the moment I took the harness from its peg and began to put it upon the mother the little miss ran out of doors. I thought I had scared her in some way and paid no particular attention, but when I was ready to drive away and tried to get her back into the barn she positively refused to go or be driven. She was as resolved to stay out as I was to have her go in, and it was only when I secured additional help that I was able to get her inside.

The same thing occurred on the following day, and then I began to suspect that the colt knew as well as I did what was going on and was resolved not to be left behind. So I called to my wife to come and watch with me, while we experimented. So long as I merely fussed around with the mare, cleaning her, etc., it was all right, but the moment I touched the harness and made it appear I was going to hitch up, out shot the colt from the barn in a moment. We tried this out a dozen times and always with the same result. This occurred when she was nine days old, and with conviction I turned to my wife and exclaimed: "She'll do, the little Trixie; she's got brains, and I'll begin to train her right away." Thus she got her name, and I started upon her education.

In my past experience I had taught many horses to respond to questions with a Yes or No, to paw out numbers, to kiss me, to sit down, lie down, roll over, and other similar simple tricks. I would ask if they would like a drink, a feed of oats, a lump of sugar, etc., and teach them how to answer with a nod of the head, and with a shake when I asked: "Shall I whip you?" or "I guess you don't want any feed today," but with Trixie I determined to go further than this and see if she really could be trained, or, better still, *educated* in any degree.

Thus began Trixie's education, which continued persistently for eighteen months. Every day I kept at it, and it might be interesting here to state that while I was educating Trixie, she was educating me. I learned a great deal about horses and horse nature in those eighteen months. In due time I had trained her so that she could pick out numbers on call, colors, could add, subtract, multiply, and divide; could count with her feet, sit in a chair, on my lap, and answer questions.

I then decided to take her out on the road and give exhibitions with her. But first of all I decided to give a test exhibition at our County Fair, at Humboldt, my own town. Of course I was well known, and my horse training proclivities were the subject of conversation all throughout the country, but few knew how much I had accomplished with Trixie. Hence that first appearance was a great surprise to my neighbors. Needless to say, it was also a wonderful success. Every one was delighted with the exhibition and marveled at the intelligence the beautiful little creature displayed.

I now started to go throughout the country with confidence. I knew what Trixie could do and what the effect of the exhibition would be upon an audience. In those days an educated horse was unknown. There were a few trained circus horses, but a horse like mine excited great wonder and interest. My method was to go to county and other fairs, explain what Trixie could do, and I would undertake to exhibit her before the grandstand between races. The Fair Associations would engage me, and thus I would earn a good financial return.

Soon after we began to travel I changed the colt's name to *Princess Trixie*, and this was the name by which she was ever afterwards known. About this time I came in contact with William Harrison Barnes, of Sioux City. He had been a newspaper reporter but was naturally a showman, and shortly before I met him he had drifted into the show business. He was exhibiting such horses as "The Pacing Wonder," "Johnny, the Guideless Wonder," and when he saw the Princess there was nothing for it but that he should become my partner and go along with us. For four years we traveled together, Barnes making the business arrangements for our appearance at carnivals, state fairs, amusement parks, and under the auspices of various organizations.

Then I sold Princess Trixie to him, continuing to travel with him for four years, after which I returned to Humboldt, bought another farm, and for two or three years did a little desultory training of horses, as before. Let me here, in parenthesis, tell of Princess Trixie's unfortunate end. Barnes showed her all over the country to the great delight of all who ever saw her, until about ten years ago, when she was killed in a railway wreck at Baltimore.

Soon after my return to Humboldt I was urged by Dode Fisk, of Wonewoc, Wisconsin, to plan and organize for him a show of trained horses, dogs, monkeys, etc., with a one-ringed circus. I did so, doing all the training of the animals myself. When we were ready to travel we had a sixteen-wagon show and I was appointed the arena director. For four years I occupied this position, helping build up the show all the time, and at the end of three years we ceased traveling in wagons and became an eleven-car railway show. It was my regular duty to keep the animals in good condition, see that they were healthy and kept up to their work, and to train any new stock we might buy.

Four years of this life tired my wife, and she expressed the desire to get away from a large show. She wanted a rest at home, she said, and then, if I desired to travel she suggested I buy a young horse or a colt, train or educate it, and we would travel with that, without all the hard work, flurry, and daily excitement attendant upon a large show. In the main I agreed with my wife and, anyhow, I felt that she ought to be considered as much as myself, so I began looking out for such a horse as I had in mind. I wanted another Trixie or, better, but scarcely hoped to find one very soon, or very easily.

I was nearer to the end of my search, however, than I supposed, for almost immediately I heard of just such a colt as I was looking for at Oregon, Ill. Right away I went to see him, and there, to my unspeakable delight, I found Captain. His owner was Judge Cartwright, a great lover of and breeder of good horses. Captain was of standard bred trotting stock, and was half brother to the famous Sydney Dillon. His sire was the well-known horse Syed and his dam was the almost equally well-known Robey.

At first sight he pleased me immensely, and I sought to gain all the information possible about him. I learned that as a colt he was very friendly and playful, showing keen intelligence. He also possessed great speed, sometimes pacing in the pasture as fast as his mother could run. This had led his owner, as soon as he was two years old, to train him for ninety days for the development of speed, so that he was able to step his mile in 2:16. He undoubtedly would have made a fast pacing horse with further training. But fate had another destiny in store for him. I resolved to buy him.

Naturally Judge Cartwright hated to part with so promising an animal, but I candidly laid my heart's desire before him. I showed him the influence it would have upon the rising generation if I could demonstrate that animals can reason, that they are capable of thought. Then I expatiated upon the easier life Captain himself would live than if he were to become a regular racehorse, and I appealed to the feeling of pride he—the judge—would possess were I successful—as I knew I should be—at having introduced so world famous a horse as Captain would become, that he had bred and reared. And, finally, to clinch the matter, I produced a certified check for a thousand dollars, which I placed in his hand.

Thus the purchase was made, with the express understanding that Judge Cartwright should always be given the credit for the raising of Captain. Perhaps here I ought to state that the colt's name up to this time had been Sid Bell. As I felt my whole future life's work and fame were going to center on this beautiful, young, and intelligent creature, I renamed him, calling him by the name by which I was known to all my professional associates, Captain Sigsbee.

It was not long before we became intimately acquainted. He was a handsome fellow, a dappled chestnut, fifteen and one half hands high, with broad forehead, large, intelligent eyes, well-shaped ears, deep, sensitive nostrils, mobile mouth, strong nose, a most pleasing face, and perfectly formed in every way.

I was satisfied from the first that in Captain I had a great subject for education. Already I began to plan what I would teach him. I was assured I could go far beyond anything I had hitherto done, even with the clever Trixie. One day in conversation with a group of horse-men, among whom was Al Ringling, the great circus master, I stated some of my expectations. Ringling laughed at me, especially when I declared my intention of so educating a horse that he could do things blindfolded. He freely declared that he had no faith in horse education. He believed that horses could be trained only under the whip and spur.

Said he: "I know you've done some wonderful things with Trixie, but animals are animals, and I don't believe that you can *educate* them. Let me give you some advice. Don't waste your time. Many a man has gone crazy by allowing a fool idea like this of yours to take possession of him."

I defended my ideas, however, and argued that my years of study of the horse had revealed things of horse nature and character few even dreamed of. I was sure they could think and reason. Everybody knew that they had memory, and I was satisfied that I could educate this, or any other intelligent horse, to use his reason, no matter how small it was—in other words to think.

Ringling listened with interest but made no pretense to hide his doubts, and again said I was going crazy when I affirmed my positive conviction that I could, and would, train Captain to take and obey orders *blindfolded*. He was certain it never could be done.

How well I have succeeded the hundreds of thousands who have seen Captain can best tell. It may also be interesting to recount Mr. Ringling's expressions when he saw Captain sometime after I began to give exhibitions with him.

He said: "I confess myself beaten, Sigsbee, I take off my hat to you. What you have accomplished will be a revelation to the world, as it has been to me. In spite of my years of association with horses I never dreamed they had such powers in them. You have opened my eyes, and as others begin to see they will treat their animals with greater consideration, they will think more favorably of them, and no longer treat them as if they were mere brute instruments of their will or pleasure, without feeling or intelligence."

Mr. Ringling well stated what it has been one of my constant endeavors to bring about. I have always loved horses. I wanted to see them better treated, and it is with great satisfaction that I am learning every day that my exhibitions with Princess Trixie and now with Captain are bearing this kind of fruit.

When my purchase of the colt was completed, I took him to my training barn in Chicago and there began his education. The first thing to do was to get well acquainted and gain his affection. This was done by giving him plenty to eat, the best of care, speaking gently and kindly to him, petting him, and giving him dainties now and again, such as carrots, apples, and sugar. My friends and acquaintances often laughed at me, and said I should never accomplish what I was after, but I persevered. They knew I was wasting time, money, and energy for nothing, but "I know" that what "they knew" wasn't so.

It did not take Captain long to learn that I was kind to him; that I was his true and wise friend; and was to be relied upon. These are three things, the importance of which I cannot overestimate. Many people try to be kind to animals, but they are not wise in their treatment, and they are not to be relied upon. I knew that Captain trusted me for the little extra dainties he enjoyed. I never disappointed him. I never lied to him—that is promised him anything I did not intend to perform, and thus he soon learned I was to be trusted.

When left alone he became very uneasy. Like children he wanted companionship of some kind, so I hired a groom, Chili by name, whose duty was to remain with Captain, day and night. He was never to attempt to teach the horse anything, as that would lead to confusion, but was to care for him and be his companion at all times. Chili remained with him for several years and they became very fond of each other. I should never have parted with him, but when we came to San Francisco, he got careless and I had to let him go. Then I was fortunate enough to secure an equally good man in his present groom, Jasper.

Jasper is a natural-born horseman. He has ridden, broken, and owned some very famous horses, and has been on the track for years, hence he thoroughly understands horse-nature, and he and Captain get along famously.

As I have before explained Captain likes company. He strongly resents being left alone. Every night time before he goes to sleep he listens for the footsteps of his groom and if he is not there he signifies his disapproval by pawing, whinnying, etc., and generally keeps it up until Jasper returns and talks to him. Then, content and restful, he goes to sleep.

Once, when he was being brought south by rail, Jasper had to leave him in the Los Angeles freight yards—still in his car—to see that their tickets were properly endorsed, and he was gone for a half an hour or more. When he returned poor Captain was in a complete lather of perspiration. The unusual noises of the railroad yard in a large city, as he was shut up in a car so that he could not see, had fretted him into a frenzy. As soon as the groom returned he signified his satisfaction with whinnyings and nose-rubbings and in a very short time was cool again.

Every night before he lies down and goes to sleep, he peeks out to see if Jasper is there. If not, he awaits his return, and then stretches out with his head towards the place where Jasper sleeps.

Soon after we arrived in San Diego a lady presented Jasper with a pigeon. The bird was taken to the stable, and Captain became much interested in her. As the pigeon perched on the partition he reached up and nuzzled it in the most affectionate manner. Not only did the pigeon not resent it, but she seemed actually to enjoy it, showing no fear or desire to get away. Now they are almost inseparable friends, and Captain spends hours with his head upon the partition, snuggling close up to the bird. Prior to its coming, Captain often showed considerable nervousness when he heard strange footsteps approaching his stable, or just before a performance, but the presence of the pigeon has changed this. Its mere presence is a soothing influence, and when the show is over he goes back to the stable and greets his bird friend with evident pleasure and affection.

One of my experiences with Captain demonstrated his superior intelligence over most horses. My training barn was two stories high, and a wide pair of stairs led from the ground to the second floor. When my grandson was born Captain took a great liking for him. He loved to "kiss" him and nuzzle him while he was in the cradle, or baby-buggy, or even in his nurse's arms. As the child grew older we used to place him on Captain's back and Captain would march back and forth, as proudly as a king, apparently conscious of the trust we placed in him.

One day while I was working with Captain the child was in the barn, and he kept going up and down the stairs. I noticed that Captain's attention was more often fixed upon the child than upon me and he seemed much interested. Someone called me away for a few moments, and when I returned there was no Captain to be seen. Then I heard a peculiar noise from above, and looking up, what should I see but Captain following the child up the stairs. I am free to confess I got scared, for I couldn't see how I could get him down. But I went up, controlled my fears, and then quietly talked to Captain and told him he'd come up the stairs and now he'd have to go down them. And I backed him down, a step at a time, as easily and as safely as could be. And, strange to say, ever after that, whenever he wanted to go upstairs

I let him, and he came down alone. I never had to back him down again. He comes down that way of his own volition.

People often ask me how I train an animal. Personally I would not use the word "train," in speaking of such a horse as Captain, not because it is the wrong word, but because it conveys a wrong idea. I would say "educate," for I firmly believe that horses and dogs and elephants and other animals possess the power of reason, though, of course, in a limited degree. And I believe that by patient and kindly treatment we can "draw out"—educate—the intelligence possessed.

I have no set rules or fixed system by which I work. There are a few principles that control me. First of all I study the animal's nature and disposition. No two animals are alike, any more than any two children are alike. Some animals are very nervous, are easily excited, while others are placid and docile and nothing seems to disturb them. But whatever the natural disposition nothing can be done without gaining the animal's complete confidence.

This I do by uniformly kind treatment. I always speak gently, mildly, never angrily or impatiently. Then I pet the animal at every opportunity, though with some, one must approach them at first, cautiously. As soon as possible get an animal accustomed to the feel of your hands, and to know that they always come gently, and with soothing effect. Find out what they particularly like to eat, and every once in a while, give this to them as a relish, a luxury, a reward for something well done. As I have explained elsewhere horses like carrots, apples, and sugar. Too much of any of these, however, is not good, as their natural food is grass, hay, cereals, and the like. Yet it should never be overlooked that a horse, like a man, can more easily be reached through his stomach than any other way.

Though you must be kind you must also be firm. Many people confound and confuse kindness with mushiness. No animal must be allowed to have his own way, when that way conflicts with his master's will. (Yet a caution, here, is necessary. One who is training either a horse or a child should remember his natural proclivities and tendencies. There should be no attempt to "break the will." It is to be trained, disciplined, brought under control. Hence, never set your will against the will of your animal unless it is in a matter where you know you are right.) For instance, if a horse wants to cut up and frolic when you wish him to attend to business, there are two ways of doing.

One is to leave him alone for a while and then firmly bring him to attention, even though he still desires to continue his fun. Another is to crush the spirit of fun and frolic and not allow him to play at all. This latter method is unnatural, unreasonable, and cruel, and therefore not to be thought of for one moment by any rational or kind man. The former is both kind and *disciplinary*. The horse is allowed to follow his natural instincts, but is also taught to control them at his master's word. This is training and education. A third method is to allow the horse to frolic to his heart's content and then get him to do what you desire. Here there is no discipline whatever. This is the way of "mushiness," and it is often followed by parents and others in handling their children. It is about as bad as the cruel method of suppressing the natural instincts, for an uncontrolled will or appetite soon becomes the child's, animal's, or man's master, and nothing is more disastrous than such a bondage.

Hence be firm in control. It is not necessary to whip to punish. A horse, as well as a child, will learn self-control through appetite, or the giving of something that is a pleasure. Where you have trouble in gaining control, or where the animal is lazy, hold back on the tidbit, or the free run, or something of the kind the horse enjoys. He will soon learn to associate the loss with his disobedience. Equally so be prompt and certain in rewarding his good conduct. It is a good thing in dealing with a stubborn or refractory animal (or child) to let him get "good and hungry." It does not take him long to learn to associate obedience with food, or disobedience with hunger.

Then it is most important that you never lie to an animal. Be strictly truthful. When you promise anything—or by forming a habit imply a promise—do not fail to keep that promise. If your animal expects an apple, a carrot, a piece of sugar, or a frolic at the close of his hour's training, *do not disappoint him.* A horse, a child, instinctively hates a liar. One soon loses confidence, and where there is no confidence there can be no pleasure in working together, and as soon as pleasure goes, the work becomes a burden, a labor, a penalty, and a curse, to be dreaded, shunned, avoided. So win your animal's confidence and then be sure to keep it.

When it comes to actual teaching always be very patient, never excited, always talk gently and keep your voice pitched low, and remember that all animals are curious, possess more or less of the imitative faculty, and have good memories. To remember these things is of great importance. Never lose sight of them. Talk to your animal as you would to a child. Whether you think or believe he understands you, or not, act and talk as if he did. Then *show* him what you want him to do. Do it before him, again and again. Thus you will excite his imitative faculties and at the same time, train his memory.

Occasionally you may be able to give him extra aid. For instance, you want to teach your horse to shake his head to express the idea No! When you say No! tickle the horse's ear, and he will shake his head. Then you also shake your head, and say with emphasis, No! Repeat this several times, and you will find that when you say No! the horse will shake his head without your having to tickle his ear. As soon as he responds to your question with a shake of the head be sure to pet and reward him with a lump of sugar, at the same time talking encouragingly to him.

Then repeat the process, again and again, until it is well fixed in his memory.

Every day go over this same thing; for, if you neglect what he learns today for a week or two, it is very possible he will forget and you will have to begin afresh. Review perpetually, until you know that *he knows*.

In assisting him to nod his head when you want him to signify Yes! when you use the word tap him under the chin. This leads him to throw his head up and down. Soon he will nod at the mere saying of Yes! and later, he will respond with a nod when you ask him a question to which he should reply with the affirmative.

Remember always, in all you do, that you are dealing with an animal whose brainpower is far less than that of an ordinary child, and be *patient, kind, and persevering*. Never allow yourself to believe the animal does not possess intelligence. *Believe* he has it, *hope* he has it, *trust God* that he has it, and work in that belief, hope, trust, and you will accomplish wonders. Faith, hope, and love are the abiding and moving powers of life. With them there is no limit to what can be done, for they belong to the infinite.

23

IN WHICH TRUE BECOMES JUSTIN MORGAN

BY ELEANOR WARING BURNHAM

The Morgan horse emerged in New England during the first quarter of the nineteenth century in a time and place where good agricultural records were kept, particularly of horses that proved to be useful and valuable. We know something of the second generation and a great deal about later generations of Morgans but comparatively little about the father of the breed, even though he became well known during his own lifetime.

The mysterious origins of the first Morgan horse led to fiction and nonfiction accounts of his early life. In Eleanor Waring Burnham's book Justin Morgan, Founder of his Race, *readers got some of both approaches. Burnham produced a fictionalized narrative of one of the several versions of the horse's early years. It was a technique that Burnham had successfully used in her previous novels.*

In her story, Burnham begins with a mare she names Gipsey, who has produced a handsome bay colt, the son of a stallion named True Briton. Their owner, a farmer in West Springfield, Massachusetts, names the colt True Briton the Second, soon shortened to True. Gipsey has a prophetic message for True. "When other horses now famous are forgotten," she says, "your memory will live on."

True becomes a favorite pet of his owner, especially when he saves his master's life by running for help when the elderly farmer is injured. But the farmer reluctantly sells True to a singing teacher from Vermont, a kindly young man named Justin Morgan.

After a sojourn among well-bred horses and distinguished people in Hartford, Connecticut, True travels to Vermont with his new master, who is proud to show off the sturdy little horse to his hardworking neighbors. Illness and financial problems force the singing teacher to rent True to Robert Evans for fifteen dollars so the farmer can clear a new field.

It was hard work but True revels in it, enjoying the admiration from Evans and his neighbors for the amount of work he could do. Evans enjoyed the admiration just as much. In this chapter, True receives a new name.

Once or twice a week it was the custom among the farmers waiting at Chase's Mill to pass the time testing their strength or that of their horses. It was healthful sport and kept them and their beasts in trim. Many were the jugs of Medford rum consumed on these occasions, and anyone having a horse to try, or a new test of strength for the men, was welcomed.

Running their horses short distances for small stakes came to be very popular. A course of eighty rods was measured, starting at the mill and extending along the highway; a line was drawn across the road, called a "scratch," the horses were ranged in a row, and at the drop of a hat away they went, cheered by the crowd.

It so happened that Evans and True, who never finished their work until dusk, were rarely at these tests. Evans, himself, was too tired to join in the sports, but True often thought he would like to try his strength against the larger, heavier horses.

One day, coming along the River Road to the mill, his heavy farm harness and tug chains still dangling on True, they passed Master Justin Morgan—he stood under a maple tree and was lilting an old French song learned from the Canadian lumbermen, called "A la Claire Fontaine." True and Evans paused to listen. Everyone liked Master Morgan for his sweet voice and gentle manners.

When the song was finished Evans gave the singer a neighborly greeting and strode on to the mill, True following him, more like a dog than a horse. The sun was gone and the evening shadows were beginning to fall, but there were still lingering along the horizon long streaks of crimson and gold that tinged the river with color.

In evident discussion, near a log at the mill, stood a group of farmers. Evans and True approached. Nathan Nye, friendly and jovial, whittling a birch stick, looked up as Evans said: "How be ye all?"

"Why not give Bob's horse a show?" he asked, a twinkle in his keen blue eyes, a smile brightening his genial face.

Horses and oxen were hitched to the limbs of trees or grazed near at hand, quite without interest in whatever was taking place. Sledges and wagons rested their shafts on the ground, seeming to wait patiently.

"Is it a pulling bee?" asked Evans, leaning against True's side.

"Yaas, but I guess it's about over, now," drawled a lank youth, coming out of the mill with a sack of meal on his shoulder.

"Anybody but you in a hurry to be going homealong?" questioned Nye, crushingly.

The youth did not answer, but went on to his sledge.

"There's a jug of Medford rum in the store for the owner of the horse that can get that there log on my runway this evening," explained Miller Chase to Evans.

"Now I want to know!" exclaimed Evans, carelessly, "Why didn't you say so before? You seem to be making quite a chore of a very simple thing; I'll just have my little horse do it for you in a jiffy!"

A shout of derisive laughter greeted his remark.

"Now do tell!" cried Hiram Sage, sarcastically.

"That pony pull a log my Jim refused?" scoffed another.

"My 'pony,' as you call him," laughed Evans, good-naturedly, "has never refused me yet." He placed his arm over True's neck; the horse rattled his chains musically, and reached for a low-handing bough.

"Work is play for this animal," Evans went on. "We've been in the logging field all day, but that don't make a mite o' difference to the Morgan horse. Come, show us your log!" True shook himself again and went on chewing leaves.

"Why, that beast's naught but a colt!" said Jim's owner, scornfully.

"Colt or no, he's the finest bit o' horseflesh this side of The Plains of Abraham!" Evans contended, hotly. "Give him his head and he goes like a shot and doesn't pull an ounce, and as for drawing a load—when this horse starts, *something's* got to come! That is," he added with a laugh, "as long as the tugs last!"

"Well, stop your bragging," said the sarcastic Hiram; "actions speak louder than words. Hitch him up that there 'something' and let us see it 'come.'" Miller Chase stepped forward, hospitably.

"First come in, men, and fix up your bets over a mug," he said.

They went inside the shop, all talking at once, and left True nibbling among the grasses and weeds. When they had disappeared he glanced at the log which the other horses had refused—horses much larger and heavier than he. The opportunity he had hoped for had come!

"But can I do it?" he asked himself.

The answer was, he *could*, and *would*. He was spurred to the greatest effort of his life by the taunt that he was a "pony." At any rate he was over fourteen hands and weighed nine hundred and fifty pounds!

"As I understand it," Evans was saying, as the men came out of the shop, "the agreement is that my horse has got to pull that big log ten rods onto the logway, *in three pulls*, or I lose?"

"That's the idea, exactly," assented Miller Chase.

Evans took hold of True's bridle confidently, and led him to the enormous log, where he fastened the tugs properly. Then he stepped one side and looked the young horse straight in the eye.

True returned his look—they might almost have been said to have exchanged a wink.

At this thought, Evans shouted with laughter.

"Gentlemen," he said, when he could speak seriously, "I am ashamed to ask my horse to pull a little weight like that *on a test*—couldn't two or three of you get on and ride?"

Then Evans was *sure* he saw a twinkle in True's eye.

A loud laugh greeted the proposal. "But, man, that there's a dead lift!" expostulated the miller.

"Well, mine's a live horse," Evans cried, with a grin. "Get on there! Justin Morgan's waitin' for to take you to drive!"

From this day the young horse was called *Justin Morgan's*. It was an easy transition to drop the possessive "s," after a while, and call him "Justin Morgan." With much hilarity three men climbed up on the log.

By this time darkness had fallen and Master Chase ran to get his lanthorn, swinging it back and forth, as he returned.

"Mind you don't fall off," Evans warned the men. "'Something' is about to 'come.'"

And "something" did!

Justin Morgan's horse gathered himself together, almost crouching, and waited for the word to start. When it was given, his chest muscles strained, his wide nostrils were scarlet and dilated, and this scion of Arabia's proud breed moved off as if inspired by Allah himself for an almost miraculous feat.

The bystanders, craning their necks to see, ran alongside; the men, perched on the log, fell off as it rocked from side to side, and then the young horse paused for breath—or to recover his strength.

Utter silence was over all. There was no jeering now. The second pull landed the log on the logway, and the amazed men broke into the wildest cheers ever heard at Chase's Mill.

~~~~~~

Burnham continues the fictionalized story of the first Morgan horse. Justin Morgan the man becomes increasingly ill and is forced to sell Justin Morgan the horse. With his new owners he finds kind treatment, satisfying work, cheerful conversations with interesting horses, and, improbably, a role as an equine Paul Revere in the War of 1812. Except for a brief period late in life he lives out his years in comfort and honor. Burnham makes little mention of what really made Justin Morgan famous—the hundreds of offspring that created the Morgan breed.

~~~~~~

24

WHITE HORSE WINTER

BY WILBUR DANIEL STEELE

Wilbur Daniel Steele was among the most popular short story writers in the United States at a time when almost every literate person at least occasionally read short stories. Although he was born in North Carolina, Steele lived for many years in Provincetown, Massachusetts, where he discovered some of his favorite themes and settings. He found special inspiration in the lives of the Portuguese fishermen of Cape Cod.

"White Horse Winter," one of Steele's best stories, does center on Portuguese Americans, but at its heart is the magnificent horse of the title. At first, neither the characters nor the readers are quite sure whether the white horse is a dream or a ghost or an illusion. Or could he be real?

The little house where I was born, and in which I passed the earlier years of my life, stands about a hundred yards back from the beach and a little more than a mile down shore from Old Harbor. What we always knew as the "Creek" runs in there, with plenty of water even at low tide to float my father's dory; and the flawless yellow face of a dune used to stand up behind the house, sheltering us from the northerlies that pick the scud from the ocean, a mile back across the Neck, and spatter it in the bay at our front door. My father and mother still live in the house, but the dune has shifted to the westward, and it is colder there on a winter night.

My older sister was born before my father and mother came from the Western Islands, so she had a recollection of green country; but we younger children knew nothing but the water and the sand. Strangely enough, my most vivid remembrance of the water is not from any of its wilder moods: I picture it with the tide out at evening, reflecting the face of the western sky, flat, garish-colored, silent, with a spur of mute fire reaching out at me along the surface of the Creek.

The dunes were the magic land, full of shifting shadows, and deceptive, where a little covey of beach plums made themselves out as a far-away and impenetrable forest, especially when the mist came inland, and a footprint in the sand across a hollow appeared a vast convulsion of nature at the other end of a day's journey. And one felt the dunes always moving, rising up out of the sea, marching silently across the Neck, and advancing upon the little house. I can remember the spring when the sand ate up a pear-tree my father had brought from the Islands.

The dunes entered our lives, and became a part of them. Even now the sight of a strip of sand gets a queer grip on me, and to this day I am apt to catch myself spying out the skyline with an indefinable and portentous dread. I cannot shake off this sensation, although I know perfectly what it is. It is a relic from that time which we have always called, in our family, White Horse Winter.

I remember my father's coming in one October day and standing a long time before the barometer which always hung behind the kitchen door. After a while he said to my mother in his broken English,—

"It weel be ver' bad weather tonight—tomorrow."

That night when I was trying to get to sleep, I heard the skirmishers of a great wind feeling at the shingles above my head.

My next recollection is of the tumult of a gale outside, mingled with beating on the door downstairs, and distracted fragments of men's voices calling to one another of a vessel come ashore. I knew it must be at Round Hill or they would not have come past our house.

Then I was out myself, where no boy of ten had any business to be, isolated in the center of a vast disruption, except when an occasional agitated phantom passed in the rocking darkness toward Round Hill Bars. I had an acute consciousness of doing wrong, and with all the fight to keep my feet in the chaos of sand and wind and scud, the thought of what my father would do if he came upon me lay heavy on my mind.

After a time one of the shore dunes came up before me, black, with an aura of distracted sand about its crest and the sky behind it gray with the labor of dawn. The silhouettes of men, and of a few women, were running about over it and pointing to sea with jerking arms. But I was afraid to go up there—still with the fear of my father's anger—so I ran to the northward in the hollow a hundred yards or so before I felt it safe to venture upon the ridge, where I cowered down, a very small and very tired-out boy.

It was a full-rigged ship. Her main and mizzen were already gone, and her foremast writhed in dismal and contorted circles toward the sky, a frail, sensitive needle point marking every onslaught and repulse of the fight below, where the vessel wallowed in the smother between the outer and inner bars. Inshore, on the torn and clamorous beach, the figures of the lifesaving crew moved about their boat with futile gestures, lifting cursed hands to their faces to scream soundless words at one another. The wind was like a blast from the colossal explosion that flared behind the eastern clouds.

But it was the water that fascinated me that morning. The Round Hill Bars make a talking, even in a moderate breeze, which can be heard in our kitchen across the Neck. Now their shouting seemed to me to fill up the whole bowl of the visible world, rumbling around its misty confines in tangled reverberations. I could see the outer bar only as a white, distorted line athwart the gray, but the shoreward shallows were writhing, living things, gnawing at the sky with venomous teeth of spume, and giving birth in agony to the legions which advanced forever and forever upon the land.

My mother used sometimes to sing a little Portuguese song to my brother Antone, the baby. It had a part which ran:

> The herd of the Sea King's White Horses
> Comes up on the shore to graze . . .

It pleased my boy mind, on this morning, to figure them as ravening, stung to frenzy by the lash of the gale, tossing maddened manes, and bellowing, for horses were not common in that fisher country. Try as I might, my eyes would not stay on the wreck, but returned inevitably to those squadrons of white horses advancing out of the mist. They were very fearsome things to me at that time, although I was old enough to know that they were not alive and could not possibly get at me.

Then a tremendous wave broke and flattened out in a smother on the beach, and I was sure for a moment I had seen an actual horse struggling there. The next breaker overwhelmed the place, swirling, thunderous, shot its thin mottled tongue far up the sand and withdrew it seething into the undertow—and now there could be no doubt that a horse was there, screaming, pawing at the treacherous sand, his wide glistening back horribly convulsed, and eyes and nostrils of flame.

Many and many a time since then I have had it all in a dream; and in the dream, even now, I am swept back into something of the elemental terror that held the boy cowering on the ridge of sand while the great white stallion staggered up the face of the dune and stood against the sky, coughing and coughing and coughing.

Of a sudden, I knew that I must run away from that thing, and I scrambled out of my little burrow and ran, not daring to look back, not daring to ease my pace when the sand dragged too cruelly at my shoes—ran and ran—till I found myself in the safe haven of the front room at the little house, and my mother stirring a pan over the kitchen stove.

I staggered out to her, crying that a horse had come out of the water and run after me. She thought that I was feverish, had had a bad dream, and it occurred to me that I need not let her know I had been where I should not have been that morning. She packed me off to bed again, and when I woke in the afternoon I was of even minds myself whether I had dreamed it all or not. Certainly it was cut from the cloth of a dream.

During the weeks that followed I heard a deal about the wreck, from my father and from others who came past on the state road, and stopped to chat. It was a bad affair, that wreck. The shore people could see her men, now and then when the rack drifted aside for a moment, swarming over the deck like ants disturbed by a pail of water. One of these glimpses showed them the crew clustered about the boats on the lee side, and then the lifesavers burned in vain the signal which means, "Do not attempt to leave in your own boats"; the next lifting of the curtain discovered the ship's decks bare of life, and seventeen bodies were dragged from the surf that day.

But a strange thing happened when the lifesavers rowed out to the hulk after the sea had gone down. In the cabin they came upon a young man, dry-clothed, sitting before a fire in the stove, plainly much shaken by the experiences of the night, but still with a grip on himself. He asked if the boats had come ashore all right, and when Captain Hall told him, he seemed taken aback.

"Nothing come ashore?" he asked.

"Nothing alive," said the captain. The other looked into the fire a while, white, and shaking a little. "I was afeared to go with the sailors," he said, after a time.

Of course the story did not come to me in this straight sequence, but merely as haphazard snatches from the gossip of my elders, some of it not clearly till years afterwards—for the details of a great wreck are treasured among people of the sea so long as the generation lasts.

It was almost a week before I went out on the dunes again. Although I was now convinced that I had seen something that was not, still even a bad dream is not a thing for a child to shake off lightly. But my sister Agnes's eighteenth birthday was coming soon now, and it was always a custom in our family to signalize such events with a cake and bayberry candles. So I was off this day to the north of Snail Road, where the bottom of a certain hollow is covered with a mat of bayberry bushes. It takes a good many bayberries to make even a small candle, and the dark was beginning to come down when the basket was filled and I started back across the sand hills toward home.

The dunes were very silent and very misty and very lonely that evening; I trudged along with my small head going about like the mythical owl's, but the dusk remained empty of any horror till I had come across Snail Road and into the region of black sand where one may scoop out a little hole and drink fresh water. I almost always did this, whether I was thirsty or not, but that night I was saved the trouble of scooping the hole—or would have been had I cared to take advantage of the great glistening gash that lay in my path. It was no work of human hands. All about the place the sand was churned and scarred by enormous, deep tracks, and a double thread of them led away over the eastern skyline. Then I was running again, as I had that other morning, running all the way to the little house, careless of the bayberries that strewed my backward trail.

Two nights after, we were all sitting around the fire in our kitchen. There was no wind that evening and the tide was down beyond the flats, so that all was very quiet outside the little house, and a note of distant trumpeting came plain to us through the crisp night. It was surely a queer sound for our country, but its significance passed me till my father spoke to my mother.

"It's the white horse again," he said. My mother nodded, without curiosity or surprise.

"Yes," she answered, "we must keep Zhoe"—that was I, Joe—"off the dunes more."

But they could not keep me off the dunes entirely, now that the white horse had become actual and an object of common gossip. I took an adventurous pleasure in climbing to the top of the hill behind the house and overlooking the country of hummocks. Especially was this fine to do of an early evening, when the light had left the sand and the ridges stood out black against the sky.

I saw him many times from this point of security—always as a dark, far-away silhouette, tremendous, laboring over the back of a dune or standing with his great head flung up and tail streaming on the wind. His presence there gave the whole dune land a new aspect for me—as of a familiar country grown sinister and full of the shadow of disaster.

Nights when the wind was northerly, his racketing sometimes came to me in the loft where my cot stood; then I would shiver under the clothes and fall asleep to dream of being lost in a wilderness of shifting dunes, and that great shaggy white beast above me on a ridge, coughing and coughing and coughing. Once he must have come plunging down the face of our own hill, because we were startled by a splashing of sand on the shingles of an outhouse, followed by a great snorting and a ripping of fence timbers. That night even my father and mother were pale.

For I was not the only one who was afraid. Some of the men came out from Old Harbor with lines one day to take the animal, and at first sight of him, suddenly, over the angle of a dune, dropped their entanglements and fled back past our house, running heavily. And that was in the flat sun light of midday. After that men went over to Round Hill Station by other and circuitous routes.

One of these evenings, while I was crouching on the hill with a delightful shiver playing along my spine, a strange man came up and stood a few yards to one side of me, looking out to the eastward. The white horse was there, perhaps a half-mile off, outlined against a bank of silver that came rolling in from the ocean. The newcomer regarded him a long time without moving; then I, being a little afraid of the man, slipped out of the bushes and down the hill to the little house.

The dusk was already thick when he came down the dune and stopped to pass a word with my father, who was working over a net near the gate. I remember my sister Agnes peering curiously at the figure indistinct in the gloom, and my mother whispering to her that it was the man they had taken off the wreck. That made a tremendous impression on me. I was glad when my father asked him to sit a while by the fire.

From my vantage-point behind my mother's chair, I could examine him better than I dared do on the ridge. He was a smallish man, of a wiry build rather uncommon among our own people, whose strength is apt to come upon them with an amount of flesh. His skin was not brown but red, hairy about the wrists,—I thought of it as brittle. His hair was almost the color of his skin, his features were heavy. He sat or stood with elbows out and thumbs tucked in his belt, and he had little to say. I can give his age definitely as twenty-eight at that time.

From the moment he entered, the stranger seemed unable to keep his slow-moving gray eyes away from my sister Agnes, who stood leaning against the door which led into the front room. Those two were as far apart as the two poles. It is hard for a small boy to know how his brothers and sisters really appear, but looking back out of later years I remember her as rather tall for a girl, full-formed, straight, dark as the rest of us, and with a look of contempt in her black eyes for this alien whom she had no means of comprehending.

For a time my father talked about the wreck, putting questions, hazarding technical opinions in the jargon of the sea. The stranger's replies were monosyllabic and vague. Then in a pause the neighing of the white horse came in to us, and the man started up with an abrupt scraping of his shoes on the boards. I am sure that Agnes believed he was frightened, and that she took no pains to hide it. After that the talk turned naturally on the white horse, going back and forth between my father and mother, for the stranger had even less to say now than before.

Jem Hodges (that was the stranger's name) came the following day and sat on the front porch, watching father who was tarring weir twine in the yard. He had nothing to say—simply sat there with his thumbs tucked in his belt.

Agnes came in and said to my mother, "He's a dummy—I never seen such a dummy, ma."

"I don' know, Aggie," my mother answered her. "He ain't our kind, and you can't tell about things you ain't used to." That was my mother's way.

Agnes flounced out of the kitchen in a manner which had no significance to me then, for my rudimentary wits could perceive no possible connection between her action and the silence of the little man on the porch outside.

I think I can say now what the connection was. Among other things the world has taught me this—that no two men do the same thing in exactly the same way. Jem Hodges was wooing my sister Agnes. Little wonder that her spirit was restive under that wooing, when all the blood of the race in her veins sang of the lover's fervor, the quick eye, the heart speaking in words, the abandon of caresses. And here was a man, fulfilling none of our conventions of beauty, who sat imperturbable, impassive, saying nothing, and making her come to him. I am sure that he did it without planning or analyzing—I think half of it was constraint and all of it instinct. And Agnes might flounce out of the room as she would: sooner or later I saw her again at the front of the house.

This went on for two or three weeks. Jem Hodges came almost every day to sit on the porch a while, after which he sometimes wandered away in the growing evening over our own dune. Again and again I saw him standing there, as on the first evening, for a long time without motion, looking over the hummocks. Sometimes I could hear him whistling under his breath an air that was very strange and outlandish to me, then, who had never heard the like. Many years later I heard one of the great tenors of the world sing the same air, and it thrilled me, but not in the same way.

On the evening of the twenty-eighth of November (I have the date from Agnes) I was ensconced in my bushy retreat, watching the night take hold of the world of sand. Jem Hodges stood on the ridge to the east of me. Every minute that passed robbed his motionless figure of some detail, and lent to it a portion of the flat mystery of the night. I had seen the white horse once that evening, topping a rise far off to the northward, and then no more till I was suddenly aware of a gigantic, indistinct form moving up hill toward me amid a vast *shuf-shuf* of troubled sand.

I was terribly frightened for the instant; then I knew it was a matter only of hopping over the bank behind me and sliding down to the very back door of the little house. I had slipped from the bushes and was almost to the bottom of the smothering slope, when I heard such a plunging in the sand above that my wits came near leaving me again; I made wild and futile plunges, and cried out to my sister, whom I saw in the open doorway. I had no thought in the world but that it was the white horse charging down. I had almost gained the house, a pathetic small figure of panic, when I felt myself brushed aside with a violence which left me sprawling, terrified, on my back in the sand, with a confused impression as of something passing through the doorway where my sister had stood. It was not beyond me at that moment to imagine the white horse, overcarried by the impetus of his charge, blundering right on into the kitchen of the little house.

Jem Hodges had passed completely out of my mind, and it was Jem whom I found in the kitchen, ill at ease, confronted by my sister. Agnes I hardly knew that evening—she was like a new and strange person, aflame with anger and a high, emphatic beauty, speaking tensely, with the nerve twanging upward slur at the end of the phrase which discovered the blood of the Island race through all the veneer of public school. The accumulated unrest of weeks had found a vent at last.

"You—you—oh, you coward!" she reviled him, "you little sneaking coward, you!—an' they call you a man !" Her voice was a whispered shriek, her clenched hands moved before her as though to do him harm.

Jem was white, and still breathing hard.

"A man," Agnes went on. "They call you a man—an' you knock over little children so's you can save your own little hairy hide. You lose your eyesight—and your mind—from seein' a horse walkin' over some sand . . . Agh!"

Then she turned to me with a fierce gesture of protection.

"Zhoe—poor little Zhoe—he hurt you, didn't he? There, don't cry no more—you're more of a man 'n he is, ain't you Little Zhoe?"

My face was in the folds of her skirt and I still sobbed out the after-swell of the terror, but I could hear Jem's voice speaking. He always seemed to me, when talking, to be expending his words with immense care.

"The horse wouldn't harm Joe," he pronounced.

That was a signal for Agnes to fly at him once more.

"No—won't harm him—you slip that out easy because Zhoe's no folks of yourn—an' never will be either. Agh!—God!—I could kill you if you weren't such a worm!"

"He wouldn't harm Joe, nor nobody."

The man's words were unsteady but assured. Agnes's voice went from her control completely; she came close to him and screamed in his face.

"Harm nobody?—Oh!—Oh!—Little man, go an' bring me that white horse—You been makin' eyes at me—Oh, I seen 'em!—Now if you want me—*me*—go out an' get the white horse that won't harm nobody—with your two bare hands—an' bring him to me."

For that moment, my sister was out of her mind.

Jem came over and laid an absent hand on my shoulder, as if he had thought to comfort me, and then had fallen into abstraction before the act was accomplished. After a moment of vacant quiet he looked up at Agnes.

"An' you tell me that, too," he said.

All that evening I was haunted by a picture of the silent man, with his hard red thumbs tucked in his belt, pursuing a shadow of horror through the black dune country. This distressed me so much that I finally crawled out from beneath the table, where I had been lying, and whispered my fears in my sister's ear. She had been very quiet all evening, but when she understood what I was saying she gave a little bitter laugh and put her arm around me.

"Don't be afeared, Zhoe," she whispered her answer. "The little man is tight behind his own door this night." Then she fell to brooding once more.

When Jem came to the little house the following day he carried a piece of line in one hand. He sat down as usual on the front steps. The picture of him that evening has remained to me the most vivid memory of my young days—why, I cannot say. I peeped out of the front window and saw him there, silhouetted against the blazing waters of the bay—the vast, silent, and expressive shout of the departing day casting out at me the unexpressive man.

Agnes came around a corner and stood, looking down at the line in Jem's hand. He looked down at it, too.

"I been thinkin' it over," he said.

"You're a-scared to do it!" she answered. For a long time they remained there without moving or speaking, both looking down at the line.

"You're a-scared to do it!" Agnes repeated at length, and Jem got up from the steps and went out through the gate toward the dunes. Never have I seen the whole world so saturated with passive flame as it seemed to me, peering from the gloom of the front room that evening.

At supper Agnes talked feverishly of many things, but ate nothing. All of us noticed it, and my mother remarked upon it. The silence outside was so complete that the riffle of the coming tide was audible in the pauses, and once I heard the note of the stallion, far away over the sand. Then my sister broke out into a humming tune—the first and last time I ever knew her to sing at table. I remember wondering why her eyes, which were usually so steady and straight seeing, turned here and there without rest, and why, after the meal, she wandered from window to window, and never stopped to look out at any.

That was to be a gala night for me. My father had been raking up the brush and leaves about the place for a week, heaping them, together with bits of old net and tarry shreds of canvas, in half a dozen piles before the house, and tonight I was allowed to set them off. I had them blazing soon after supper was over, and a fine monstrous spectacle they made for me, who danced up and down the lines full of elemental exultation, and then ran off to call Agnes to see my handiwork.

I could not find her anywhere in the house; I went through all the rooms and out and around the yard. No one knew where she was. My mother thought she had seen her with a shawl over her head, but had taken no particular notice at the time. It didn't matter, at any rate— Agnes often wandered out toward town in the early evening. The rest of us sat on the steps and watched the fires, baby brother and all, but they had lost something of their enchantment for me. I was pursuing an idea, an obscure apprehension.

"I b'lieve Aggie's gone to the dunes," I proclaimed, at length.

"Dunes!" my mother cried out. "No—you're foolish, Zhoe. Why?"

Thus confronted by the direct question, I found my reasonings too diaphanous for a logical answer.

"I dunno," I answered, abashed.

But I had set them worrying. It is a strange fact that fisher-folk are at once the bravest and the most apprehensive people I have any knowledge of. When worried, my mother was generally restless with her hands, while my father betrayed his anxiety by unwonted profanity and by aimless expeditions to inspect the dory mooring in the creek.

These things they did tonight, my mother on the steps, impassive save for her writhing fingers, my father visible in peripatetic red glimpses as he wandered, muttering, about the yard. He called out that he was going to step down and take a look at the boat.

After that, he was gone a long time—half an hour I should say—while the flames died down over the fires, replacing the uncertain flicker in the yard with a smooth pervasive glow. When he at length appeared, I wondered to see sand burrs clinging about the edges of his trousers. The nearest sand burrs I knew of were half a mile off toward Snail Road.

I don't know how long we waited after that. My mother put the baby to bed, and returned to sit with restless hands; my father, muttering curses the while, added bits of driftwood to the fires, with the instinct inbred in sea-people of keeping a beacon alight.

Their coming was as the coming of an apparition seen suddenly in the firelight, tottering forward on limbs too frail for its inexplicable and uncouth frame. Then my mother cried out, and my father's oath was a prayer, and it came to me that the apparition was not one but two figures, one bearing the other.

Jem staggered up between the fires and laid his burden down with her head in my mother's lap. My sister's face was a queer color, her eyes were closed. I was bewildered and afraid.

"Scared," Jem panted. He collapsed rather than sat upon the lowest step. "He never touched her—just scared her—out of her head."

None of us doubted for an instant who "he" was. I ran into the kitchen under my mother's order for water. She worked with a sort of feverish calm over the girl in her lap, while Jem sat, head in hands, and back heaving. After a little he got up and regarded my sister's face.

"She'll come around," he said.

It may have been a question. If it was the answer was at its heels.

Agnes's eyes opened at the sound of the words with a shadow of unutterable horror behind them—her hands went out to him in an agony of rigid appeal. Jem knelt down with an arm about her shoulders.

"You're all right," he comforted her, still expending his words, as it were, with care.

"He came out of the sand—right up out of the sand at me."— there was a certain queer quality of raving in Agnes's whisper. She clung to him with the impossible strength of terror. "He came out of the sand—his eyes were red—oh, red—I could see them—and—an' I couldn't run—couldn't step—not step—"

"Yes—yes—Home now, Miss Aggie." Jem's red hand was on her hair, soothing, as one might a child.

"How did I come here?" She put the question abruptly—in her own voice now—took her arms from his neck with a gesture of shame and laid them across my mother's shoulders. It was my mother who answered her query.

"Meester Hodges bring you, Aggie girl." Agnes's eyes went to the little man, but he was lost in abstract contemplation of the nearest fire bed. My mother went on, "Ain't you goin' to thank Meester Hodges, Aggie?" Jem turned at that, lifting an imperative hand.

"Wait!" said he. "'Wait! You told me—to bring the horse."

Agnes cried out, "No!—no!—Oh, please—"

"You told me. Wait—an' don't be afeared." He leaned against a post of the railing, his red skin seeming to take to itself all the dying light of the embers, and began to whistle, low at first, then filling out clear and high and throbbing. He whistled in a peculiar way which I have never observed in any other.

The air was half familiar to me, the one he had played with softly on the dune behind the house. But to me and to my people, bred to the cloying accents of the South, that clear, soaring, sweet thread of Northern melody came as strange and alien and tingling, filling our own familiar night with a quality of expectancy. Jem Hodges was a new man before our eyes; for the first time in our knowledge of him, he was giving utterance to himself. He swept through the melody once, and twice, and paused.

"He's far," he said, and a note of whickering came to us from the eastward dunes. He caught up the air again, playing with it wonderful things, sweeping the little huddled family of us out of our intimate house and glowing, familiar yard, into a strange, wind-troubled country of his own.

And this time it was the night, not the sea, that gave up the great white stallion, rising to our fence in majestic flight, exploding from the flat darkness.

Jem cried, "No!—no!—don't be afeared!"—for we were making the gestures of panic. The animal came to him, picking a dainty way about the coals for all his tremendous weight, making a wonderfully fine picture with the fiery sheen over his vast deep chest, along the glistening flanks where the sweat stood, turning the four white fetlocks to agitated pinions of flame. Thus, I believe, the horses of the gods came to the ancients.

He stood over us there, heaving, mountainous, filling half the sphere of our sight. But his nose was in the bosom of Jem Hodges's coat, and his ears pricked forward to the breathing of Jem Hodges's song without words. The little man wandered on and on, picking a phrase from here and from there, wooing, recounting, laughing, exulting, weeping, never hating. When he suddenly began to speak in words, it was as though he had come down a great way, out of his own element.

"It had to be—after all," he said. "After all.—Now I suppose I've got to take you on to the rich American leddy? She'll keep you fine—in a fine paddock—you—you of the big wide moorland—free gentleman of half an English county. Ah, it's bad, Baron boy."

Then he was talking to us—to Agnes. "I been lying' to myself—tryin' to make myself believe Baron was away off and wild—I wanted to have him free like the air—long as he could. The rich leddy will pay five hundred pounds. Why do I need it? We're comfortable on our little place at home. Why?—because father says so an' a man must do what his father says—till he gets a wife an' family of his own. I thought Baron was gone when the ship got wrecked—I was near glad of it—he's no boy to pen up—in a paddock—with a ribbon on, mebbe. An' when I knew he wasn't gone—why—I fair couldn't do it—put it off an' off an' off. Ah, Baron, Baron,—they gave me you when I could pick you up in the meadow—but a man's got to do what his father says—"

He fell to musing, then, running his hand over the broad forehead, combing out the silk of the forelock, caressing a fine ear. Then, as to himself—

"Till he gets a wife of his own!"

He spoke to my sister.

"Come here, Miss Aggie."

Agnes went to him and, at his command, laid her fingers on Baron's nose. The animal arched his great neck—oh, an indescribable gesture!—and mouthed the back of her hand. I thought of Agnes at that moment as the bravest girl in all the world. Agnes was a stranger to me that night.

After a little time my mother got up, saying that I ought to have been in my bed long ago. My father came in with us, so that we left only the white horse and my sister and Jem Hodges, standing in a black group against the glow of the fires.

SOURCES

Chapters 23, 33, and 34 from *Memoirs of Conquistador Bernal Díaz del Castillo,* 1569 (translated by John I. Lockhart, 1844).

"The Dun Horse," from *Pawnee Hero Stories and Folk-Tales,* by George Bird Grinnell, 1890.

"The Woman Who Became a Horse," from *Traditions of the Skidi Pawnee: Memoirs of the American Folk-Lore Society,* vol. 8, by George A. Dorsey, 1904.

"The Comanches' Manner of Capturing Wild Horses," from *The Delahoydes: Boy Life on the Old Santa Fe Trail,* by Henry Inman, 1899.

"The Camp of the Wild Horse," from *A Tour on the Prairies,* by Washington Irving, 1832.

"Chu Chu," from *The Bell-Ringer of Angel's and Other Stories,* by Bret Harte, 1894.

"A Chestnut Pony," from *Out of Drowning Valley,* by S. Carleton Jones, 1910.

Chapter 7 from *Wildfire,* by Zane Grey, 1916.

"His Love for his Old Gray Horse," from *Ladies' Home Journal,* by Laura Spencer Portor and Charles Marshall Graves, January 1908.

"How Miss Lake's Circus Horses Were Restored," from *Horse Stories and Stories of Other Animals,* by Thomas Wallace Knox, 1890.

"A Ride with a Mad Horse in a Freight-Car," from *Atlantic Monthly,* by W. H. H. Murray, April 1869.

"How Comanche Came Into Camp," from *The Master of the Strong Hearts: A Story of Custer's Last Rally,* by Elbridge Streeter Brooks, 1898.

"Soldier Boy—Privately to Himself," "Soldier Boy and the Mexican Plug," "Soldier Boy and Shekels," "Soldier Boy and Shekels Again," "Mongrel and the Other Horse," "Soldier Boy—To Himself," from *A Horse's Tale,* by Mark Twain, 1907.

"The American Cavalry Horse," from *Munsey's Magazine*, by Wilmot E. Ellis, April 1905.

"Anecdotes of American Horses," from *The Family Magazine or Monthly Abstract of General Knowledge*, unknown author, 1841.

"The Cumbersome Horse," from *More Short Sixes*, by H. C. Bunner, 1894.

"A Drummer's Horse," from *Our Dumb Animals*, by R. M. Lockhart, 1912.

Chapter 11 from *White Dandy: Master and I—A Horse's Story*, by Velma Caldwell Melville, 1898.

"The Great Match Race between Eclipse and Sir Henry," from the *American Sporting Magazine*, by "An Old Turfman" (Calwallader R. Colden), July 3, 1830.

"The Story of a Jockey," from *Stories for Boys*, by Richard Harding Davis, 1916.

"World Record Is Set by Man o' War," from the *New York Times*, June 13, 1920.

"How I Bought and Trained Captain," by W. A. Sigsbee, from *The Story of Captain: The Horse with a Human Brain*, by George Wharton James, 1917.

"In Which True Becomes Justin Morgan," from *Justin Morgan, Founder of his Race: The Romantic History of a Horse*, by Eleanor Waring Burnham, 1911.

"White Horse Winter," from *Atlantic Monthly*, by Wilbur Daniel Steele, April 1912.

INDEX

Californios, 33. *See also* Saltello,
Consuelo; Saltello, Enriquez
camping, ix; in "A Chestnut Pony," 61,
67; *The Delahoydes: Boy Life on the
Old Santa Fe Trail* and, 24; in "The
Dun Horse," 10–11; in "His Love
for his Old Gray Horse," 96–97;
in "A Ride with a Mad Horse in a
Freight-Car," 107–10, 119–20. *See
also* "How Comanche Came Into
Camp"
"The Camp of the Wild Horse" (Irving):
hunting in, 26–27; lassos in, 30;
wild horse ancestry in, 27–28; wild
horse capture in, 27–32; wild horse
taming in, 29, 31–32
Captain (horse): acquisition of, 244–45;
as colt, 244–45, 247; companionship
needed by, 247, 248–49; grooms
of, 247–48; intelligence of,
245–47; Panama-Pacific Exposition
performance by, 238–39; Sigsbee
training of, 247; stairs climbed by,
249–50
Carm (fictional character), 194
Cartwright (judge) (character), 244–45
Cavalry Drill Regulations (U.S.), 167–68
Chadwick, Charley (fictional character):
affection between Heroine and,
220–21; Behren hiring of, 222; bet
fixing and, 226–28, 229, 230–31;
family farm of, 219–20; Heroine
feed and, 223–26; Heroine reunited
with, 221–22, 231
Charlie (horse), 173–75
Chase's Mill, 255–59
"A Chestnut Pony" (Jones): Athol
conceals pony in, 60, 69; camping
in, 61, 67; Eldon discovers of pony
in, 69; Eldon gang begins pursuit
in, 60–61; Eldon investigates Athol
in, 66–69, 70; Eldon investigates

Janesville in, 61–63; Eldon
suspects Sabarin in, 63–64, 66;
events following, 71; gold deposits
discovered in, 59; horse illness in,
60; Inkster questions Eldon in,
61–62, 63, 64, 65–66; mining town
in, 60, 61–63; Sabarin sighting of
Athol in, 64–65; Scarlett in, 59,
60–61, 63, 71; shooting in, 67, 68;
Welsh in, 67–70
Chet (fictional character), 194–95; horse
racing and, 196–98; murder of
horse and, 197–98; Topsy taming
and, 199–201
children: horse racing by, 147–48;
in "Soldier Boy—Privately to
Himself," 143–44. *See also* Alison,
Cathy; juvenile literature; "White
Horse Winter"
"Chu Chu" (Harte): eye contact
in, 33–34, 35, 37, 42, 55; horse
human affection in, 33–34, 35,
36, 38, 48–49; lassos in, 34–35,
47; Madroño tree in, 44–46,
48; mounting in, 42; neighbor
confrontations in, 35, 36–37;
Saltello, C., adoption of horse in,
48–49; Saltello, C., elopement in,
55–57, 58; Saltello, C., flight in,
49–55; Saltello, C., introduction to
horse in, 43–48; Saltello, E., horse
acquaintance made in, 37–38;
Saltello, E., mounting in, 40–41;
Saltello, E., saddling in, 38–39, 41
Cintla, 5–7
circuses: in Civil War, 103–5; in "How I
Bought and Trained Captain," 240,
243–44
Civil War: Battle of Malvern Hill
in, 110–15; circuses in, 103–5;
conscription of horses in, 96–97,
103–5; end of, 117–20; freight car

return from, 121–27; horse racing and, 206–7; Knoxville midnight ride in, 122. *See also* "His Love for his Old Gray Horse"

Clemens, Samuel. *See* Twain, Mark

Cloverdale Stock Farm, 220

Cody, Buffalo Bill. *See* Buffalo Bill

Coe, W. R., 235

Colden, Cadwallader R. *See* "The Great Match Race between Eclipse and Sir Henry"

colts: Captain as, 244–45, 247; in "The Story of a Jockey," 220; taming of wild, 112. *See also* Traveller

Columbus, Christopher, 2

"The Comanches' Manner of Capturing Wild Horses" (Inman): battle in, 21–22; buffalo in, 20–21; hunting in, 22; wild horse capture in, 22–24; wild horse taming in, 23, 24. *See also* "How Comanche Came Into Camp"

communication, nonverbal: in "A Drummer's Horse," 190; in "A Ride with a Mad Horse in a Freight-Car," 116–17, 120; in "Soldier Boy and the Mexican Plug," 150–51. *See also* talking, by horse; whistling

Companion (animal welfare publication), 189

conquistadores, Spanish: Native Americans battle with, 4–7; North America horse reintroduction by, vii–ix, 2, 163. *See also Memoirs of Conquistador Bernal Díaz del Castillo*

conscription, of horses, 164–66; in Civil War, 96–97, 103–5

Cordts (horse thief in *Wildfire*), 73, 91; Bostil, J., encounters, 82–83; Bostil, L., eyed by, 85; horse race gambling by, 82

Cortes, Hernan, 2–7

Crafts, William (jockey), 211; Purdy replacement of, 214; riding position of, 213; whipping by, 212, 213–14

Crazy Horse, 137, 138

Creech (fictional characters), 91; flood and, 74, 78–80

Creech, Joel (fictional character), 73, 79

Crook, George, 137

crowds, 208–9, 216

"The Cumbersome Horse" (Bunner): Brimmington commissions Skinner in, 186–87; Brimmington home invasion and, 181–82, 185–86, 187–88; farmhouse in, 176–78, 182–83; horse discovered in, 179–81; Skinner persuades Brimmington in, 184–85; Sparhawk in, 179–81, 187–88

Curtis (fictional character), 223, 224–25, 229, 230

Custer, George Armstrong. *See* "How Comanche Came Into Camp"; *Master of the Strong Hearts*

David Harum (horse), 235

Davis, Richard Harding, 219. *See also* "The Story of a Jockey"

The Delahoydes (Inman), 20–24. *See also* "The Comanches' Manner of Capturing Wild Horses"

detective work. *See* "A Chestnut Pony"

Díaz del Castillo, Bernal, 2–7

A Dog's Tale (Twain), 140. *See also* Potter; Shekels

Donnacona (horse), 235–36

Dorsey, George Amos, 18–19

dreams: of horse washing ashore, 264, 265; interruption of, 181–82, 185–86

drowning, 105. *See also Out of Drowning Valley*

"A Drummer's Horse" (Lockhart), 189; affection in, 190–91; blinders in,

military horses. *See* "The American Cavalry Horse"; conquistadores, Spanish; "His Love for his Old Gray Horse"; *A Horse's Tale*; "How Comanche Came Into Camp"; "How Miss Lake's Circus Horses were Restored"; "A Ride with a Mad Horse in a Freight-Car"

mining, 33; Janesville town of, 60, 61–63. *See also* "A Chestnut Pony"

"Mongrel and the Other Horse" (Twain), 159–60

Monmouth Park race track, 220, 221, 222; bet fixing at, 226–28, 229, 230–31; horse feed problems at, 223–26

Morgan, Justin (fictional character), 255, 256, 259

Morgan horses, 254–59

mounting, of horses, 40–41, 42

murder of horse, 197–98

Murray, William Henry Harrison "Adirondack," 106–7. *See also* "A Ride with a Mad Horse in a Freight-Car"

music: horse performance of, 238; in *A Horse's Tale*, 148, 150, 153–54, 157, 159, 161; in "How Comanche Came Into Camp," 131, 133–34; in "In Which True Becomes Justin Morgan," 256; in "White Horse Winter," 269, 276, 277. *See also* bugle music; whistling

Nashville, Tennessee, 103–5

Native American horses. *See* "The Comanches' Manner of Capturing Wild Horses"; "The Dun Horse"; "The Woman Who Became a Horse"

Native Americans: horse knowledge about, 142; mobility of, 28; Spanish conquistadores battle with, 4–7; in *Wildfire*, 78, 79, 81, 84, 85. *See also* "The Comanches' Manner of Capturing Wild Horses"; Lakota tribe; Pawnee tribe; Sioux tribe; Skidi Pawnee tribe; wild horses, Native American capture of

"Nearer My God to Thee" (Captain), 238

neighbor confrontations with horse, 35, 36–37

New York Evening Post, 216

New York Times, 94, 232–36

Niagara River: ferryboat across, 171–72; horse swims across, 172–73

Ninth Dragoons (U.S.), 143, 146, 149

nooses. *See* lassos

North America, horse reintroduction to, 163; by Spanish conquistadores, vii–ix, 2, 163; wild horse ancestry and, 27–28. *See also Memoirs of Conquistador Bernal Díaz del Castillo*

Nye, Nathan (fictional character), 256–57

Oklahoma, 26–32

Oli, Christobal de, 3, 5

Our Dumb Animals (animal welfare publication), 189–91

Out of Drowning Valley (Jones), 59–60, 71. *See also* "A Chestnut Pony"

Paddy (fictional character), 204

Paiutes. *See* Piutes

Panama-Pacific Exposition (1915), 238–39

Pawnee tribe, 10–13, 16–17; Sioux battle with, 14–15. *See also* Skidi Pawnee tribe

The Perfect Horse (Murray), 106

Piutes, 79

pony, spotted, 18–19. *See also* "A Chestnut Pony"

Portor, Laura Spencer, 94. *See also* "His Love for his Old Gray Horse"

Portuguese Americans, 260. *See also* "White Horse Winter"

Potonchán attack, 4–5

Potter (dog) (fictional character), 144, 152–53

prairies. *See A Tour on the Prairies*

Prince (horse): buggy horse mismatch with, 196–97; horse racing of, 197; murder of, 197–98

Princess Trixie (horse), 240–43

pseudonyms, author, 33, 59, 72, 140

Puck Magazine, 176

Puertocarrero, Alonso Hernandez, 3, 5

purchase, of horses. *See* conscription, of horses

Purdy (jockey): Crafts replacement by, 214; inside pass by, 215–17

race times: in "The Great Match Race between Eclipse and Sir Henry," 213, 217, 218; in "World Record Is Set by Man o' War," 233–34

racing, horse: bet fixing and, 226–28, 229, 230–31; Civil War and, 206–7; in "In Which True Becomes Justin Morgan," 255–56; journalism and, x, 232–33; preliminaries for, 81–88; in "Soldier Boy and the Mexican Plug," 147–48; virtues in, 220; virtues in, 220; in *White Dandy*, 196–98; in *Wildfire*, 76–77, 80–81, 88–91. *See also* gambling and horse racing; "The Great Match Race between Eclipse and Sir Henry"; "The Story of a Jockey"; "World Record Is Set by Man o' War"

Racquette Lake, 107–10

Rarey, John S., 167–68

Red Top (fictional character), 128, 135; burial of, 129–30

religion, 52, 160

Reno, Marcus Albert, 134–35

riatas. *See* lassos

Riddle, Samuel D., 232–36

"A Ride with a Mad Horse in a Freight-Car" (Murray), 106; affection between human and horse in, 112–13, 115–16, 117; Battle of Malvern Hill in, 110–15; boating stealth in, 107–9; camping in, 107–10, 119–20; Civil War ending in, 117–20; freight car ride in, 121–27; groom in, 115–17; horse anxieties in, 119–20; horse injuries in, 119, 120; hospital in, 115–17; Knoxville midnight ride in, 122; master chosen by horse in, 114–15; nonverbal communication in, 116–17, 120; phrenitis in, 120, 123–27; veterinary practices in, 123–24

Ringling, Al, 246–47

romance. *See* "A Chestnut Pony"; "Chu Chu"; "White Horse Winter"; *Wildfire*; "The Woman Who Became a Horse"

Sabarin (fictional character), 60–61, 71; Athol sighting by, 64–65; Eldon suspects, 63–64, 66

Sage King (horse), 73, 86, 88–89, 91

salesman, traveling, 189–91

Saltello, Consuelo (fictional character), 37; adoption of horse by, 48–49; elopement of, 55–57, 58; horse flight of, 49–55; introduction of horse to, 43–48

Saltello, Enriquez (fictional character): elopement of sister and, 55–56; flight of sister and, 53, 54; horse acquaintance made by, 37–38; mounting of horse by, 40–41; saddling of horse by, 38–39, 41

also *A Horse's Tale*; "Soldier Boy and the Mexican Plug"

Union Course, Long Island. *See* "The Great Match Race between Eclipse and Sir Henry"

United States (U.S.): branding horses, 165; Cavalry Drill Regulations of, 167–68; health inspection of horses, 164–65; Massachusetts Regiment of, 110–15; Ninth Dragoons of, 143, 146, 149; Tenth Dragoons of, 142–43. *See also* "The American Cavalry Horse"; Civil War; North America, horse reintroduction to; Seventh Cavalry

Van (fictional character), 77–80, 86, 88, 89

Velasquez de Leon, Juan, 3, 5

veterinary practices: in "The American Cavalry Horse," 164; in "His Love for his Old Gray Horse," 102; in "A Ride with a Mad Horse in a Freight-Car," 123–24; in *White Dandy*, 195, 201–2. *See also* medication, for horses

Virginia. *See* "The Great Match Race between Eclipse and Sir Henry"; West Virginia

Walden, John (Sir Henry jockey), 211; Taylor replacement of, 217

Wallace, Fred (fictional character), 193, 198; horseshoeing and, 202–4; medication prescribed by, 195

Wallace, Richard (fictional character), 193, 204

Washington, D.C., 115–19

weight: of Eclipse, 211; of Sir Henry, 211; of Taylor, 217

Welsh, Jim (fictional character), 67–70

the West, 20, 59, 72, 129, 193; European expansion to, ix; Native American mobility in, 28

western horses. *See* "The Camp of the Wild Horse"; "A Chestnut Pony"; "Chu Chu"; *Wildfire*

West Point, 166–68

West Virginia, 95–96, 97, 101

whipping: of Eclipse, 212, 213–14; in *White Dandy*, 194, 195, 196; in "World Record Is Set by Man o' War," 236

whistling: in "A Drummer's Horse," 190; in "White Horse Winter," 269, 276, 277

White Dandy (Melville): alcohol in, 194–95; bitting and horse tongue health in, 201–2; *Black Beauty* influence on, 192; buggy horse mismatch in, 196–97; grooms in, 195, 196, 198, 202, 203, 204; hitching in, 194–96, 203; horse blanket in, 195–96; horse illness in, 195, 196; horse racing in, 196–98; horseshoeing in, 202–4; murder of horse in, 197–98; Prince in, 196–98; taming of Topsy in, 199–201; Wallace, F., prescribes horse medicine in, 195; Wallace, R., in, 193, 204; whipping in, 194, 195, 196

"White Horse Winter" (Steele): Agnes confronts Hodges in, 270–72; Agnes disappearance in, 273; Agnes fainting in, 274–75; bayberries in, 265, 266; bonfire in, 273; dunes in, 260–61, 262, 265–66; fear of horses in, 267, 270–71, 272, 276; Hodges knocks over protagonist in, 270–71; Hodges wooing of Agnes in, 268–69, 277–78; horse presence